MARRIAGE IN MOTION
A Study on the Social Context and Processes of Marital Satisfaction

SOCIOLOGIE VANDAAG / SOCIOLOGY TODAY

Volume 10

MARRIAGE IN MOTION

A study on the social context and processes of marital satisfaction

Ann Van den Troost

Leuven University Press
2005

The research in this book was supported by the Flemish Organization of Scientific Research (FWO grant: G.0204.02)

Published with the support of the K.U.Leuven Commissie voor Publicaties

ISBN 90 5867 464 9
D / 2005 / 1869 / 22
NUR : 756

Cover: Mai Grietens, Dorien Coussement en Els Vandervoort
Layout: Margot Van Baelen

Acknowledgments

This book bears the stamp of many people. First, I owe many thanks to my promoters Koen Matthijs, Jan Gerris and Ad Vermulst for sharing their scientific and methodological expertise with me. Koen, Jan en Ad, each of you have inspired me to push out my frontiers. Thank you!

I would also like to thank the 'women' of the secretary for relieving me of administrative and practical tasks. Thanks, Carla, Marina, Martine and Kristien. My chats with you all have certainly cheered up my working life at the Department of Sociology. Special thanks further to Margot who was there until the final minute for the professionally lay-outing of the text.

Writing a book is often a lonely endeavor. Many (former) colleagues however have turned it into a heart-warming and pleasant activity. Thank you Anja, Ann, Annelies, Astrid, Axel, Bart, Bartjes, Caroline, Dirk, Elke, Hanne, Hilde, Ine, Gert, Greet, Greet, Hans, Hedwig, Indra, Inge, Ilse, Jan, Jan, Jef, Jeroen, Jerry, Koen, Kristine, Kurt, Leen, Lesley, Michaël, Michel, Nadia, Sara, Sofie, Steven, Stijn, Silke, Veerle, Vicky and Wouter.

All the years I have been surrounded by many friends who each (in their own way) have conquered a place in my heart. Not only because of their emotional support during the research process but also because of so much more, I want to thank Peter, Muriel en Bart, Ilse en Koen, Tim, Sybiel and Koen, Karlien and Hans, Kurt, Annelies and Stijn, Katelijne and Christoph, Lieve and Jochen, Lieve, Ilse, Monic and Hugo, Patrice and Jo. That you are still beside me after all these years is a great feeling. I also want to mention here my "new coming" club of friends, Lieve and Steven, Lieve and Maarten, Lieve and Herman, and Sabine and Kristof for sharing all kinds of pleasant moments with me.

I am grateful to Maike, Ivo and Koen for all their (culinary) help and support during the last two years. Thank you so much!

I also owe special thanks to my family and my parents in particular. They have always supported me in the choices I have made. Without their encouragements and assistance I would probably never finished this book. Mum and dad, I am truly thankful to you.

Finally, Hans. You have had the patience of a saint with me and had to miss me during so many hours while I was finishing this book. Know that your never ending love and sense of humor has given me the strength to go on. Hans, thank you so much for being in my life.

Ann Van den Troost
December 2004

Table of Contents

List of Tables

List of Figures

Introduction

Late 20th-century family sociology is faced with new and interesting challenges related to intimate realities barely known half a century ago. Society swarms with unfamiliar social manners and life forms such as *TINS*-couples (two incomes, no sex), *DINK*-couples (double income, no kids), *LAT*-relations and the *new man*. However, more familiar social models such as marriage continue to arouse family researchers' interest, the more so since marital relationships are increasingly prone to failure. This proneness is due to macro-level shifts such as the expansion of the welfare state, individualization and the emancipation of women, turning marriage into a risky business. The socially prescribed 'ought' to marry, as well as to stay married, has lost its compelling character. Hence, we do not only marry less and later but also get divorced more and earlier. The normative uncertainty ensuing from this behavior makes our intimate relationships less predictable and more diverse than ever (Cheal, 1991).

For some, this self-ruled private scenery is not only the most in-depth social change of the past decades but also the most problematic one. Prophets of doom such as Popenoe (1993) even identify this private turmoil as a 'great disruption' or a 'dramatic change'. Intimate partners are suspected of enforced hedonism, turning them into economical utility calculators weighing up self-interests and desires against the costs and rewards offered by a marital relationship. Others, such as Cheal (1991) and van Stokkom (1997), refute this cultural pessimism and interpret the same evolution as a process of *re*-integration instead of *de*-integration and even as moral progress. It is striking, though, that both logics revolve around the same issue of *relationship quality* and *satisfaction*. While some argue that the quality of partnership has considerably deteriorated, others put forward exactly the reverse argumentation, emphasizing partners' motivation to develop satisfying marriages. This puzzlement poses the question whether marital quality has actually changed during the past decades. The answer, however, is not obvious since several and diverse social transformations all clot together in individuals' personal experiences. Positive and negative social forces might largely offset one another as well, resulting in apparent stable marital quality throughout time while actually considerable changes have been taken place. In fact, asking the question about changes in marital quality may be irrelevant because of the risk to judge past reality according to current standards and vice versa.

Nevertheless, the present circumstances in many Western countries attest to a vulnerable marital institution. More than ever in history, the survival of marriage seems to depend on the *quality* and *satisfaction* it can offer for the parties involved. Therefore, the question as why some partners are more satisfied with their marriage than others became increasingly significant in light of the profound social and cultural transformations of the past century. If the degree of satisfaction with one's partnership is indeed substantial and even of utmost importance in partners' legitimation of partnership, gaining insight in this evaluation criterion is vital for understanding the nature of contemporary marital bounds.

The present study aims to contribute to this understanding by examining spousal marital satisfaction in the Netherlands. Although an overwhelming body of research on marital satisfaction and its determinants exists, our knowledge on this theme is primarily based on American studies. For the Netherlands, however, this field is still unexplored. Moreover, previous studies leave important questions unaddressed as to long-term associations, spillover effects, and the different manifestations of marital experiences in higher and lower social groups. Therefore, the *central aim* of this study is to examine the underlying processes and correlates of Dutch spouses' satisfaction with marriage, about 40 years after the onset of the so-called second demographic transition. The latter term is usually reserved for referring to the interlinked demographic developments observed in Western Europe in the sixties and seventies (Lesthaeghe & Van de Kaa, 1986; Van de Kaa, 2001), resulting in both external and internal transformations of partnership.

For our research purpose, data of a Dutch longitudinal project "Family and Child-Rearing in the Netherlands" (Gerris et al., 1992; 1993; 1998) is used. Husbands and wives included in this project are generally born at the end of World War II. Thus, the present study is directed towards a specific social group, i.e. the pioneers of the current demographic conditions. It was the baby boom generation, born between 1940 and 1955, and socialized with the ideal type of the nuclear family, that instigated enormous quantitative and qualitative changes in the private sphere. Hence, this generation has inherited a whole other private story than the one they would write down themselves. This experience might have important sociological consequences for the intimate relations this generation would develop later in their life. Actually, they were a generation confronted with *old realities* and *new ideals*. Precisely this tension makes the study of their marital experiences very interesting.

The work presented here is a collection of the studies that were conducted over the past four years on the determinants and processes underlying marital satisfaction. Three major parts are distinguished.

Part I is conceived as the societal background and scientific impetus of the present study. By drawing attention to the broader social context fuelling the micro-level experiences of husbands and wives, the social significance of a micro-sociological phenomenon like marital satisfaction is clarified. In particular, attention is drawn to the Dutch context. Part I also discusses the theoretical and methodological background of the present study and the distinct research questions formulated to gain insight in Dutch husbands' and wives' marital satisfaction. This part is concluded with a description of the data, the sampling procedure and the validation of the sample.

Part II of this study consists of six chapters. Each chapter addresses a particular research question on marital satisfaction covering four broad themes: gender, communication, parenting and, spousal social and cultural position. Since an attempt was made to preserve the possibility that each chapter can be read on its own, some degree of repetition inevitably exists. The overlap predominantly concerns the description of the method and the theories that are applied. Doing so, the reader can choose a chapter of interest without lacking information already addressed in another chapter.

Part III of the present study summarizes the key findings of individual chapters and endeavors to go beyond these findings in order to arrive at a broader reconsideration of research results. The different studies are also evaluated in terms of the theoretical approaches and methodology used. To conclude, future directions for research are delineated.

PART I

Social Background and Research Agenda

1. Marriage and Partnership in a Changing Social Landscape

Marital partners initiate and develop their current relationships in a societal climate that is very different from mid 20th century's context. In the same way, marital and intimate life underwent several external and internal changes during the past decades. By marking these broad social contours, this chapter aims to illuminate the social forces being at work in spousal daily experiences and evaluations of their partnership.

Because marital experiences at the micro-level cannot be fully captured without taking the larger social context into consideration, the first section of this chapter draws attention to major socio-demographic changes characterizing the second half of the 20th century as well as to the structural and cultural factors put forward to explain it. Since the present study deals with Dutch couples, Dutch material is used to illustrate the demographic trends.[1]

In the second section, the socio-demographic discussion is situated within the broader theoretical perspective of individualization and emotionalisation. Specific emphasis is placed on the vulnerable character of marriages today as well as on the identity-building function of current partnership.

The third section addresses the consequences of the described demographic and social transformations for spousal experiences at the micro-level. Specifically, attention is paid to gender-specific and parental issues prevalent in contemporary marriage.

---

[1] The evolution of Dutch partnership throughout the past three decades is extensively described in the Family Report [Gezinsrapport], which was published in 1997 by the Dutch Secretary of State of Public Health, Welfare and Sport and the Social and Cultural Planning Office of the Netherlands (SCPON) (Van Praag & Niphuis-Nell, 1997). In this section the contributions of various authors to this Family Report will be overviewed to highlight the findings of interest for the present study. Main attention will be paid to married couples with children, as the latter constitutes the sample of this research.

1.1. DEMOGRAPHICAL ISSUES

The first paragraph deals with recent external and internal transformations characterizing Dutch family and marital life. The interpretations of these transformations are discussed in the second paragraph. Because the shifts in family and marital life are a source of serious social concern, the third paragraph endeavors to put this social debate in the proper perspective.

1.1.1. The 'New' Outlook of Dutch Partnership

Half a century ago, the landscape of private life was less diverse than it is now. The ideal construct of the typical family dovetailed more or less with the empirical reality; most people left the parental home to get married young, promptly had several children and stayed with their partner until death. All sociological and demographic indicators pointed to what later would be identified as the *standard life course* (Dumon, 1997). Within this standard course, there was little room for individual experimentation: gender roles and expectations were clearly delineated and socially accepted. (Matthijs & Van den Troost, 1998).

Since the seventies, this standard family pattern underwent rapid quantitative and qualitative transformations. Almost all Western countries witnessed a downturn in fertility and in the intensity of (re)marriage. Whereas in the Netherlands married couples with children still represented 56% of the households in 1960, today they account for about one out of three households.

This evolution can be partially put down to the total *fertility* rate, decreasing from 3.11 children in 1960 to 1.53 in 1995. Dutch couples do not only opt for fewer children but they also prefer to have them later in life. Of the female cohort born in 1945, 59% had their first child at the age of 25 whereas this is only true for 19% of the women born in 1970. Moreover, it appears that nowhere in Western Europe the mean age of mothers at the birth of their first child - i.e. 28.5 years in 1995 - is as high as in Dutch society (Kuijsten & Schulze, 1997). According to van Praag (1997) postponement of child bearing is so strongly pronounced in the Netherlands due to a strong existent ideology of individual self-development and the relatively lack of the necessary social provisions to fulfill this cultural desire.

Besides the decrease in fertility rates, the numerical and social popularity of marriage began to wane in the '70s. Although van Praag (1997) asserts that marriage remains by far the most common tool through which families are formed in the Netherlands, the preamble to marriage has changed since the seventies (Van Praag, 1997). The evolution of age at first marriage attests for this changed prelude. For men, the mean age at first marriage increased substantially from 26.8 years in 1960 to 29.7 in 1995. For women, these figures are respectively 24.5 and 27.3 years. These statistics echo a tendency to delay marriage and to initiate intimate relationships in different ways than fifty years ago (Kuijsten & Schulze, 1997).

This quantitative decline of marriage was, however, not indicative of a diminished enthusiasm towards relationships. On the contrary, it was largely compensated by the social desire to *cohabit*. Today, unmarried cohabitation is a phenomenon occurring at all social levels. This "*normalization*" of the cohabitation phenomenon does not only play an important part in couples' postponement of marriage but also increasingly functions as a durable alternative to it. Therefore, public marriage seems concurring with informal marriage (Latten & De Graaf, 1997; Latten, 2004).

Alongside the rise in cohabitation, the institution of marriage further wanes in importance due to rising *divorce* rates. Whereas in 1960 only 5.7% of Dutch marital dissolutions were ended by divorce, this figure raised to 37% in 1995. Although these statistics demonstrate that the majority of marriages still end by the death of one of the partners, the divorce risk (i.e. the likelihood that a marriage will be ended by divorce considering the contemporary divorce figures) considerably increased to about one out of three marriages ending in divorce. In the last decade of the 20th century, divorced couples had been married for about 12 to 13 years when they broke up. The mean age of men at the time of divorce was 42,7 in 2002. At the beginning of the nineties this was 39,9 years. During this period the mean age of women at divorce increased from 37,1 to 39,8. Experiencing a divorce is also socially influenced. Highly-educated women in the Netherlands are more likely to break up than lower-educated women. This holds for women born in the period 1945-1954 as well as for those born ten years later and might be due to the higher economic independence of these women or to the less likely presence of children (de Graaf, 2000).

The divorce explosion is historically a completely new phenomenon with a plethora of individual and social outcomes (Matthijs & Van den Troost, 1998; Vanhove & Matthijs, 2002). One of these outcomes is the effect of imitation or *social contagion*. Because divorce has become so common, more people take advantage of the opportunity. Hence, people now enter marriage with a set of risks and choices unknown to their parents.

These quantitative transformations are also associated with qualitative shifts. The greater involvement of women in education and employment during the '70s and '80s meant a real challenge for couples in harmonizing professional and family responsibilities. In the Netherlands, women's participation in the labor market was a slowly progressing phenomenon and until recently, it was low as compared to other West-European countries. This situation has changed. Whereas in 1960 only 7% of married women had a paid job, this figure increased to about one out of two in 1995 (Alders, Latten, Pool, & Esveldt, 2003; Niphuis-Nell & de Beer, 1997). With a participation level of 53%, Dutch women now leave Spanish, Italian, Greek, Irish and Belgian women behind them.

Despite the increase in female employment, husbands' and wives' earnings continue to be unequal due to women's high level of part-time labor (Niphuis-Nell & de Beer, 1997). Compared to other Western countries, part-time employment in the Netherlands is by far the highest (see Table 1.1.). Whereas at the end of the seventies, Swedish and Norwegian women still surpassed their Dutch counterparts with respect to part-time employment, two decades later the latter largely outnumbered them. Halfway the nineties, about two out of three Dutch women were employed on a part-time contract whereas this is only true for 16% of men (Kuijsten & Schulze, 1997). These figures indicate that the increase in Dutch women's employment during the last decades is mainly due to their strong part-time employment. Apparently, women 'benefited' more from the relative strong growth of part-time jobs in the Netherlands (Latten & De Graaf, 1997). It is unclear, however, whether women's participation is cause or consequence. Did women decide to participate more in the labor market because of the availability of part-time jobs or did employers create more part-time jobs because their employees preferred it?

Table 1.1
**Part-time Employed Women in Some Western Countries, 1979-1995
(% of the Labor Force)**

	1979	1983	1995
Norway	51.7	54.9	46.6
Sweden	46.0	45.9	40.3
Belgium	16.5	19.7	29.8
France	17.0	20.1	28.9
Netherlands	44.0	50.3	67.2
Italy	10.6	9.4	12.7

Source: OECD, 1996

Thus far, we have not specifically focused on women with children. When considering *mothers* in particular, it appears that in the last two decades of the 20th century their employment levels show a continuous rise as well, indicating the weakening of the barrier of parenthood for women's participation in the labor market (Kuijsten & Schulze, 1997). In accordance with the general trend, women with children seldom work full-time (Kuijsten & Schulze, 1997). Apparently, they solve the compatibility problem between a paid job and childcare by working part-time.

Besides the increased possibility of part-time employment, the rise in mothers' labor participation might also reflect the larger supply of informal childcare arrangements. Until the eighties, the Netherlands endorsed a *non-interventionist* or *implicit* family policy (Dumon, 1991; Jonker, 1990). Instead of encouraging women to enter and remain in the work force, policy in the Netherlands rather induced mothers to stay home (Mills, 2000). It was only at the beginning of the nineties that an *emancipation* policy was established, resulting in the availability of formal (subsidized) childcare and more flexible regulations of maternity leave (Kuijsten & Schulze, 1997; Niphuis-Nell & de Beer, 1997). Thus until then, the steady increase in mothers' employment was therefore a phenomenon that evolved in spite of the absence of structural incentives, rather than because of incentives[2].

At the couple level, Dutch mothers' employment situation implies that the two-income family does not frequently occur among couples with children (Niphuis-Nell & de Beer, 1997). With the arrival of children, the typical 'one-earning family', with the husband as major provider, or the 'one and a half-earner model', with the husband as main provider, become the dominant models. This is especially true for lower educated couples but although in lesser extent for middle- and higher-educated pairs.

The unequal participation of the sexes in full-time and part-time employment may be a significant impediment to implementing labor division *inside* the family and to usher in new forms of social pressure such as shifting power balances between men and women. Therefore, the question arises to what degree external divisions of labor in the Netherlands have an internal pendant as regards household and childrearing tasks. From Table 1.2 it becomes clear that in all stages of the family life cycle, the time mothers spend on household and childrearing tasks sharply exceeds that of fathers (Van der Lippe, 1997). As children become older, Dutch mothers seem to spend more time at childrearing tasks but less on household chores. Fathers, in contrast, spend less time on both household and childrearing tasks as children grow up.

---

[2] This policy as regards to the (lack of) availability of public services making family life compatible with women's demand for economic independence caused Esping-Andersen (1999) to classify the Dutch welfare state as a conservative regime. Nonetheless, the Netherlands cannot be totally subsumed under a conservative heading as Dutch policy also emphasizes income maintenance (Esping-Andersen, 1999).

Table 1.2
Hours per Week and Trend (1975-1995) in Spending Household and Childrearing Tasks of (Married) Cohabitating Husbands and Wives in the Netherlands, According to Age of the Youngest Child

	Women		Men	
	1995	Trend [a]	1995	Trend [a]
Youngest child 0-5 years				
Household tasks	26.0	--	8.6	++
Childrearing	19.6	++	8.4	++
Youngest child 6-14 years				
Household tasks	28.3	--	9.9	++
Childrearing	6.7	--	2.6	no change
Youngest child > 14 years				
Household tasks	30.4	-	7.7	no change
Childrearing	2.7	no change	0.5	no change

Source: Van der Lippe, 1997
[a] --/++ significant at 1%-level, +/- significant at 5%-level

The conclusions about the evolution in husbands and wives' participation in family labor are somewhat more optimistic. By means of '+' or '-', Table 1.2 also indicates whether significantly more or less time is spent at that specific task during the period 1975-1995. As can be seen, the past decades have witnessed a decrease in women doing family tasks while men spend more time at these tasks than twenty years ago. At least this is true for fathers of which the youngest child is 5 years old maximum. When the youngest child is at least 14 years old, no significant change shows up. For women, largest 'positive' change took place with respect to childrearing tasks when the youngest child is between 0 and 5 years old. Overall, these findings support the idea that young fathers and mothers significantly changed their behavior with respect to childcare, paving the way for propagating the phenomenon of the 'new father' in the next generations.

1.1.2. Transitions in Partnership Interpreted

The aforementioned family changes were accompanied by other major shifts in society such as secularization, birth control, expansion of the welfare state and the emancipation of women (Beck, 1992; Espenshade, 1985; Van de Kaa, 1987). At a theoretical level, demographers have usually defined the structural and cultural family changes since the '60s as the *second demographic transition* (Lesthaeghe & Surkyn, 1988; Lesthaeghe & Van de Kaa, 1986).

According to several authors (Ariès, 1980; Lesthaeghe, 1993; 1999; Shorter, 1975), clear distinctions can be identified between the demographic changes that took place prior to the 1950s and those brought about by the baby boom generation since the 1960s. In contrast to the *first demographic transition*[3] during which the 'traditional' family model became dominant, the second transition was associated with a more individualistic partnership model, directed towards self-fulfillment and quality of partnership. Compared to spouses in the first half of the 20th century, marital partners increasingly sought getting more personal satisfaction out of a relationship (Lesthaeghe, 1993). In this way, a considerable part of the second demographic transition does not relate to classical demographic orientation points such as birth and death, but rather to changes in partnership and family functions. Therefore, it can be identified as a qualitative rather than a quantitative transformation (Matthijs, 2001).

It is definitely not a sinecure to establish causal lines in the transformations within the private sphere. One of the reasons is that family functions and behavior reflect individual, dyadic as well as broader social tensions and desires (Matthijs, 2001). As a result, explanations put forward in the literature to understand individuals' private behavior remain limited and can merely offer general frameworks rather than claiming strong explanatory power (Straver, van der Heiden, & van der Vliet, 1994). The explanatory efforts revolve around economic or cultural aspects as forces of change.

Economic explanations contend that the labor division between women and men provides the primary incentive to form stable unions (Becker, 1981). The economic emancipation of women is therefore argued

---

[3] The first demographic transition (period between 1880 and 1930) was characterized by a decrease in mortality as well as a decrease in marital fertility.

to be the cause of the weakening of marriage, leading to a reduction of women's economic gains in marriage and simultaneously to an increase in opportunity costs. The time women once spent on household labor now represents a high cost given the fact that they can exploit this time in the labor market. According to this economic line of reasoning, the shift in marital behavior is the outcome of micro-economical utility calculations driven by changing sex roles, female labor market participation and the increased cost of children. This economic reasoning, however, has been criticized by some authors, among them Oppenheimer (1994; 2001). She states that, although it is closely connected to long-held views of traditional family functioning, this economic theory of marriage encounters, among other difficulties, the problem that the assumed beneficial effect of sex-role specialization, i.e. the traditional division of labor, is also related to individ-ual and social costs. A traditional labor division may be disadvantageous because a temporary or permanent loss of one 'specialist' may endanger the well-being of the whole family.

Besides economically oriented explanations, the demographic changes since the '60s cannot be separated from Inglehart's (1977) *silent revolution.* Inglehart stresses a shift in dominant values as the force behind family change. This shift from 'materialist' values towards 'post-materialism' reflects a Maslowian evolution in which growing welfare and economical security resulted in emphasizing self-expression and quality of life. As such, concerns about 'having', are replaced by concerns about 'being' (Lesthaeghe, 1987).

This dynamic is associated with the erosion of normative prescriptions and the emergence of individual autonomy (Lesthaeghe, 1999). The latter, however, does not point to egocentric behavior but to the fact that external norms are no longer taken for granted. Everyone 'makes' his/her own life. This manifestation of individual independence and the associated change in values is illustrated by Dutch trend data (see Table 1.3), showing that non-traditional and egalitarian values gradually emerged and spread after World War II. The new set of values of increased individual autonomy concerning norms, values and life styles along with a waning influence of traditional institutions was the breeding ground for the pluralization and informaliza-tion of living forms (Halman, 1991; Latten, 2004).

However, instead of pinning down the recent family transitions to either an economic or a cultural explanation, Lesthaeghe (1999) pleads for not solely relying on one set of factors but instead considering both the economic and cultural aspects in tandem to capture the current state of intimate affairs.

Table 1.3

Value Changes in the Netherlands: 1965-1984 (% of Survey Respondents Agreeing with Value Statements)

	'65 –69	'70 -74	'75-'79	'80 -84
Sexual relations permitted if intention is to marry	21	60	59	72
Husbands' unfaithfulness acceptable	20	46	49	/
Virginity not to be preserved before marriage	29	62	/	/
Tolerance for homosexuality	56	69	84	/
Divorce inadmissible if children still home	48	13	9	6
Voluntary childlessness is acceptable	22	60	70	83

Source: Lesthaeghe, 1999

1.1.3. Much Ado About What?

Sociologists use 'big words' like *de-standardization* of family patterns or the *pluralization* of family life to indicate the breakdown of traditionally pre-scribed foundations and the emancipation of the private sphere (Beck & Beck-Gernsheim, 1995; Mills, 2000). The latter have caused marriage to become one among others. Strong pillars, however, are not easily removed. The current social 'playground' and in specific the vulnerable character of marriage is a considerable cause for concern and *fin de siècle* anxiety. The concern is mainly centered on the functional loss of the family as well as on the pursuit of self-fulfillment at the expense of private commitment (Lewis, 2001; Popenoe, 1993).

The former is the result of a social process of *functional differentiation*, which developed with the transition from a traditional to a (post)modern society. In this structural process, previous multifunctional institutions are split up into unifunctional institutions (Felling, Peters & Scheepers, 2000). In this way, a multitude of social systems developed side by side; each with their own finality. The family system became a specialized agency with demarcated sex roles, i.e. instrumental roles for men and expressive roles for women. Also within one system such as the family, different subsystems developed autonomously and hence the parental and the spousal system are increasingly split up too. Matthijs (2000) typifies this emancipation within the private sphere as *expressive segmentation*. It essentially concerns a similar process as functional differentiation at the broad social level, which carves its way at lower levels and even at the individual level. Actually, it is the cultural pendant of functional differentiation: individuals within the new unifunctional and specialized institutions increasingly function as independent subjects who are relatively free to decide on their own life project.

Through this differentiation process the family as a social system has lost some of its previous functions. From its original functions, such as the economical, socializing, religious, and affective/procreative function, only the latter has remained as vigorous as in prior eras. Popenoe (1993) is one of the strong adherents of the idea that this functional loss is detrimental[4]. He raises great concern about the family as a weakening institution in carrying out its traditional functions and claims that "Families have lost power functions, social power and authority over their members. They have grown smaller in size, less stable and shorter in life span. People have become less willing to invest time, money and energy in the family, turning instead to investments in themselves" (Popenoe, 1993, p. 528).

Apparently, the social worry does not only relate to the de-institutionalization and differentiation of family life, but also to the de-investment and higher valorization of the individual. In line with the latter, a recurring theme in this debate is the negative effect of women's employment and its consequences for the partner, children and the organization of family life. Other authors, however, accentuate the new opportunities and functional gains that modern family life has to offer. According to Kellerhals (1998),

---

[4] The conclusion that the family would have lost is production function is contested. According to Esping-Andersen (1999, p. 48) the family might no longer represent the main unit of production, but it surely does provide non-monetarized goods and services.

for example, the importance of the contemporary family lies in its personal identification dimension. Since many of the choices family members currently make are merely options instead of socially prescribed patterns, it has become difficult to find coherence in the development of one's identity (Giddens, 1991). Within the affective climate of the family, individuals can create their unity and their self-identity (see also § 1.2.2).

Table 1.4
Reasons for Divorce Retrospectively Reported by Dutch Husbands and Wives (%)

	Men	Women
Communicational problems	59	64
Incompatible characters	57	56
Sexual problems	24	29
Incompatible plans for the future	27	34
Disagreement about having children	8	9
Financial problems	14	24
Addiction problems	5	20
Infidelity	37	35
Other reasons	29	34
Among which: Loss of interest in partner	5	5
Social differences	4	3
Physical or mental problems	6	3
Job situation	4	1
Started the relationship too young	1	2
Family/children	1	2
Abuse	/	7

Source: de Graaf, 2000

Families also fulfill the essential function of offering emotional care and well-being to its members. The undeniable significance of this function, however, is at the same time endangered as the family increasingly stands or falls with the quality of the marital relationship. The cultural norm of romantic love and high qualitative relationships may inflate partners' expectations to levels that are hardly feasible. Paradoxically, *individuals* may attach greater value to the importance of a close relationship while its *social* importance seems to decrease.

The qualitative character of intimate bonds also become manifest in the prerequisites for a successful marriage as reported in values studies. Factors such as 'mutual understanding and respect', 'marital fidelity' and 'understanding and tolerance' are considered the most important conditions for successful partnership (Van den Troost, 2000). Also spouses' reported reasons for divorce reveal the qualitative nature of partnership. As can be derived from Table 1.4, more than half of the Dutch divorced men and women indicated, 'incompatible characters' or communicational problems as important reasons for their broken marriage. In summary, these findings indicate that the survival of partnership increasingly hinges on the willingness to take the other partner's well-being into consideration.

According to Dumon (1974) and Scanzoni (1987) the functionality and the mutual dependency between partners should become the central point of social orientation instead of the institutional bounds or prescribed behaviors. Because intimate life is no longer a standardized but rather a *makeable* project, other models than the nuclear family can be conceived to fulfill individual needs. Not the form but the content and nature of interactions should be the criterion of differentiation.

This also becomes clear in studies on family definition. Using a sample of university students, Matthijs & Van den Troost (1998) demonstrate that by subtle weighing up of elements such as the parent-child relationship, living situation, sexual inclination or marital status, students distinguish clearly between a more emotional concept of 'family' and a more de facto or material perception of 'household'. Interpersonal configurations consisting of a parent-child relationship and of cohabitation are mostly considered as a family. Marital status, for example, appears to be less important in this consideration. The reason why a plurality of configurations is considered to be a family should be sought in their common characteristic. Apparently, they all function as person-supporting systems (Dumon, 1997).

Indeed, it appears that families, be it in different forms, continue to fulfill several emotional, psychological, social and economical functions. Intimate relationships even appear to be the key to individual happiness. In his study *Conditions of Happiness*, Veenhoven (1984) confirms that people with a steady life partner are happier than people who live alone. In the US and the Netherlands, the differences have even grown in the post-war decades. As to marriages in specific, recent analyses demonstrate that the strong association between marriage and well-being is not primarily due to social selection processes - i.e. individuals with particular characteristics are more prone to marry - but rather to the protective effect of the relationship on individuals (Gove et al., 2000; Kim & McKenry, 2002). According to Gove et al. (2000) the strong association between marital relations and general happiness is caused by the intimate and expressive characteristics of a relationship rather than by the instrumental ones.

This brings us back to the aforementioned qualitative nature of the second demographic transition. Lesthaeghe (1999) identifies the *quality of dyadic relations* as an important motivation underlying this transition. "Quality" can be defined as characteristics of an object that are valued by the user (Lesthaeghe, 1993). Since it is an essential feature of a relationship that not one but two users are involved, its quality evaluation depends on the fulfillment of both partners' desires. The belief that recent family changes are motivated by relationship quality may be derived from the fact that the early rise of divorce was borne by the baby boom generation, being socialized in the conviction that marriage is a lifelong commitment "for better or for worse" (Lesthaeghe, 1999).

In conclusion, relationships in general and marriages in specific still fulfill vital functions, contributing to individuals' general well-being. More than ever, the expressive side of the marital picture came to the fore. Therefore, the foundations of social worry regarding marital and family life seem to be dictated by the loss of traditional institutions and habits, rather than by the validity of claiming moral deterioration or decline. This argument will be further elaborated in the next section.

1.2. THEORETICAL ISSUES

As indicated above, the modernization of society is characterized by many interdependent processes such as industrialization, specialization, urbanization and geographic mobility. These structural processes also have a cultural pendant of secularization and growing individualization, mirroring a transition from tradition- and religion-based values towards an emphasis on personal autonomy and individual preference (Halman & Ester, 1995). In this respect, it is often mistakenly assumed that individualization equals egoism. In contrast, though, individualization refers to the process in which traditional meaning-delivering systems diminish in importance. Hence, this concept needs to be distinguished from individualism as individual autonomy in decision making. However, the loss of social prescriptions along with the broad pattern of options that has become available for individuals in different areas of life has created both risks and opportunities for the marital relationship. Theoretical thinking about these risks and opportunities will be described below in function of the consequences for the intimate and marital sphere. The discussion elucidates that alongside new living forms and options, 'traditional' marriage is also in motion.

1.2.1. The Homo Optionis: Choice, Risk and Partnership

In the *standard biography* of the 50s, sexuality, reproduction, partnership and marriage were inextricably bound up with each other (Giddens, 1992). Everyone traveled along the same roads of intimate life, guided by clear and externally controlled expectations (Beck & Beck-Gernsheim, 1995). This standard biography has now been replaced by a *choice biography* (Wouters, 1985). Few aspects of individual action follow a socially preordained path. Whether one marries or not and how one shapes his/her intimate relationships have largely become matters of choice. In this respect, partners' mental horizons are broadened. This is not to say that individuals cannot make decisions based on traditional norms and prescriptions. They can. The difference is that this decision is no longer obvious and that a plethora of options have become available: one can reproduce without sex or have sex without reproduction or partnership (Giddens, 1992). All these agreements depend on the partners legitimating them. As a result, personal life consists of an endless chain of decisions. The individual has actually become an actor.

The source for acting also increasingly becomes the individual and not a social collectivity. This idea is precisely the meaning of the concept individualization. Individualization does not refer to the content but to the source of meaning (Beck, 1992; Laermans, 1993; Lewis, 2001). Therefore, in an individualized society, individuals must learn to conceive themselves as the center of action, as the planning office of their own biography, relationships and so on (Beck, 1992, p. 135). Paradoxically, this freedom of action and choice also creates new constraints; everyone is now obliged to make and justify his or her choices. In this way, there is now a 'new' social pressure for self-constraint (Beck, 1992; Lammertyn, 1998).

The image of the 'active actor' also applies to partners choosing a life-long marital commitment. Marital partners are confronted with multiple options and choices that direct them to one or another outcome at a particular point in time. Because one can walk along non-institutionalized and therefore various roads, choices and decisions are potentially insecure and uncertain. By analogy with Beck's (1992) *Risk Society*, the choice biography is essentially a *risk biography*. This risk culture implies that individuals (are forced to) reflexively organize and 'calculate' the pros and cons of their (future) actions. For example, some individuals may decide not to marry because of their awareness of high divorce rates or the experience of their parents' divorce; whereas others can choose to enter the institution with the idea that leaving it is much easier than half a century ago.

The choice to marry, however, enrolls individuals in a changed 'traditional' institution that is now part of a risk society. The inside character of marriage is changed and its meaning is evolved because marriage no longer *establishes* a couple (Mills, 2000). To marry has become an individual and risky decision today. The reasons are well known. First of all, the stability of marriage is not as externally controlled as five decades ago (Giddens & Pierson, 1998). Society has created ways of leaving this institution. Even the presence of children does no longer strongly cement the marital system. Second, it seems that relationships in general and marital relationships in particular need to prove their value *hic et nunc*. Duration depends on the energy invested by the partners. In this way, breaking up a relationship is a 'forced' or 'obliged' choice. Those who do not succeed in developing a successful relationship are now held responsible for this outcome. What is more, they have to justify their pursuit of a less successful arrangement, since other choices and options are possible. This results in new social mechanisms coming to the fore. Apparently, cohabitators now upgrade their partnership at the expense of marriage. Since they engage in a 'non-institutionalized' partnership, they feel the need to choose more consciously for their partner.

The social fact that relationships cannot be taken for granted implies that they have to be continually made explicit and actively maintained from within (van der Avort, 1987). This is what Giddens (1992) defines as the *pure relationship*. This type of relationship is not socially anchored to kinship networks or tradition, but reflexively organized by the couple itself. Key sustaining dynamics are mutual intimacy, open communication and the appreciation of each other's unique qualities (Giddens, 1992; Jamieson, 1999). In essence, the pure relationship is a democratic system because it is supposed to be a reciprocal and open relationship between equals who are freed from the ballast of rigid expectations (Giddens, 1992).

However, the strong emphasis on individual's responsibility in Beck's and Giddens's view, might obscure the social construction of risks that continue to exist. Therefore, intimacy and relational satisfaction are still social products. Beyond the uniqueness of each relationship, the evaluations and emotional states associated with private life have their roots in social definitions and meanings. The social, economic and cultural contexts in which partners act, outline the options that are recognized and the choices that are made (Allan, 1993). Therefore, developing satisfactory relationships involves knowledge of appropriate relationship models. This is not to say that socially agreed scripts regarding relationships are overly specified and deterministic, rather it points towards the social boundaries in which partners can 'freely' act and make 'risky' decisions.

According to Comaille (1998) the persisting existence of social boundaries results in a contradictory situation. Even though current private constellation can be seen as liberation from traditional constraints, individuals have an unequal access to new private arrangements. Due to unequal personal resources (social class, age or gender), individuals are differently exposed to risks. Risks are not democratic but inscribed in social hierarchy and power relationships. We do not take decisions and choices in a social vacuum but need to bear for example, working conditions or policy decisions in mind, when making our own biographies. This points to the close tie between private life and structural factors outside our reach. Hence, we are faced with difficulties and risks that we can hardly deal with.

Especially less advantaged groups in our society are proportionally more affected by cumulative risks fostered by this new climate (Mills, 2000).

1.2.2. Emotionality, Identity, Stability and Vulnerability

As a consequence of increased individual freedom of choice and due to the self-produced biography, it is sometimes asserted that the meaning of existence has been lost. People experience a loss of inner stability because identities are less pre-given and many reference frames have become candidates in providing meaning and offering a personal anchoring place (Beck & Beck-Gernsheim, 1995). Individuals should have lost their well-steering vehicle to find their place in a complex and socially wider environment.

Things were different in pre-industrial societies, providing individuals with a consistent view of life and a stable self-definition. Personal identity was tied up to the roles and specific functions of individuals (Pattyn & Van Liedekerke, 2001). In the transition to a more complex and mobile society, however, individuals have become more self-reliant and independent. This freeing of the individual implies that one has to develop his/her own personal identity. Thus not roles and functions of an individual but the human behind them are central (Pattyn & Van Liedekerke, 2001). The social identity is replaced by a self-identity.

It appears that the private sphere represents an important area for individuals to seek psychological stability and to develop their self-identity (Giddens, 1992; Gove et al., 2000). Beck & Beck-Gernsheim (1995) identify this historically new identity as *person-related stability*. This term refers to the fact that our emotional and mental stability has become increasingly dependent on the close support and love of others. To the degree that traditional anchor points are disappearing 'the other' increasingly represents a reference point to give meaning to our lives.

Against this background, marriage plays a crucial part in what Berger and Kellner (1964) already described in the 60s as *nomos*-building, referring to the process through which individuals construct a meaningful and consistent reality. In this process each partner's definitions and interpretations of reality must be continually correlated with the other partner's. Berger and Kellner (1964, p. 64) state that "this process [...] is ideal-typically one in which reality is crystallized, narrowed and stabilized. Ambivalences are converted into certainties. Typifications of self and of others become settled." To put it simply, through continuous and intense dialogue with the other, men and women build up their own subworld with shared expectations, beliefs, habits and experiences. Therefore, the development of close relationships increasingly relies upon the internalization of another persons' view of the world. By lack of external standards and outside authorities, partners' selves are increasingly defined and (re)created by internal standards This creation of an intimate *nomos* world facilitates the quest for finding one's self.

The statement coined by Berger and Kellner (1964), has been critisized, however, for ignoring the issue of power in intimate relationships and for neglecting the tension between identity and stability (Askham, 1976; Ferree, 1990). With respect to the former, it must be stressed that marital business is not symmetrical but rather asymmetrical. Therefore, Berger and Kellner have overemphasized the autonomy that men and women have in creating their self-identity within marriage. Whereas the authors might be correct in their understanding of marriage as an ongoing-process and open dialogue, they ignore the fact that not everything needs to be discussed in a relationship (Askham, 1976). Although the search for identity might require open communication, the search for stability might require the reverse, i.e. not every preference is articulated and some conversations are avoided. Hence, the tension between identity and stability - i.e. between the creation of a sense of self and the importance of continuation of the relationship - substantially pervades the marital dialogue (Lewis, 2001).

It is precisely this tension that touches the fragility of current partnership. Societies with a strong hierarchical structure leave little room for this kind of dialogue and for the freeing of individuals' emotional households. Actually, love and emotions are a threat to social hierarchy (Borscheid, 1986; Shorter, 1975). That is the reason why economic considerations and property concerns, which primarily regulated marriages in a more traditional society, provided more stability for marriage than love, which is intrinsically unstable. Love is a risk.

The love between men and women is prone to failure. Therefore, marriage became a risky business (Beck & Beck-Gernsheim, 1995). This is not to say that husbands and wives attach less importance to intimate relationships or that they are less committed (Beck & Beck-Gernsheim, 1995).

On the contrary, expectations are high; often so high that it surpasses the capabilities of the other partner. Thus, it is not the lack of consideration of the partners but rather the high standards set on living together that might explain current vulnerability in the intimate sphere (Jacobs, 2000). Because relationships are justified by their bilateral and emotional character, it is legitimate that they are also broken up when the emotional basis becomes weaker (Latten, 2004). "People marry for the sake of love and they get divorced for the sake of love" (Beck & Beck-Gernsheim, 1995, p. 11).

1.3. GENDER ISSUES

In the previous sections it became clear that traditional cementing blocks are eroding to the advantage of individual experimentation. Because marriages are less externally controlled, they are increasingly established from within. Therefore, the question arises how the main figures, i.e. husbands and wives themselves, experience their intimate life and the changes it underwent. If they have distinct perceptions of their marital relationship and use different criteria to evaluate it, then marital satisfaction is not only a social product but also a gender-specific product.

1.3.1. Who Gets the Best Deal?

About thirty years ago, Bernard (1972) speculated that there are two marriages, *his* and *her* marriage, with his marital experiences more positive than hers. According to the author, the statistical basis for the argument that marriage is more beneficial for men than for women is convincing. Support might be found in the lower rates of mental illness of married men (see also Gove et al., 2000) and the higher scores of depression and anxiety reported by married women (see also Dempsey, 2002). Bernard (2002) demonstrates that these differences are related to the marital status of husbands and wives and thus not are merely sex differences.

Besides these health problems, women also report more marital problems, more negative marital feelings and less positive companionship (Bernard, 2002). This may be why women are less likely to remarry than men (Walker, 1999). Moreover, research on divorce motives illustrates that

women blame their partners more often for the breakdown of their marriage than vice versa (Matthijs, 1986).

Hence, there are indications that marriage is more advantageous for
men than for women. An interesting study in this respect is that of
Dempsey (2002). Husbands and wives were interviewed about their view
on who gets the best deal from marriage. About three-quarters of the
women and almost one out of two men reported that men got the best deal
whereas only a minority of the respondents asserted that women were
better off than men. Table 1.5 presents the different arguments formulated
by men and women in support of their opinion. From this list it becomes
clear that both husbands' and wives' arguments revolve around men's burden of being the main financial provider and women's burden of permanently delivering both emotional and household services.

Table 1.5
Arguments Formulated by Husbands and Wives on Who Gets the Best Deal from Marriage

Men get the best deal	Women get the best deal
Women's explanations	**Women's explanations**
Women's double burden: paid and unpaid work	Men serve as main economic provider
Women are expected to be always available	Women have opportunity to raise children
Men are looked after more than women	
Men are free from emotional and physical homework	
Men have more freedom	
Men's explanations	**Men's explanations**
Women's responsibilities at home never stop	Women are more in need of support
Mothering activity	Women are economically dependent on men
Men have more autonomy	

The contrast between the emotional labor of women and that of men (see §
1.3.2) also became clear in Rubin's (1983) study *Intimate Strangers*. In this
study, Rubin (1983) vividly illustrates how men's rational instead of emotional expressions takes its toll in intimate relationships. Women complain
that their partners give too little emotional support and hardly, if ever, talk
about their personal emotional experiences. The connotation of men and
women as *intimate strangers* is derived from the conclusion that the sexes
have incompatible goals in marriage with women seeking for an empathetic
partner more than men, and with men non-disclosing as a central part of
their masculine identity.

Women's emotional complaints are socially significant because emotional factors play an essential part in spousal marital quality and stability
with little or no constraints to stay in a less successful marriage. Therefore,
women have become important social actors as to marital instability. Actually, the exploding divorce phenomenon has largely been driven by women.
Women seem to initiate a divorce more often than men and they are also
more deliberate in their decision (Matthijs, 1986). Beck & Beck-Gernsheim
(1995, p. 62) put it this way, "If they were disappointed, women used to
give up their hopes; nowadays they cling to their hopes and abandon their
marriage".

1.3.2. The Gender Division of Emotion

The structural position of men and women seems to be at the heart of the
explanation why women are more dissatisfied with marriage than men.
About half a century ago, the position of men was strongly tied up to a specific role repertoire, which sociologists refer to as instrumental roles. Men
were expected to provide the means and instruments to develop and maintain the family. A side effect of this position was that men not only brought
in money but also derived their social status and that of their family from
this external position (Dumon, 1977).

This strongly contrasts with the expressive roles traditionally associated with the female position. Women were considered to be responsible
for caring, loving and parental tasks in the private sphere. The fact that
women were the main suppliers of affection and emotion is sometimes
referred to as the *emotional division of labor* (Duncombe & Marsden, 1993;

1995). At present, however, the gender divisions in emotional and in domestic labor continue to exist (Duncombe & Marsden, 1993; 1995). Women still take the burden of household and childrearing to their account (Glorieux & Vandeweyer, 2002; Van Praag & Niphuis-Nell, 1997); they still supply more emotional care than they obtain and are the family member par excellence to whom other members vent their feelings (Duncombe & Marsden, 1993).

In reaction to this gender bias, there is a cry for 'new men' and 'new fathers'. These new male humans are now socially allowed to carry out formerly female tasks, domestic as well as expressive ones. It is striking, however, that the scientific, and in Belgium and the Netherlands also public discourse[5], is mainly concerned with husbands' domestic labor and to a lesser degree with their emotional labor in relationships. This might support Duncombe and Marsden's (1995) assertion that the gendered emotional labor is the *last frontier of gender inequality.*

Emotional asymmetry apparently accounts for the fact that in marital and divorce literature, women's marital complaints concentrate primarily on affective factors such as poor communication and lack of attention, while instrumental factors such as disagreement about household labor is less frequently mentioned (Amato & Rogers, 1997, Dempsey, 2002; Matthijs, 1986). The study of Duncombe and Marsden (1993) on longer-term relationships illustrates the argument of asymmetry and marital misunderstandings. In their interviews with 60 married or cohabiting couples, a woman affirmed that, "It is not that you necessarily want them to do the housework; it is that you want them to understand that you do it" (Duncombe & Marsden, 1993, p. 227). The pervasiveness of emotional asymmetry also becomes clear in the following citation of a male respondent "Sometimes it is easier to help more in domestic work and childcare than it is to change the tone and character of our emotional and sexual relationships" (Duncombe & Marsden, 1993, p. 232).

---

[5] In Belgium a large public discourse on the 'new man' was held as a result of Glorieux's study on the division of labor within the family. Popular magazines paid a lot of attention to the research findings and Mieke Vogels, the former Flemish Minister qualified for family affairs opened up a public forum on the internet as a result of the study. In the Dutch campaign "Who does what?" emphasis is also primarily put on household rather than on childrearing tasks.

Historical family research explains the gender-specific division in emotional labor as the outcome of the interplay between biology and social institutions. The emotional division of labor is socially channeled and its roots date back to the 19th century. According to Matthijs (2003), the accentuation of the affective and expressive functions of the family and the dyadic power of women became possible through women's economical exclusion in the 19th century. Women's marginalization in public life evoked a counter reaction by developing a separate female identity in the domestic sphere. Women developed a range of skills to recognize and meet the emotional needs of family members (Matthijs, 2003). They became the relational specialists. Over time, the persistence of the gender-specific arrangement led to the social reproduction of two different emotional cultures, one for men and another for women.

In this way, the historical explanation of emotional asymmetry goes further than explanations merely focusing on socialization, such as Chodorow's (1978) theory, which stresses the different separational experiences of men and women in earlier childhood. For the current discussion, the historical explanation is important because it cautions us to conclude that women's incorporation of emotional themes in their discourse occurs because women *are* relational (Fisher, 2000). Since women were excluded from the privileges of men, through which the latter confirm their identity and status, they looked for their own identity and validation in close relationships. That may also explain why men assert that they show their love in an instrumental way through shared physical activity and being a good provider (Rubin, 1983). Ignoring the social steering of this discourse, risks assessing men by feminine criteria, and hence overemphasizing emotion to the expense of instrumentality (Cancian, 1989). Men just like women are social products and changing men will imply changing broader social and economic structures (Segal, 1990).

This situation might change to the extent that women gain more equality through paid work and its consequences cannot be foreseen at the moment. Some assert that we move towards an androgynous individual adopting both feminine and masculine qualities (Vannoy-Hiller & Philliber, 1989). This would imply that it is socially accepted that men become more feminine, as advocated in the 'new man' discourse, but also that women become more masculine. It is striking to note, however, that the existent discourse on the 'new woman' is less strongly pronounced given the fact that her role in the public sphere is socially increasingly approved.

Perhaps the break-through of the masculine/feminine transfer in stereotypical qualities is made difficult because of the loss of power that might be associated with it. The socially managed suppression of men showing their emotional needs openly represents a source of male power. Reversely, women can derive power from holding back their emotional services for men, indicating that not only economic sources but also emotional sources function as power mechanisms (Lewis, 2001). The latter is especially apparent in divorce motives. Women seem to be prepared to leave a marriage for emotional reasons. Therefore, the ability to fulfill the other partner's emotional needs and desires might have become a significant resource in current partnership.

The reason why women's ability to exert emotional power over their men remains limited, is due to the social steering of both men's suppression of their emotional needs and women's reserve to withhold emotional services for men (Duncombe & Marsden, 1995). Both are at the core of the stereotypical masculine and feminine identity. Precisely this stereotypical identity does not seem to fit very well in a social environment emphasizing emotional communication in partnership. The difficulties men might have with this behavior may emerge as a significant source of private trouble, underlying the statistics of rising divorce rates. In the near future, it seems that sustaining partnerships will increasingly demand the emotional labor of *both* partners. Or to voice Vansteenwegen (1988), "Love is a Verb".

1.3.3. The Gendered Impact of Children

Spousal marital experiences can also be illustrated by means of the role and impact of children. Notwithstanding the social fact that motherhood is a central feature of the traditional feminine identity, having children is no longer obvious and subjected to personal legitimation (Knijn, 1997). Because of the increasing spectrum of options available in one's personal life, motherhood has to compete with other roles such as women's labor market participation. Women are now forced to make choices within both realms. This choice is not evident, all the more because the meaning of having children underwent qualitative changes. In pre-industrial society, children contributed to the economical well-being of the family, whereas the exact opposite is the case in post-industrial society (Beck & Beck-Gernsheim, 1995). Children are no longer the *raison d' être* of marriage. Today, their rewarding aspect rather needs to be sought in their psychological and emotional (added) value (Knijn, 1997). This is reminiscent of the nature of current partnership as well. For both parenthood and partnership, economical motives are decreasing or disappearing and are replaced by the emotional needs of the parties involved. In this way, children may become a threat to partnership unless they can make significant contributions to the emotional well-being or self-actualization of husbands and wives (Mills, 2000).

Children may also serve as an important anchor point. Whereas other close relationships have become increasingly arbitrary and revocable bounds, the parent-child bond is non-interchangeable and permanent, not including the risk of being abandoned (Beck & Beck-Gernsheim, 1995). Parenthood cannot fail in the same way as love relations can. At least it would be considered deviant if it does. The different social and personal meaning attached to parenthood and partnership also becomes clear in the fact that marriage is increasingly chosen as a living form with the orientation on the child and not primarily on the partnership (Tyrell & Schulze, 1997).

This does not imply that children are beneficial for marital well-being. In contrast, parents seem to report lower marital satisfaction than non-parents and the decrease in parents' marital satisfaction often coincide with the transition to parenthood (Hooghiemstra, 1997; Twenge, Campbell & Foster, 2003). This might be due, among other things, to the reorganization of roles, the restriction of freedom clashing with one's personal development, or the expensiveness of having children. Besides, the high hopes individuals set on raising children, makes childrearing a difficult and complex task. Not only the demands placed on our intimate partners and on ourselves have risen, but so did the standards of raising children, turning parenthood into a tough psychological job (Hooghiemstra, 1997). This saddles individuals up with the difficult task of how to combine the objectives of 'wanting the best for my child', 'being a good partner' and 'living a life of my own'.

Women in particular are confronted with this dilemma and its effects, as they are still the main figures in rearing children. Moreover, in the Netherlands a strong belief in the importance of the 'always-available' mother still exists (Knijn, 1997). Along with the fact that mothers are also important relational gatekeepers, marriage and motherhood have increasingly become a balancing act for women. Indeed, the more energy poured in by one family member, the less energy is left for the other (Beck & Beck-Gernsheim, 1995). Despite the fact that fathers hardly sacrifice labor time for raising their children, they also increasingly attach importance to an emotional-affective relationship with their children (Knijn, 1997). Society even expects them to do this.

1.4. CONCLUSION

The above discussion of social forces driving the everyday marital reality of couples unequivocally demonstrates the social relevance of our study object. Particularly, two mutual reinforcing forces meet each other within marriage. Marital partners do not only want to get more out of a relationship than fifty years ago, they are also embedded in a social climate simplifying the possibilities to leave a marriage not fulfilling their needs. The vanguard of these transformations in partnership was the baby boom generation, born between 1940 and 1955. They grew up with a relational scheme built around the complementary public and private roles of men and women. Sex role expectations were clearly delineated and individuals' identity was nourished by or even reduced to the roles one was expected to play.

Due to broad structural and cultural transformations, described in this first chapter, this clear-cut social reality has been undermined, broadening the package of options available to husbands and wives in working out their life trajectory. As a consequence, contemporary couples are now faced with new marital realities barely known half a century ago and for which they have no established models at their disposal. This may account for the difficulty of developing marriages that satisfy the needs and desires of both partners.

Four factors attract our attention in this discussion, representing a lead of departure for the present research. First, the erosion of 'tradition' resulted in changes with respect to *gender practices* and *values*. Because both relate to an upgrading of women's social position, they may represent a potential source of marital problems. This chapter, however, also demonstrates that the *economic* position of Dutch women remains limited due to prevailing part-time labor. Related to the erosion of tradition, is the weakening impact of individuals' sex role position in building a personal identity. As husbands' and wives' *identity* is no longer exclusively based on the performance of expressive and instrumental roles, it can be supposed for the same reason as with respect to gender role behavior and attitudes, that the endorsement of a non-stereotypical identity may be a potential source of marital stress.

A second striking element is the paramount role of *communication*. Since marital relationships are increasingly maintained by the partners themselves, marital communication lies at the heart of partnerships. Its significance also becomes clear in couples' divorce motives and marital narratives. These learn that communicational problems are an important stumbling block in maintaining marital relationships. More specifically, marriages seem to be taxed by a gender-specific communication style accounting for wives more negative evaluations of their relationship.

Third, its significance notwithstanding, *parenthood* is no longer an intrinsic need in marital relationships but rather an option among many others. In this way, the presence of children may even be a threat to the relationship because other options must be given up. Because women are still held responsible for taking primary care of children, they may feel more hindered in exploiting other opportunities offering themselves, than men. These gender-specific parental experiences may put marital relationships under pressure.

A fourth noteworthy factor characterizing the transformations in partnerships is the structural inequalities that continue to exist. Not everyone acts on the basis of the same relational model. Individuals have even 'unequal' access to new relational schemata put forward by some authors. Therefore, marital satisfaction may not only be a gender-specific but also a class-specific phenomenon.

These four concerns ensuing from the social discussion introduced in this first chapter steer the present study on marital satisfaction and its underlying processes. In the following chapter, the theoretical and methodological background from this study is elaborated and the research questions are specified.

2. Towards a Research Design for Marital Satisfaction

The present research consists of six different studies examining the determinants and underlying processes of husbands and wives' satisfaction with marriage. In the first section of this chapter a general theoretical framework covering the complete set of studies is introduced. This framework, along with the themes introduced in the previous chapter, leads to the specification of six major questions. These research questions are presented in the second section. The third section gives an overview of the structure of the different studies.

2.1. IMPETUS OF THE STUDY

Research on the factors that contribute to marital satisfaction is prolific and dispersed among various disciplines. To organize this myriad of determinants, several authors have attempted to develop comprehensive classification schemes. These efforts proved to result in the distinction of three groups of determinants: (a) individual factors, (b) social and economic factors, and (c) dyadic factors (Holman, 2001; Lewis and Spanier, 1979).

Such classification runs parallel to the levels of analysis as distinguished in an ecological thinking on marriage (Bubolz & Sontag, 1993). In his social ecology model of marriage, Huston (2000) considers three levels of analysis: (a) the individuals characterized by their own physical, psychological and cultural attributes or resources, (b) the marital relationship as a behavioral system embedded within a larger network of relationships and (c) the social context in terms of macro-social forces but also in terms of smaller ecological niches in which individuals and couples function (e.g. neighborhood). The latter is already extensively dealt with in the first chapter. The two other levels are addressed throughout the present research. As can be seen in Figure 2.1 all three levels mutually influence each other and operate in complex and interdependent ways.

As indicated above, the central aim of the present study is to examine the degree to which these individual, contextual (i.e. approximate context) and dyadic factors account for variation in spousal marital experiences. Because this objective covers a broad research agenda, a particular set of factors or topics need to be selected. This selection is primarily made on the ground that the topics must significantly concern the everyday life of married couples and thus being consequential for spousal marital experiences. In the social definition of our research problem, as described in Chapter 1, four themes were put forward as stumbling blocks in developing intimate relations in general and a marital relationship in particular: (a) spousal social position and cultural orientations, (b) communication, (c) gender attitudes, identity and behavior, and (d) parental experiences. These themes lay the foundation of our specific research questions, addressed below.

Figure 2.1
A Three-Level Model for Viewing Marriage

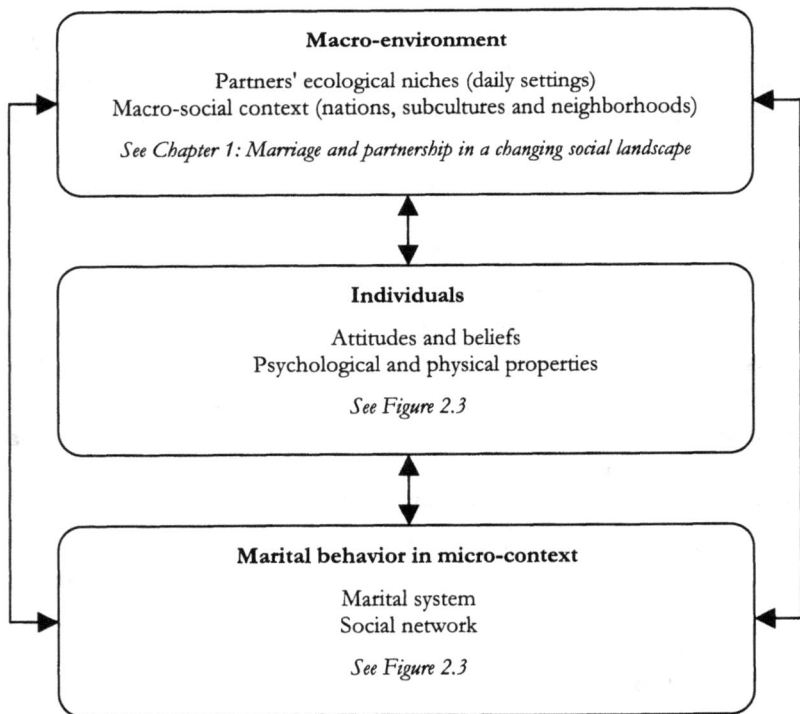

Macro-environment

Partners' ecological niches (daily settings)
Macro-social context (nations, subcultures and neighborhoods)

See Chapter 1: Marriage and partnership in a changing social landscape

Individuals

Attitudes and beliefs
Psychological and physical properties

See Figure 2.3

Marital behavior in micro-context

Marital system
Social network

See Figure 2.3

Beyond the integration of issues that are assumed to significantly affect people's marital experiences, a secondary goal of this study is to make methodological as well as theoretical contributions to current marital scholarship. The proceeding of this aim involves two steps. First, the separate narratives as regards the above selected topics must be subsumed under a new overarching theory that should enable us to develop new hypotheses about the interrelationships between the distinct groups of determinants. A theory that is qualified for meeting this requirement is the Vulnerability-Stress-Adaptation model of marriage, hereafter referred to as the VSA-model. Second, gaining insight into husbands' and wives' marital satisfaction involves, among other things, a methodological approach that can model the dyadic dependency of husbands and wives. In the remainder of this section both issues are addressed.

2.1.1. The Vulnerability-Stress-Adaptation Model of Marriage

The VSA-model of marriage is a theoretical framework that became prominent in recent thinking on marital relationships. To develop this model, the authors reviewed 115 longitudinal studies of marriage in combination with four major theoretical perspectives used to explain marital quality and stability: (a) social exchange theory, (b) behavioral theory, (c) crisis theory, and (d) attachment theory.

These four theories were evaluated in terms of three distinct criteria. First, it is questioned to what degree the theory encompasses a full set of predictors for marital outcomes and whether it provides links between different levels of analysis. Second, the theories are evaluated on their capacity to specify mechanisms of change within marriage. By stressing this feature, the authors attach great importance to *explain* how marriages accomplish different outcomes, rather than limiting oneself to *predict* why they succeed or fail. Third, it is required that the theory accounts for variability in marital outcomes, between couples as well as within couples over time.

Table 2.1

Evaluation of Theoretical Perspectives on Marriage

Criterion	Social exchange theory	Behavioral theory	Attachment theory	Crisis theory
Link micro-macro?	Barriers such as social norms may be macro whereas attractions such as interaction may be micro.	Main focus is on interaction between spouses.	Focus is on the link between childhood and adult relationships.	Links external life events to adaptation within marriage.
Mechanism for change?	Not clear how couples may change over time	Each interaction affects global marital evaluations, which in turn affect subsequent interactions.	Not clear how couples may change over time	Resources and adaptation may change in response to life events.
Within and between couple variation?	No within variation but addresses how some couples may be unhappy but stable and others happy but unstable.	Within-variation in one direction but no between-variation	No within- and between- variation	Partners with inadequate coping resources will dissolve when crises occur but may endure until then.

Source: Karney & Bradbury, 1995

Table 2.1 summarizes the results of their critical analysis, showing that no theoretical perspective satisfies all criteria. A more in-depth discussion of the similarities and differences between the distinguished theories is addressed in Karney and Bradbury (1995). Based on this theoretical analysis, the authors integrated the distinct strengths of the theoretical perspectives along with the results of their meta-analysis into a new framework, the VSA-model (see Figure 2.2). The model claims that "couples with effective adaptive processes who encounter relatively few stressful events and have few enduring vulnerabilities will experience a satisfying and stable marriage, whereas couples with ineffective adaptive processes who must cope with many stressful events and have many enduring vulnerabilities will experience declining marital quality, separation or divorce" (Karney & Bradbury, 1995, p. 25). In the following the different relationships, as visualized in Figure 2.2, will be explained in greater detail to show the integrative nature of this framework

The authors define a reciprocal relationship between the ongoing processes of adaptation within marriage and the marital satisfaction experienced by the spouses. The concept of adaptation or adaptive processes is defined as the ways individuals and couples contend with differences of opinion, with individual and marital difficulties and transitions (Bradbury, 1995). It refers to how spouses regulate and manage (non) marital events (Bradbury, Cohan & Karney, 1998). Thus, adaptation primarily concerns the positive and negative marital interaction styles but may also point, for example, towards the capacity to provide social support. So far, however, marital researchers paid an almost exclusive attention to the effect of interaction on marital satisfaction, leaving open the possibility that the strength of the effect from satisfaction on interaction might be stronger than the opposite effect.

The degree to which spouses adapt depends on the stressful life events they encounter. Stressful life events refer to the developmental transitions, situations, incidents, and chronic or acute circumstances that impinge on a couple's relationship and create tension or stress (Bradbury, 1995). Among others, examples are health problems, unemployment and concerns over raising children. The attention paid to this component highlights how circumstances external to the couple affect the longitudinal course of marriage by means of spouses' adaptive processes. In line with crisis theory, it is also presumed that adaptive processes may determine the stressful experiences spouses encounter. Indeed, unsuccessful recovery may provide a context for stressful events to continue or even exacerbate.

Partners' adaptive capacity is not only related to the stressful events they encounter but also to the enduring vulnerabilities that each spouse brings into marriage. Bradbury (1995, p. 461) defines vulnerabilities as "stable demographic, historical, personality and experiential factors that individuals bring to marriage", such as educational attainments and experiences in the family of origin. These characteristics are expected to be relatively stable and to 'set the stage' for marriage. In this way, they may contribute to stressful experiences encountered by the spouses and to their adaptive processes (Bradbury, Cohan & Karney, 1998). For example, some personality characteristics are associated with the arousal of stressful situations but may also cause individuals to experience events as more stressful (Karney & Bradbury, 1995). Finally, an effect of marital quality on marital stability is presupposed. Declining marital quality should result in higher marital instability[6].

Figure 2.2
The Vulnerability-Stress-Adaptation Model of Marriage

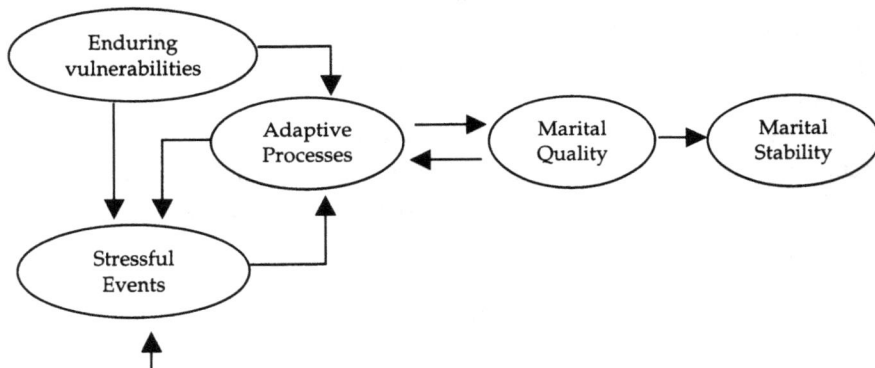

Because of the close integration of theory and empirical research, the model is amenable to empirical application. The VSA-model provides a framework to pose specific questions as regards marital satisfaction and to develop a more in-depth understanding of the processes underlying marital experiences. Hence, the model endows us with a conceptual toolkit to translate the selected topics in well-delineated research problems.

---

[6] Note, that despite this well-replicated finding, the effect is not strong (Karney & Bradbury, 1995). This might be due to social exchange assumptions, predicting that the path from quality to stability is likely to be influenced by the barriers to leave the relationship and by attractive alternatives outside the relationship. Hence, spousal alternatives must outweigh the barriers to stay in the relationship before one decides to leave an unhappy marriage.

2.1.2. From a Conceptual to a Methodological Toolkit

Before arriving at the specification of our research questions, it is necessary to take note of the methodological implications of the VSA-model as well as the sidetracks it leaves open.

First, the added value of the VSA-model must be sought in its dynamic character. Attention is shifting away from *predicting* marital satisfaction to *explain* the processes through which marriages arrive at different outcomes. By identifying adaptive processes as a key mechanism through which external events and individual characteristics impinge on the marital system, the model includes the opportunity to examine processes underlying marital satisfaction. However, it leaves open the possibility to examine whether different processes underlie the marital experiences of husbands and wives in different social contexts (see Figure 2.1). Beyond the consideration of communication as a mediating mechanism, the present study also endeavors to grasp the dynamic character of marriage by considering moderating social contexts.

Second, the VSA-model is conceived as an abstract model that is adaptable to the specific research context in which it is used. In the present study explicit attention will be paid to the applicability of the model as regards husbands and wives' marital experiences. The reason for this emphasis relates to the shortcomings that characterize current scholarship in this respect. For the most part, research looses sight of an in-depth consideration of gender in marriage. The latter can be thought on two distinct levels. For one, a specific variable may affect men and women's marital satisfaction differently and for another, men's variables may affect the marriage in a different way than are women's. However, because in the majority of research designs data were only gathered by one of the partners, studies fail to address these specific gender questions.

Moreover, to capture the complex and dynamic nature of partnerships, the evaluation of one spouse's marital experiences, should be controlled for the characteristics of the other partner. Indeed, a defining feature of relationship research is that measurements of one partner not solely refer to the individual him/herself but also to an interpersonal system. Hence, pooling men and women's information may mask interesting interpersonal aspects of marriage. Therefore, this study attempts to capture the sheer nature of marriage by including both partners' characteristics in the models to be tested and by evaluating the different marital experiences of husbands and wives.

2.2. RESEARCH QUESTIONS

Our central research objective is directed towards examining the degree to which contextual, individual and dyad characteristics influence spousal marital satisfaction. This objective is translated into six research questions. In the subsequent chapters of Part II, each research question is discussed in-depth and situated within the marital research field. The following section introduces the six major questions and their sub-questions.

Research question 1: How to measure marital satisfaction and communication in a valid and reliable way?

1a. *Does the Dutch Marital Satisfaction and Communication Questionnaire, measuring marital satisfaction, open communication and destructive communication, represent a three factor structure?*
1b. *Can this factor pattern be replicated in an independent sample?*
1c. *Is this factor pattern stable across time?*

Our first research question is addressed in Chapter 4 and is directed towards the measurement of our central object of interest. In response to both the controversial debate on the measurement of marital quality and the lack of attention paid to the measurement invariance of instruments, we examine the validity and stability of a Dutch instrument measuring (a) marital satisfaction, (b) negative communication and (c) open communication. This self-report instrument consisted initially of 24 items that were derived from the Marital Satisfaction and Stability Inventory and the Communication Inventory developed by Kerkstra (1985). The advantage of this instrument is that it covers the most frequently used indicators of marital quality, i.e. marital satisfaction and marital communication.

Using exploratory factor analysis, the factorial structure of the items is examined in a sample of Dutch husbands and wives. The reproducibility of the factor structure is explored in another independent sample by means of confirmatory factor analysis. To demonstrate the measurement invariance of the scales, the factor structure is examined in the first sample of couples participating in the same research project five years later. Both the internal consistency of the identified scales as well as their construct validity is demonstrated.

Research question 2: What is the long-term association between communication and marital satisfaction?

2a. To what degree is communication a predictor or an outcome of marital satisfaction?
2b. Is the direction of the relation between satisfaction and communication the same for both sexes?

Chapter 5 deals with the second research question, which relates to the importance of communication in shaping current partnership. The importance and difficulties of communication are inherently associated with new images of intimate relationships in terms of individual needs and egalitarianism. The significance of communication for marital well-being has been well established both at the theoretical and the empirical level. However, in the VSA-model of Karney and Bradbury (1995), a reciprocal relationship between marital satisfaction and communication is assumed. Thus far, the opposite relationship, i.e. the degree to which marital satisfaction affects communication has received less attention and therefore the reciprocity between marital satisfaction and communication remains elusive.

Moreover, the question arises to what extent this relationship might be sex-specific. Because marriage and marital communication are shaped by two individuals, each with a particular social position, the direction of the relation between marital satisfaction and communication may be different for husbands and wives. These questions will be examined with the help of cross-lagged panel analysis.

Research question 3: How and to what degree do economic and cultural indicators relate to marital satisfaction?

3a. To what degree do spousal economic resources affect marital satisfaction?

3b. To what degree does spousal cultural orientation affect marital satisfaction, controlling for economic indicators?

3c. Do spouses' cultural orientations moderate the effect of women's employment on marital satisfaction?

3d. Do changes in economic and cultural variables relate to changes in marital satisfaction?

The third research question relates to the economic and cultural factors involved in marital experiences. At the macro-level, both economic and cultural factors are used to understand contemporary partnership (see Chapter 1). The question now arises to what degree these factors are also important in understanding husbands and wives' marital satisfaction at the micro level. Therefore, both economic and cultural dimensions are included to predict current as well as subsequent marital satisfaction and to examine the degree to which cultural variables significantly add to a model already including economic characteristics.

Besides their relative importance, we are also interested in the interaction of economic and cultural variables. In the economic debate on marital quality and stability, cultural variables are often neglected, therefore it remains unclear to what extent the effect of women's labor market participation is moderated by the attitudes held by the spouses. These questions are addressed in Chapter 6. Hierarchical regression analysis is used to examine question 3a, 3b and 3c. The last question is studied using multiple regression analysis.

Research question 4: How do stereotypical feminine and masculine qualities relate to marital satisfaction?

4a. To what degree is one's gender role identity associated with marital satisfaction and do these associations differ for husbands and wives?

4b. To what degree does gender role identity affect marital satisfaction in relation to different social contexts?

Gender roles and gender role identities have become uncertain in our rapidly changing culture (see Chapter 1). Gender role identity is part of one's personality and refers to the extent to which one incorporates stereotypical feminine and/or masculine qualities into his or her self-concept. In this part of the study we are interested in the consequences of one's gender role identity for spousal satisfaction.

As a result of the increased emotionalisation of partnership it might be expected that feminine expressive qualities contribute more positively to marital satisfaction than masculine qualities. The question arises, however, whether this assumed association is equally strong for both sexes. Moreover, it remains unclear to what extent gender role identity, which is social in nature, yields different outcomes for husbands and wives in different social contexts. These contexts are indicated by marital stage, family income, spousal educational level and whether wives are employed or not. The results of the regression analyses are described in Chapter 7.

Research question 5: Are different gender characteristics consistently related to different marital outcomes?

5a. Are distinct gender-related characteristics consistently related to marital satisfaction and marital communication, and do these associations differ between husbands and wives?

5b. Do associations between gender and marriage differ for husbands and wives in higher or lower income groups?

In the previous research question, gender role identity was conceptualized as a self-definition, i.e. the incorporation of stereotypical feminine and/or masculine qualities into one's self-concept. Some argue that this is a too limited definition of someone's gender. Attitudes towards sex roles or role behavior such as performing household labor can also be considered as indications of one's gendered position in the social structure.

Moreover, the fourth research question limited marital outcomes to marital satisfaction whereas marital communication is a significant indicator as well. The latter is interesting because identity theorists presume that a feminine identity is associated with more positive communication behavior whereas a masculine identity implies dominant and negative behavior. In this study theoretical identity assumptions are extended to other gender characteristics than feminine and masculine qualities and to other marital outcomes than marital communication.

Because previous work only paid limited or no attention to the possibility that the complex relations between gender and marriage differ according to spouses' social position, it is additionally questioned if and how gender differently operates in different income groups. The elaboration and results of these research questions are discussed in Chapter 8.

Research question 6: If and how does parenting spill over to marital relationships?

6a. To what degree can negative communication be considered a spillover mechanism between parenting and marital satisfaction?

6b. To what degree do parents' resources and role demands affect their experiences of parenting?

6c. To what degree do parents' resources and role demands affect their experiences of marriage?

6d. To what degree can parenting be seen as a predictor or an outcome of marital satisfaction?

Drawing upon the VSA-model of Karney & Bradbury (1995) we finally examine the effects of parenting on spouses' marital experiences. As indicated in the first chapter, parents need to combine parenthood with other important objectives in life such as partnership and personal fulfillment. In Chapter 9 we examine the impact of parenting experiences on spouses' satisfaction with marriage. This relationship is addressed cross-sectionally as well as longitudinally. In the short-term analysis (cross-sectional) the aim is to predict marital satisfaction by husbands and wives' parenting experiences. More specifically, it is questioned to what degree negative communication functions as a spillover mechanism between parental experiences and spousal marital satisfaction. Three indicators of parenting will be considered: (1) parental satisfaction, (2) parental stress and (3) parental role restriction. By discerning three domains of parenting, it can be identified which aspects are an important source of marital (dis)satisfaction.

Because the experience of parenting as well as one's marriage may depend on available resources, we also assess which resources alleviate or aggravate husbands' and wives' parenting and marital experiences. The inclusion of mothers and fathers in the same analysis, allows for the assessment of the relative influence and sex-specificity of the distinct paths.

In addition to the short-term interrelationship between parenting and marital satisfaction, the long-term associations will also be considered. Including the distinct parental aspects in different cross-lagged models, this study examines whether parenting can be seen as a predictor or an outcome of marital satisfaction and whether this association is different for fathers and mothers.

2.3. STRUCTURE OF THIS STUDY

In the following, the exploration of the aforementioned topics is presented in individual chapters. The general outline of these chapters is visualized in Figure 2.3. Chapter 1 is also depicted in this Figure because it functions as a broad preamble to our study of marital satisfaction. It dealt with the (changing) social context in which husbands and wives develop their current relationships and in which spousal marital satisfaction crystallizes.

Packed with this social baggage, we turn in Chapter 4 to the measurement of our central study object. Using exploratory and confirmatory factor analysis, the factorial structure of marital satisfaction, open and negative communication is evaluated. Demonstrating the uniqueness of these concepts is a prerequisite for discussing the long-term relationship between marital communication and spousal marital satisfaction in Chapter 5.

As can be seen in Figure 2.3, the fourth chapter makes use of *dyadic analysis*. This term is used in the present study to specifically refer to analyses testing significant differences between husbands and wives belonging to the same dyad. Dyadic analysis needs to be distinguished from an analysis with *partner effects*. The latter is used to refer to analyses in which it is evaluated whether the characteristics of one partner affect the marital experiences of the other partner. This was for example the case in Chapter 6. This chapter examines whether spousal economic and cultural characteristics impact spousal marital satisfaction as well as the changes in satisfaction between 1990 and 1995. Specific attention is paid to the question whether cultural attitudes mitigate the effect of wives' employment on both husbands' and wives' marital satisfaction.

Figure 2.3
General Outline of This Study According to Topic and Method

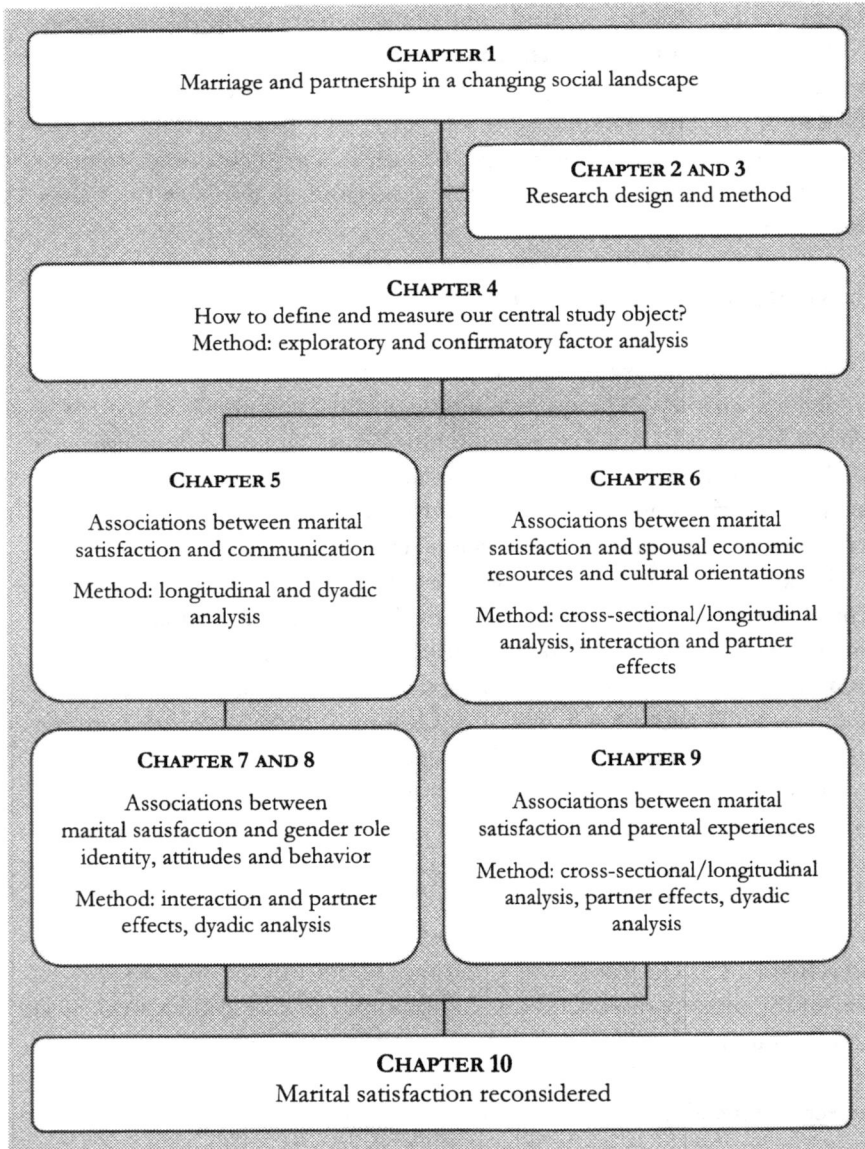

CHAPTER 1
Marriage and partnership in a changing social landscape

CHAPTER 2 AND 3
Research design and method

CHAPTER 4
How to define and measure our central study object?
Method: exploratory and confirmatory factor analysis

CHAPTER 5

Associations between marital satisfaction and communication

Method: longitudinal and dyadic analysis

CHAPTER 6

Associations between marital satisfaction and spousal economic resources and cultural orientations

Method: cross-sectional/longitudinal analysis, interaction and partner effects

CHAPTER 7 AND 8

Associations between marital satisfaction and gender role identity, attitudes and behavior

Method: interaction and partner effects, dyadic analysis

CHAPTER 9

Associations between marital satisfaction and parental experiences

Method: cross-sectional/longitudinal analysis, partner effects, dyadic analysis

CHAPTER 10
Marital satisfaction reconsidered

Chapter 7 and 8 cover the exploration of gender in relation to spousal marital experiences. The seventh chapter explores the significance of husbands and wives' self-definitions in terms of instrumental and expressive traits. More specifically, it is attempted to investigate how and to what extent this influence varies according to marital duration and social class. Because instrumental and expressive qualities are only a limited indication for understanding how gender operates in marriage, the analysis is extended in Chapter 8 with gender role attitudes and role behavior in terms of household and childrearing tasks. Both marital satisfaction and marital communication are considered as outcomes in this analysis. Couple's income position is used as an indicator for distinguishing between higher and lower social layers in order to examine whether these gender-related characteristics play a different part in different social strata when considering distinct marital outcomes. Chapter 7 and 8 both assess differences between husbands and wives as regards gender and marital outcomes, and include the characteristics of the partner in examining the other partner's marital outcomes.

In Chapter 9 the short-term and long-term spillover of parenting experiences on marital experiences is addressed. It is examined to what degree marital communication can be considered as a mediating mechanism by means of which the parental system affects the spousal system. Moreover, structural sources that may help couples to deal more effectively with the stress and strain associated with rearing (young) adolescents are considered. Because of the reciprocal nature of both the parental and the marital system, longitudinal analyses are additionally used to investigate whether three indicators of parenting, (a) parental satisfaction, (b) parental stress and (c) parental role restriction are antecedents or rather consequences of marital satisfaction.

To conclude, Chapter 10 summarizes the key findings of the present study and critically assesses the theoretical approaches and methods that were used. By bringing the different research findings together, our findings are interpreted in light of the discussion presented in Chapter 1.

Before presenting the results of the subsequent chapters, Chapter 3 firstly deals with the method of the present study. It discusses the longitudinal data that were used, the procedure of data gathering that was followed as well as the internal and external validation of the sample.

3. Method

The six major research questions described in Chapter 1 are addressed using secondary data. The option of using secondary data is inextricably linked with the financial advantages it offers. However, disadvantages of data gathered by other research teams such as operationalisation of concepts or the specific sample composition must also be taken into account. Therefore, the decision to make use of secondary data for the present study was the result of careful consideration of the drawbacks and the advantages offered by the available data. In the first and second section of this chapter the longitudinal dataset and the procedure of data gathering are described. Because only married couples are eligible for our research purpose, the third section discusses the selection of this sub-sample. Since non-response is a pervasive problem in longitudinal datasets, the fourth section evaluates the external and internal validation of the sample. However, besides non-response of respondents, item non-response might also pose difficulties. The fourth section therefore additionally addresses the procedure that was used to save cases with missing values.

3.1. DUTCH PANEL DATA

The present study makes use of cross-sectional and longitudinal data from the research project "Child-rearing and family in the Netherlands". This national survey was undertaken to examine Dutch familial and marital life (Gerris et al, 1992; 1993). The focus is upon subjective characteristics of primary relationships as actualized in parent-child and husband-wife interactions. Properties of the broader social environment are measured both in more objective as well as subjective terms. The central aim is to relate characteristics of the environment to the internal functioning of the family.

To select the families, a multi-stage sampling method was followed. In a first stage, a sample was taken of all Dutch municipalities distinguished by regional zone and degree of urbanization. Four regional zones were distinguished: (1) the North, comprising the provinces of Groningen, Friesland and Drenthe; (2) the East comprising the provinces of Overijssel, Flevoland and Gelderland; (3) the South comprising the provinces of Zeeland, Noord-Brabant and Limburg and (4) the West, comprising the provinces of Utrecht, Zuid-Holland and Noord-Holland.

To measure the degree of urbanization, the classification of the Centraal Bureau van de Statistiek was employed (Gerris et al, 1992). Category "A" refers to rural municipalities with 20-50% of the economically active population employed in the agrarian sector. Category "B" represents the urbanized rural municipalities with a maximum of 20.000 inhabitants, in which more than half of its active population works in the manufacturing industry. Also included in this category are the resident municipalities of commuters where 30% of the economically active population is commuter and where 60% of the resident male population (of at least 14 years old) has been born elsewhere. Categories "C1" to "C4" include country towns, small or medium sized, with a population of 20.000 up to 100.000 inhabitants in the urban center, containing urban institutions and services. The final category "C5" comprises large towns with over 100.000 inhabitants in the urban center. For a more extended description of this classification see Gerris et al. (1992).

The number of inhabitants in the specific combination of regional zone and degree of urbanization was divided by the sample fraction, indicating the number of families to select. The sample fraction equals the population divided by one thousand; for the Netherlands this is 14.804. For practical reasons it was decided to approach a minimum of 10 families in each selected city.

Families were selected on the basis of their target child. Therefore, in a second stage, a random sample of children was taken from the municipal registers in the selected municipalities. The target children were selected in such a way that in each city as many boys as girls and as many children aged 9 to 12 as aged 13 to 16 were selected. The parents were automatically selected via the target child. In most cases, the parents are the biological father and mother of the target child, but also stepparents and one-parent families were recruited. Twice as many families than ultimately intended were chosen. If the address of the child and the parents was not the same, for example because the child lived in an institution, the family was replaced by the next one on the list. The same principle was used when a family refused to participate. In total, 1829 families were selected for an interview.

Initially the interview time was calculated to be one and a half hour but finally turned out to be two hours and fifteen minutes. That might be the reason why more families than expected refused to participate in the study or failed to finish the interview. This increased the cost of the field-work, and therefore it was decided to eliminate part of the interview and decrease the number of families to be included. In the end, 788 families participated in the project, which is a response rate of 43 % (1.829/788). This ratio is comparable to the response rate in other panel studies such as the Panel Study of Belgian Households (PSBH) but indicates the difficulty of attracting families to participate in a longitudinal research project.

Families who refused to participate were asked for their reasons. The reasons are presented in Table 3.1. As can be seen, the majority of the non-participants reported not to be interested or having no time.

Table 3.1
Reasons Why Families Refused to Participate In the Research Project in 1990 and 1995

Reasons to refuse	Number of families in 1990	Number of families in 1995
Family was not interested or no time	761	72
Family was approached three times without success	79	10
Address is unknown or not correct	43	6
Respondent was died, ill or on holiday	32	7
The child was too young or too old for being eligible	22	0
Linguistic problem	76	1
Invasion of privacy	0	7
Couple was divorced or problems in the family	0	8
Prior research was too long ago	0	9
Otherwise	28	23
Total	1.041	143

Source: Gerris et al., 1992; 1998

However, despite the reduction in the number of families, the sample was representative regarding regional zone and degree of urbanization. In the upper line of Table 3.2, the number (left column) and percentages (right column) of families that had to participate to guarantee a representative sample are presented. The bottom line shows the number and percentages of families that actually participated.

Table 3.2
Number and Percentage of Families that Should Have Participated and that Actually Participated in the Research Project

	North		East		South		West		Total	
	N	%	N	%	N	%	N	%	N	%
A	25	3.2	21	2.7	17	2.1	27	3.4	90	11.4
	33	4.1	26	3.3	11	1.4	17	2.2	87	11.0
B	24	3.0	65	8.2	91	11.5	119	15.1	298	37.8
	15	1.9	64	8.1	101	12.8	132	16.8	312	39.6
C1-C4	27	3.4	44	5.6	55	7.0	86	10.9	212	26.9
	33	4.2	29	3.7	49	6.2	96	12.2	207	26.3
C5	9	1.2	30	3.8	32	4.0	118	15.0	188	23.9
	11	1.4	36	4.6	30	3.8	105	13.3	182	23.1
Total	84	10.7	160	20.3	194	24.6	350	44.4	788	100
	92	11.6	155	19.7	191	24.2	350	44.5	788	100

Source: Gerris et al., 1992

Of the 656 families who agreed in 1990 to participate in the second wave, 627 could be traced five years later. The other families had moved or were untraceable. 484 of the contacted families agreed to participate again (1356 of the 1881 contacted family members). This adds up to a response rate of 77% at the household level (Gerris et al., 1998). The reasons for refusal are presented in Table 3.1. As in the first wave, the most frequently reported argument is "no time" or "not interested".

This sample still proved to be representative for regional zone but not for degree of urbanization. It appeared that primarily participants from the bigger cities refused to participate for the second time in the research project.

3.2. PROCEDURE

The interviewers responsible for the collection of the data were selected on the basis of their experience with administering surveys. Instruction meetings were organized to extensively inform the interviewers about the project in general and specifically about the interview and the questionnaires. The fieldwork started in August 1990 and lasted until January 1991. The selected families received a letter in which the purpose of the study was explained (Gerris et al., 1992). Within three days after receiving this letter, the interviewer contacted the families and made an appointment with both parents and the target child.

Various kinds of data were gathered during the interview. Demographic information on the parents as well as on the family as a whole was asked to both parents together by means of structured interviews. Background information such as spousal age, age of the target child, marital duration, educational level, employment status and whether or not one's parents had been divorced were included in the demographic questionnaire.

Other variables regarding attitudes, family characteristics and personal properties were measured with questionnaires consisting of 7-point Likert scale items. Most of the scales range from "not at all applicable" to "completely applicable".

Both husband and wife had to fill in separately a questionnaire about parenting including among others, parental satisfaction, parental stress and feelings of restriction imposed by the parental role. They also filled in a questionnaire about characteristics of the marital relationship. Items measuring marital satisfaction, negative communication as well as open communication were included.

Socio-cultural orientations on diverse aspects such as gender roles, autonomy and work orientations, were measured by means of 5-point

Likert scales ranging from 1 = "very important" to 5 = "unimportant" or 1 = "totally agree" to 5 = "totally disagree". The questionnaires on cultural orientation were left with the family. The interviewer explained how to fill out these questionnaires and requested that the family members completed them separately. After sending these questionnaires back frank, the target child received a reward of 25 Dutch Guilders.

In the second wave of the research project, some additional measures were included. Of interest for the purpose of this study is the Personal Attributes Questionnaire measuring femininity and masculinity as well as a questionnaire on task allocation in the household.

Each of the aforementioned instruments and measures will be described in depth in the subsequent studies addressed in the following chapters.

3.3. SELECTION AND CHARACTERISTICS OF THE MARRIED SUB-SAMPLE

In order to examine married couples, a sub-sample from the Dutch dataset had to be selected. Because the original dataset also includes cohabitating and one-parent households, we removed these observations from the sample. The resulting sample of married couples, however, still included first and higher order marriages. Although their relational satisfaction may not be that different, previous studies have found that the marital processes and characteristics in first and higher order marriages may differ (Booth & Edwards, 1992). Therefore, only first marriages were selected. Because no question was directed to the issue of first and higher order marriages, we reconstructed the first married couples by using indicators about the number of times the child experienced divorce or death of (one of) the parents.

In the next step, ethnic mixed marriages were removed from the sample.[7] Hondius (2003) has shown that couples consisting of partners with a different ethnic background develop specific strategies to cope with their interpersonal differences and with the reactions from their environ-

---

[7] Because 96% of the fathers and 95% of the mothers reported to be born in the Netherlands, this selection criterion did not result in a strong reduction of the sample size.

ment (Hondius, 2003). Moreover, Dutch statistics demonstrate that marriages between autochthonous and allochthonous partners have the highest divorce risks (Janssen, 2003). In comparison to non-mixed marriages, couples in mixed marriages are more confronted with specific problems relating to differences in preferences and behavior and may therefore confound the results with respect to the factors that differentiate between more and less satisfied spouses.

In sum, first marriages consisting of husbands and wives with a Dutch nationality were eligible for the study. The selection procedure resulted in a research group of 646 couples in 1990 and 386 couples in 1995.

In 1990, the average age in our sample is 42.48 (SD = 4.88) years for husbands and 40.06 (SD = 4.17) for wives. About 90% of the husbands and wives included in our study were born between 1940 and 1955, roughly representing the baby boom generation. At the onset of the study, couples were married on average for 17 years (SD = 3.37). The range in marital duration varies from 1 year to 31 years, with about 90% married between 11 and 22 years. About 85% of the respondents report that they did not experience a parental divorce during their childhood. Couples have on average 2.48 children (SD = 1.04). In one out of two families the target child included in the study is the oldest child whereas in another 37% of the families the child is second in rank. The mean age of the target child is 12.8 years (SD = 2.20). As can be seen in Table 3.3, about a quarter of the male population enjoyed higher vocational or university education, while for women this figure was approximately one out of eight. In comparison to men, women are situated more often in the lower and middle-low educational levels. This gender pattern recurs when considering occupational status. About 16% of women are employed in unskilled jobs whereas this only holds for 4% of men. The reverse is true when considering higher occupations. It appears that 9% of the employed women occupy a higher profession; for men this is 18%. In general, the labor market participation of Dutch fathers and mothers show large discrepancies. 95% of the husbands are employed whereas less than half of the wives have a job. The discrepancy also becomes clear when taking into account the number of hours officially worked. On average, husbands work 38.4 (SD = 3.43) hours while wives work 19.5 (SD = 10.2). Hence, the couples in our study primarily represent single earner- and main-earner households. Their average monthly family income is between 1250 and 1625 euro.

Table 3.3

Distribution of Men and Women According to Educational and Occupational Level (1990) in the Research Project

	Women	Men
Educational level		
Lower	13.2	6.0
Middle-low	51.6	46.3
Middle-high	24.2	24.8
Higher	12.0	22.9
Occupational status		
Unskilled job	15.7	3.8
Skilled job	10.1	17.8
Lower employee	50.8	24.4
Small tradesman	5.6	11.6
Moderate employee	8.6	24.1
Higher professions	9.3	18.3

3.4. VALIDATION OF THE SAMPLE AND MISSING CASES

In survey research in general and in panel research in particular, non-response is an important obstacle. The difficulty lies in the fact that this non-response might not be ad random but characterized by selectivity, and hence threatening the validity of a study (Billiet, 1993; Scott, 1995, Wothke, 2000). Selectivity signifies that respondents with particular characteristics are more likely to refuse their participation than those characterized by another profile. Studies show that individuals who refuse to participate have a typical profile: male, low education and unmarried (Taris, 2000).

A sample characterized by strong bias is often more homogeneous with respect to the variables of interest, because the latter might be related with the non-response. Therefore, selective non-response can strongly distort the research results, and thus strongly reduce possibility of generalization to the entire population. Hence, one should always presuppose that the non-response is systematically associated with the research subject of interest (Billiet, 1993).

Attention to the non-response pattern is particularly relevant when using a longitudinal design. The advantages of longitudinal research and panel research in specific are offset by the risk of loosing panel members throughout the study (Dennis & Li, 2003). The possibility that lost panel members differ from all-waves-participants with respect to their attitudes and behavior towards the issue under study, cast doubt on the validity of the data (Dennis & Li, 2003). Therefore, this section aims to evaluate the non-response of our sample. In the first paragraph, characteristics of the participants of the first measurement wave are compared with characteristics of the Dutch population, i.e. the external validation of our sample. The second paragraph addresses the internal validation of our sample by evaluating the characteristics of the panel members who only participated at the first measurement wave with those of the participants who remained in the study.

3.4.1. External Validation

As mentioned before, 43% of the selected households participated at the first measurement wave, indicating a high non-response by international standards. Latten and De Graaf (1997), however, allege that the public willingness to participate in survey studies is lower in the Netherlands than in most other countries. Therefore, a response of 43% does not diverge greatly from typical rates in other Dutch studies conducted by the Netherlands Central Bureau of Statistics. For example in the Fertility and Family Survey (FFS) conducted in 1993, the response rate at the household level was 48,5%. A closer examination of the non-response in the FFS revealed that men participated less than women, younger women refused more often than older women and older men refused more often than younger men.

Because of the high refusal rate in the Netherlands, it is even more important to evaluate in depth the bias introduced by non-response in the sample used in this study. Unfortunately, the reasons for refusal notwithstanding, no registration was made of the demographic information of the refusers. Therefore an indirect method is required to gain insight in the specificity of the sample. To evaluate the non-response, characteristics of the respondents are compared with the distribution of these characteristics in the total population.

As already indicated, the representativeness of the sample in 1990 is ensured with respect to the degree of urbanization and regional zone. In 1995 the sample was no longer significant with respect to the degree of urbanization. Among other things, this may relate to the higher chance of divorce in bigger cities (Weeda, 1981).

Besides regional zone and urbanization, we are interested in background characteristics such as educational level and employment characteristics. This comparison, however, poses serious difficulties as the sample of married couples was obtained by means of a sample drawn on the basis of children's age. Hence, information is required of a very delineated subgroup of the population, i.e. first married couples with at least one child aged between 9 and 16 years old. These data are not available and therefore, as a second best solution, we use less specific data to situate our respondents according to the following characteristics: (1) age at first marriage, (2) employment status and (3) educational level of the spouses.

On average, the couples in our sample got married in 1973. In the Netherlands the mean age at first marriage in the period 1970-1975 was about 25 years for men and 23 years for women (see Chapter 1). In our sample, mean ages at marriage are 25.11 for men and 22.68 for women, which is fairly comparable with the mean age in the population.

With respect to spousal employment status, it appears that 47% of the mothers and 95% of the fathers in our sample have a paid job. To evaluate these proportions, the figures reported by Niphuis-Nell & de Beer (1997) about the labor market participation of fathers and mothers may be interesting.[8] Considering the gross labor market participation[9] of women with children in 1990, the figures show that 49% of mothers with a youngest child of 6 years or older were employed. With respect to fathers' employ-

---

[8] The figures presented by Niphuis-Nell & De Beer are computed on the basis of data of the Central Bureau of Statistics.
[9] The gross labor market participation is defined as working for at least one hour or seeking employment for at least one hour

ment, Niphuis-Nell & de Beer (1997) only discuss figures for 1995. About 90% of fathers with a youngest child between 6 and 17 years old participate in the labor market. Comparing these proportions with the figures in our sample, we can assume that the labor market participation of the couples included in our study approximates the employment situation in the population.

Of the employed spouses in our study, 5% of the husbands work less than 35 hours per week whereas this is true for 88% of the wives. Considering the figures presented by Niphuis-Nell & de Beer (1997) regarding couples with children between 6 and 17 years old, it appears that 6% of the fathers are employed for less than 35 hours whereas for mothers this is about 91%. Therefore, we can reasonably assume that the distribution of part-time versus full-time employment in our sample of employed parents reflects that of the population.

To evaluate the educational level of the respondents with that of the population, we divided the different educational levels into three categories representing lower, secondary, and higher education. The distribution is presented in Table 3.4. Since no specific cohort figures of married people with children are available, we compared our results with the distribution of educational levels within the active population aged 45-64 in 1996 as well as in 2002 (CBS, 2003). The population aged 45-64 in 1996 was born between 1932 and 1951; in 2002 they refer to the group born between 1938 and 1957. Hence, this population approximately covers the cohorts included in our study. However, in contrast to the group selected in our study, the general population also includes unmarried people or married individuals without children as well as people who do not have the Dutch nationality. Therefore, the comparison is only a rough indication and must be interpreted cautiously. Table 3.4 shows that women who are lower or higher educated appear to be underrepresented in our study in favor of women who received secondary education. In contrast, lower educated men are somewhat over represented at the expense of higher educated men. Husbands who received secondary education, however, appear to be a good reflection of the proportion in the population.

Table 3.4
Educational Level of the Active Population Aged 45-64 Years in the Netherlands, According to Sex (%)

	Sample		Active population in 1996		Active population in 2002	
	Women	Men	Women	Men	Women	Men
Lower education	42.92	38.63	56.8	36.9	49.4	34.0
Secondary education	46.07	38.47	28.7	38.9	32.1	37.9
Higher education	12.0	22.9	14.4	23.9	18.4	27.9

Source: CBS, 2003

3.4.2. Internal Validation

To assess the selectivity of the panel attrition in our study, we compare the structural, cultural and marital characteristics of the panel members who remained in the sample during the period under study – this is between 1990 and 1995 – with those who only participated at the first measurement wave. Three separate logistic regressions are conducted each testing if particular individual properties relevant to the phenomenon under study, could predict a couple's participation only at the first measurement wave. The first model assesses the degree to which *one-time* participation depends on socio-demographic characteristics of the spouses. The second model examines whether both wave participants hold different cultural orientations compared to respondents who only participated once and whether they have different network support and parental experiences. Finally, the third model tests whether differences exist with respect to spouses' marital characteristics in terms of marital satisfaction and communication.

Regarding the socio-demographic characteristics, the first logistic regression includes the following variables of both husbands and wives: age, educational level, occupational status, net family income, income satisfaction, year of marriage, parental divorce and whether one works or not.

The $\chi^2(14) = 21.4724$ with p = .0901 is not significant at a .05 level. However, three variables appeared to be significant: husbands (p = .003) and wives' income dissatisfaction (p = .02), and the educational level of the wife (p = .07). The results demonstrate that the respondents participating twice consist of husbands who are more satisfied with the family income, of wives who are less satisfied with this income and of higher educated wives.

With regard to cultural orientations, we included spousal attitudes towards (a) parenting as stressful, (b) parenting as personal restricting, (c) parenting as a rewarding task, (d) togetherness and (e) freedom in the intimate relationship, (f) sex roles, and (g) traditional family values. Moreover, the degree to which husbands and wives perceive to have access to network support is included in the model as well. This model is significant with $\chi^2(16) = 26.9396$ with p = .0422. Closer examination shows that husbands' attitudes towards sex roles (p = .01) and traditional family values (p = .01) differ significantly between the couples who remained in the study and those who dropped out. The latter endorse less traditional family values but are more traditionally orientated towards sex roles.

Regarding marital characteristics, it is of particular importance to assess whether the couples that dropped out of the study were significantly less satisfied with their marriage or display different communication behavior than those who remained in the study. The factors that tend to lower marital satisfaction may also tend to drive persons out of the married population. Therefore, it might be expected that husbands and wives who separated between Time 1 and Time 2 partially account for the dropout of the panel. To examine this assumption, we tested a model including both spouses' marital satisfaction as well as their perceptions of marital communication. This model, however, was not significant with $\chi^2(6) = 3.3468$ and p = .7642, indicating that the panel dropout is not due to the satisfaction or communication profile of the respondents.

Note that we established the nature of the panel attrition by testing three separate multivariate models. However, to fully capture the impact of our panel attrition on the various research problems and models dealt with in this study, we will reconduct the above analysis for each particular research problem. Specifically, this means that for each research problem addressed in the following chapters, a logistic regression, including all the variables of interest to that particular part of the study, will be conducted and evaluated.

3.4.3. Item Non-Response

Apart from the refusals of respondents to participate in a survey, observations can also be lost because of item non-response. The latter is a pervasive problem in empirical research because analyses rest upon a much smaller sample size than the initial number of observations selected. Therefore the question arises whether this limited number of observations is still representative. In this paragraph, we elaborate on the procedure that was followed to save cases with missing values that would be lost in common listwise deletion approaches as used in regression analysis.

Missingness can be either related or unrelated to the dependent or independent variables in the analysis. Data are considered to be *missing completely at random* (MCAR) if the missing value on a variable is unrelated to the dependent variable or to any other variable in the study (Allison, 2001; Jamshidian, 2004). A weaker variant of this assumption is *missing at random* (MAR), referring to the idea that a missing value on a variable depends on the values of variables without missings (observed characteristics). When the missingness on a variable is additionally related to the missing values on other variables, this is referred to as *missing not at random* (MNAR).

In statistical packages such as SAS, the default strategy to deal with item non-response is listwise deletion, excluding the observations with one or more missings on the variables of interest (Jamshidian, 2004). In spite of the attractive simplicity of this strategy, it is not obvious that respondents who have missing values on a particular variable are indifferent compared to those with observed variables. Listwise deletion may result in biased estimates under the conditions of MAR or MNAR (Jamshidian, 2004). Instead of ignoring observations with item non-response, one can also recycle the observation by imputing the missing value. The simplest technique is replacing the missing value by the mean of cases that have observed data on the variable of interest. However, this method may lead to biased estimates of variances (Allison, 2001; Wothke, 2000). The most advanced techniques of imputation are (1) the method of full information maximum Likelihood (FIML) using all the information of the observed data to estimate missing values, and (2) multiple imputation methods, replacing missing values on a given variable with a set of simulated values, generating different complete datasets. Each of these datasets is analyzed and the results are considered together to draw inferences (Allison, 2001; Jamshidian, 2004). It is clear that this strategy is time consuming and cumbersome and therefore not employed in this study.

To save cases with missing values, a single imputation method was used for variables with maximum 10 % missings. The imputation was conducted as follows. For a given variable that requires imputation of missing values (from here on referred to as the imputation variable), it is assumed that whether or not an observation has a missing value depends on some observed characteristics of the observation (MAR). Therefore, the first step determines predictor variables for the missingness on the imputation variable. These predictor variables are denoted matching variables. The general idea is to impute missing values on the imputation variable with values from other observations that are as similar as possible to the imputed observation with respect to their scores on the matching variables. More specifically, imputation is performed as follows.[10]

Suppose there are p matching variables, denoted $X_1, \ldots, X_p$ and that the imputation variable is denoted Y.

1. Standardize the matching variables. The standardized matching variables are denoted $Z_1, \ldots, Z_p$.

2. For every observation i with a non missing value on the imputation variable, compute:

$$SS_i = \sum_{j=1}^{p} (Z_{j,i} - Z_{j,m})^2$$

    and m denotes the observation that requires imputation on the imputation variable

3. Detect the n observations for which SS_i is minimal.

4. If $n=1$ then $Y_m=Y_i$, i.e. the observation m which requires imputation on the imputation variable receives the value of the single observation with minimal SS_i.

5. If $n>1$, then a variance ratio is calculated as follows:

---

[10] I would like to thank my former colleague Dr. Jerry Welkenhuysen-Gybels for developing and elaborating the imputation procedure.

$$V = \frac{S_{Y,n}^2}{S_{Y,total}^2}$$

where $S_{Y,n}^2$ refers to the variance of the imputation variable Y for the n observations with minimal SS_i and $S_{Y,total}^2$ denotes the variance of the imputation variable for the entire sample.

If $V < 1$ then one of the n observations with minimal SS_i is randomly selected to serve as the donor for imputing the Y value of the observation m. If $V > 1$, no imputation is performed. The latter condition is used to ensure that the variability of the Y variable among the n possible donor observations is not too high as compared to the variability of the entire sample.

Note that no imputation occurs if (1) observation m also has a missing value for at least one of the matching variables; (2) there are no donor observations without missing values on the matching variables and (3) the variance ratio V is larger than 1. The imputation was only conducted for the variables indicating individuals' score on a particular scale and not for the separate items of each scale

In comparison to imputation based on observed covariates of the imputation variable - instead of the covariates of the missingness on the imputation variable - the advantage of this imputation strategy is that the associations between the observed variables in the data set are not further strengthened by the imputation procedure.[11]

---

[11] The main conclusions drawn from the regression analyses before and after imputing the missing variables were comparable, indicating that no strong bias was caused by the imputation method.

PART II

The Study

4. The Dutch Marital Satisfaction and Communication Questionnaire. A Validation Study

4.1. INTRODUCTION

Marital communication and satisfaction represent two key elements in understanding current marital dynamics. Since the maintenance of relationships has increasingly become dependent on husbands' and wives' appreciation of marriage, gaining insight in spousal marital satisfaction is of utmost importance (Beck & Beck-Gernsheim, 1995). Several researchers and family therapists claim that one of the core elements in this appreciation of the marital relationship is communication (Becvar & Becvar, 1996; Fitzpatrick & Ritchie, 1994; Meeks, Hendrick, & Hendrick, 1998). Communication is not only instrumental for marital satisfaction but even one of the most crucial factors contributing to it (Karney & Bradbury, 1995; Noller & Fitzpatrick, 1990).

The close association between satisfaction and communication might explain the conceptual confusion about these concepts in the past. Within a Dyadic Adjustment approach, which was prominent during the seventies, satisfaction and communication are both considered as indicators of a broader concept labeled marital adjustment or marital quality (Spanier, 1976)[12]. This approach and the widely known Dyadic Adjustment Scale that was developed within this thinking received much conceptual as well methodological criticism (Fincham & Bradbury, 1987(a); Norton, 1983; Sabatelli, 1988). The major drawback relates to the confounding of descriptions of the marriage with its evaluation. As a matter of fact, the dyadic adjustment

---

[12] Spanier (1976, pp. 127-128), one of the most important representatives of the Dyadic Adjustment School, defines marital adjustment as "a process, the outcome of which is determined by the degree of (1) troublesome marital differences, (2) interspousal tensions and personal anxiety; (3) marital satisfaction; (4) dyadic cohesion; and (5) consensus on matters of importance to marital functioning." According to this definition, adjustment functions as a sort of container term consisting of diverse aspects, assumed to be necessary to build (up) a harmonious marital relation (Spanier, 1976). However, a well-founded theoretical framework that indicates why these specific five aspects need to be considered is lacking.

approach makes it difficult to examine how marital communication is related to spouses' satisfaction with marriage. Because items used to measure communication overlap in content with items used to measure marital quality, it is doubtful whether these measures assess distinct constructs.

In answer to this content overlap, a new conceptualization of marital quality, assessing only subjective evaluations of the marriage, was suggested (Fincham & Bradbury, 1987(a); Norton, 1983). The underlying assumption is that the person in question is the only expert with regard to his/her well-being. Thus instead of measuring different aspects of the marital relationship, only marital satisfaction, which is an overall evaluation toward one's partner and the relationship, is used as a referent for marital quality[13]. This approach is appealing, particularly because it allows researchers to draw inferences about how communication behavior is associated with marital satisfaction.

The latter embodies the quintessence of behavioral marriage therapy. One of the goals behavioral therapists strive to is increasing the frequency of positive communication behaviors and decreasing the frequency of negative ones. It appears that the balance rather than negative and positive interaction in itself distinguishes stable and unstable marriages. Gottman (1994) report that in stable marriages a 5:1 ratio of positivity to negativity during conflict was established whereas in unstable marriages this ratio was 8:1.

Yet, what 'good' and 'bad' or 'negative' and 'positive' communication precisely is, cannot be easily defined and is often based on global notions within the field of family and couple therapy (Kerkstra, 1985). Although an excess of 'good' communication could also work out negatively whereas not all 'bad' communication styles should be equally harmful, some negative communication styles, such as withdrawal, criticizing and blaming the other, have been systematically linked with lower marital satisfaction and higher rates of divorce (Brown & Rogers, 1991; Buunk & Nijskens, 1980;

---

[13] This specific point of view was subjected to a lot of criticism from the Dyadic Adjustment School. Spanier en Lewis (1980, p. 832) point out that "....it is unfortunate that at the time when many marriage researchers are attempting to conceptualize and measure a marriage as a unit (a dyadic relationship), [some] have chosen to employ an intrapersonal conceptualization (subjectively experienced reaction), rather than an interpersonal conceptualization."

Gottman, 1991, 1993, 1994; Gottman & Krokoff, 1989; Karney & Bradbury, 1995). Reversely, sharing thoughts and feelings about the relationship and daily event talk are considered as instrumental and functional for the relationship (Canary & Stafford, 1992; Wood, 1993). Evidence for the beneficial effect of this behavior on relationship satisfaction is obtained in several studies (Buunk & Nijskens, 1980; Canary, Stafford, & Semic, 2002; Honeycutt & Wiemann, 1999; Weigel & Ballard-Reish, 1999; 2001)

Moreover, both communication behaviors strongly correspond to two relational maintenance strategies identified by Canary and Stafford (1992). A first strategy is *openness* and includes behaviors such as discussing the relationship and sharing relational feelings. A second maintenance strategy is labeled *positivity* and refers to interacting in a polite, cheerful and uncritical manner. This behavior represents the opposite of the aforementioned negative interaction behavior.

Hence, the assessment of these communication behaviors along with spousal marital satisfaction is therefore important for therapeutical as well as theoretical aims. However, Dutch measures on this issue are scarce and the few available instruments consist of a large number of items, validated in relatively small research groups (see Kerkstra, 1985). As space is at a premium in family survey research, the availability of brief, but valid and reliable measures of marital satisfaction and communication would suit the purpose of quantitative research designs (Schumm, et al., 1986).

In addition to this, validation studies on communication and satisfaction measures are mainly directed towards internal consistencies and cross-sectional validation, failing to take into account the stability of the measures across time. Particularly, within the scope of longitudinal research, the latter is of utmost importance. When examining marital satisfaction and communication in a multiwave design, one needs to ascertain that questioning quantitative change in marital satisfaction over time is meaningful at all, i.e. the concept of interest at Time 1 should be comparable to the same concept at later points in time. Since individuals perpetually constitute and reconstitute their interpretation of reality and events, it is conceivable that at two different points in time, two different concepts are measured with the same set of indicators (Steenkamp & Baumgartner, 1998). This phenomenon is referred to as measurement variance or instability (Taris, 2000). It is therefore striking to note, though, that marriage literature is increasingly focusing on longitudinal research designs while it leaves the matter of measurement invariance undiscussed. Nonetheless, it is a logical and inevitable prerequisite to analyze longitudinal hypotheses. Therefore, in contrast to which has often been the case until now, research into concept validation should also address stability, equivalence or invariance across time.

4.2. RESEARCH AIM

To deal with the need for a valid but briefer and stable measure of the above-cited aspects, we present in this study the development and validation of the Dutch Marital Satisfaction and Communication Questionnaire (DMSCQ). The DMSCQ is an instrument designed to measure marital satisfaction and spousal negative and open communication styles. The initial 24-item questionnaire was derived from the Marital Satisfaction and Stability Inventory and the Communication Inventory developed by Kerkstra (1985).

From the former instrument, we exclusively retained those items measuring global experience of the relationship and the partner, i.e. marital satisfaction. This conceptualization precludes some difficulties expressed on previous measurements such as blending general marital satisfaction and satisfaction with specific aspects of one's marriage.

The Communication Inventory of Kerkstra (1985) assesses couples' perception of the way in which they and their partner communicate in marriage. The items are derived from several communication questionnaires such as the Communication Questionnaire of Buunk and Nijskens (1980), the Primary Communication Inventory (Navran, 1967) and the Marital Communication Inventory (Bienvenu, 1970). Using factor analysis, two dimensions prove to be paramount, i.e. destructive communication and intimacy. Although Kerkstra (1985) and Buunk and Nijskens (1980) also identified a third factor tapping 'avoidance', these items yielded low reliability.

Because it was attempted to validate a brief battery of items regarding marital communication, the items of the destructive and intimacy scales were selected for the DMSCQ. Both communication scales measure the perception of communication behavior and not individual communication skills. The Destructive Communication items measure to what degree certain forms of negative communication are characteristic of the marital relationship (e.g., "My partner often blames me when we are quarreling", or, "My partner and I interrupt each other a lot when we are talking together"). In this study, we label this scale *Negative Communication*. The intimacy scale maps out communication styles of which it is assumed that this way of communicating results in emotional closeness and intimacy between the partners. Because the items measure the openly sharing of personal experiences, we refer to this scale as the *Open Communication* scale.

Using exploratory and confirmatory factor analysis, we attempt to test the factorial structure of the DMSCQ. Both the internal consistency of the identified scales and their construct validity is demonstrated. We report on three studies to describe the psychometric properties of the DMSCQ. A first study explores the factor structure of the initial questionnaire in a sample of 646 couples followed by some validation tests. In a second study this factor solution is evaluated in a sample of 1187 couples and the correlations with five criterion variables are studied. The third study examines the stability of the factor solution over time.

4.3. STUDY 1

The objective of the first study is to evaluate the initial 24-item questionnaire in a sample of Dutch married couples. Four criterion variables will be used to assess the construct validity of the DMSCQ: (1) parental depression, (2) parenting stress, (3) conflictual family climate and (4) parental role restriction. We hypothesize that parental depression and a conflictual family climate perception is related to lower marital satisfaction, more negative communication and less open communication (Beach, Katz, Sooyeon, & Brody, 2003; Olson, McCubbin, Barness, & Hill, 1983). Because of a spillover effect between the spousal and the parental system, parenting stress is expected to be negatively correlated with marital satisfaction and to result in more negative communication (Wise, 2003). Because our measure of open communication does not refer to the dyadic system but to the individual him/herself, it is not clear whether parenting stress is strongly associated with this communication behavior. Further we hypothesize that the degree to which the parent report to feel restricted by his or her role of parenting in arranging one's personal life is negatively related to marital satisfaction and open communication and may be associated with more negative communication (Lavee & Sharlin, 1996; Rogers & White, 1998).

4.3.1. Procedure and Participants

The research sample consists of married men and women participating in the longitudinal research project "Child-Rearing and Family in the Netherlands" (Gerris et al., 1992; 1993; 1998). Families were recruited using a multi-stage sampling method. In the first stage, a sample was taken of all Dutch municipalities; in a second stage a sample of children aged 9 to 16 years was selected in these municipalities. These children as well as their parents were included in the research group. In 1990, this procedure resulted in a sample of 788 families. The sample's representativeness regarding regional zone and degree of urbanization was satisfactory. In order to establish a homogeneous research group, only first married couples were selected. This selection resulted in 646 couples with children. Data were gathered by means of structured interviews and questionnaires, completed by both the child and the parents. Mothers were 40 years (SD= 4.88) and fathers were 42,5 years old (SD= 4.17) on average. The couples had been married for about 17 years (SD=3.37)

4.3.2. Measures

All measures described below consist of 7-point Likert items, ranging from 1 = "not at all applicable" to 7 = "very applicable".

Marital satisfaction is measured by nine items referring to the degree to which parents experience the marital relationship as satisfying and positive. (e.g., "If I could choose again, I would choose the same partner").

The *Negative Communication* scale assesses the degree to which the partner reports to experience the communication and interaction with the partner as negative. The scale consists of nine items (e.g., "My partner often blames me when we are quarrelling").

The *Open Communication* scale maps out the degree to which the parent reports to exchange personal experiences in communication and interaction with the marital partner. It is a six-item scale (e.g., "I often talk to my partner about personal problems").

The *Conflictual Family climate* is a scale used to assess the extent to which conflictual interactions are characteristic of the family (e.g., "We quarrel a lot in our family"). The scale consists of 5 items with internal consistencies (Cronbach's alpha) of .66 and .70 for fathers and mothers respectively.

Parental Depression measures the degree to which the parent reports to be confused about and to feel unhappy with his functioning as a person and to be subject to feelings of depression (e.g., "Whatever I am doing, I will never manage"). It is a 7-point Likert item scale consisting of 9 items. Alpha coefficient is .79 (fathers) and .81 (mothers).

The *Parenting Stress* scale is a 3-items scale with alpha .77 for fathers and .81 for mothers. It refers to the degree to which the parent reports to experience child-rearing as a burden and as problematic (e.g., "raising my child(ren) frequently causes problems").

The *Parental Role Restriction* scale consists of 5 items measuring the degree to which the parent feels restrictions for their personal life from the parenting role (e.g., "Because of your children you cannot plan your life as you want"). Alpha is .67 (fathers) and .69 (mothers).

4.3.3. Results

Factorial structure

The factorial structure of the satisfaction and communication items was analyzed separately for husbands and wives. The central aim, however, was to obtain a similar structure for both spouses. In line with the aim to develop concepts that are empirically and conceptually clearly separated from each other, it was required that the resulting concepts were sufficiently reliable in terms of internal consistency.

Table 4.1

Completely Standardized Factor Loadings and Reliabilities of the CFA's on the Marital Satisfaction, Open and Negative Communication Items, Study 1, 2 and 3

	Study 1		Study 2		Study 3	
	Men	Women	Men	Women	Men	Women
Marital Satisfaction						
ms1 The way we treat each other now, I would like to stay with my partner forever.	.41	.54	.64	.76	.53	.56
ms2 Compared to the past I am now less satisfied with the way my partner and I treat each other.	.75	.72	.71	.66	.76	.71
ms3 I expected more from the relationship with my partner.	.76	.75	.79	.82	.84	.87
ms4 I think that the relationship with my partner is hardly a success.	.47	.64	.57	.60	.69	.80
ms5 If I could choose again, I would choose the same partner.	.46	.59	.39	.49	.59	.57
ms6 Actually, I think that the relationship with my partner should be better.	.77	.82	.77	.80	.75	.82
ms7 Generally, I am dissatisfied with the relationship with my partner.	.49	.57	.48	.53	.47	.53
Cronbach's α	.80	.77	.81	.84	.84	.86
Negative Communication						
nc1 My partner often blames me when we are quarrelling.	.72	.70	.76	.70	.80	.80
nc2 When my partner and I don't agree, we often get angry at each other.	.67	.65	.69	.62	.58	.65

	Study 1		Study 2		Study 3	
	Men	Women	Men	Women	Men	Women
nc3 My partner often pushes has his/her own way.	.54	.62	.70	.67	.65	.62
nc4 My partner and I interrupt each other a lot when we are talking together.	.53	.44	.58	.56	.49	.46
nc5 My partner often finds fault with me.	.74	.60	.68	.67	.76	.67
nc6 When talking to me my partner sometimes uses a tone of voice I don't like.	.68	.57	.62	.68	.69	.59
Cronbach's α	.81	.86	.84	.82	.83	.80
Open Communication						
oc1 I often talk to my partner about personal problems.	.41	.47	.59	.60	.65	.64
oc2 I often talk to my partner about things in which we are both interested.	.69	.75	.69	.73	.59	.63
oc3 I often talk to my partner about the nice things that happened that day.	.67	.54	.70	.68	.68	.81
Cronbach's α	.61	.62	.69	.70	.67	.71

Using principal factor analyses (PFA) with oblique rotation, the relational structure between the concepts was clarified. Items, which met the criterion of a weight of .40 or more on the factor they intended to represent and a weight of .25 or less on the other factors, were retained. This procedure yielded a clear-cut pattern of three factors, which corresponded with the hypothesized constructs. Eight items were removed from the analysis because they did not meet the retention criteria. The factor solution results in seven items loading on the factor 'marital satisfaction', six items on the factor 'negative communication' and three items load significantly on the factor 'open communication'.

Cross-loadings vary from .00 to .20, with the exception of one item from the satisfaction scale with a cross-loading of .25, indicating that we reached a simple factor structure with high loadings on the factor to be represented and low loadings on the other factors. For men, the three factors accounted for 40 % of the total variance; for women the total variance explained was 42%. The factor solution (pattern matrix) and the items are presented in Table 4.1.

Internal Consistency

Reliability coefficients (Cronbach's alpha) are reported in Table 4.1. As can be seen the marital satisfaction and negative communication scales show acceptable internal consistencies (alpha) of .77 or higher for both men and women. The open communication scale is less reliable but this may be due to the fewer items of which it is composed.

Construct Validity

Pearson correlations between the identified scales and the four criterion variables (1) parental depression, (2) parenting stress, (3) conflictual family climate and (4) parental role restriction are presented in Table 4.2. For both men and women negative associations were found between marital satisfaction and these four criterion variables. Moreover, parenting stress, parental depression, conflictual family climate and parental role restriction are associated with more negative communication. From Table 4.2 it also becomes clear that parental depression and a conflictual family climate are negatively related to open communication for both spouses. Parental role restriction shows a significant negative correlation with open communication for women but not for men. Parenting stress appears to be unrelated to the open communication.

4.4. STUDY 2

To examine whether the results of Study 1 can be replicated, a new independent sample of couples is used. The factorial structure is tested using CFA. Besides this, internal consistencies and construct validity were established. With respect to the latter, correlations between the DMSCQ and the scales of parental depression, parenting stress, conflictual family climate, life satisfaction and well-being were examined.

4.4.1. Procedure and Participants

The research sample consists of a Dutch representative sample of 1.267 families (father and/or mother with one target child with ages between 0 and 18 years old) participating in the research project "Parenting in the Netherlands" (Rispens, Hermans, & Meeus, 1996; van Ammers, et al. 1998). Families were recruited using a national family file controlled for representativeness with respect to SES, degree of urbanization and family composition (one- and two-parent families). Because 7 % of the sample consists of one-parent families, the final sample for our study consists of 1.178 two-parental families. Data were gathered by means of structured interviews and questionnaires, completed by both the child and the parents. Mean age of mothers was 38.1 years (SD= 6.2) and of fathers 40.4 years (SD= 6.0).

Table 4.2
Pearson Correlations Between the DMSCQ-Scales and Criterion Variables, Study 1, 2 and 3

Measures	Marital satisfaction		Negative communication		Open communication	
	Men	Women	Men	Women	Men	Women
Study 1						
Parental depression	-.46[a]	-.46[a]	.50[a]	.49[a]	-.14[a]	-.21[a]
Parenting stress	-.22[a]	-.17[a]	.29[a]	.22[a]	-.05	.02
Conflictual family climate	-.30[a]	-.30[a]	.37[a]	.31[a]	-.19[a]	-.13[b]
Parental role restriction	-.24[a]	-.27[a]	.29[a]	.28[a]	-.01	-.10[b]
Study 2						
Parental depression	-.32[a]	-.33[a]	.34[a]	.32[a]	-.17[a]	-.17[a]
Parenting stress	-.17[a]	-.20[a]	.16[a]	.19[a]	-.04	-.13[a]
Conflictual family climate	-.38[a]	-.40[a]	.44[a]	.44[a]	-.21[a]	-.23[a]
Parental role restriction	-.21[a]	-.19[a]	.21[a]	.20[a]	-.08[c]	-.06[c]
Life satisfaction	.42[a]	.54[a]	-.27[a]	-.30[a]	.24[a]	.34[a]
Well-being	.27[a]	.33[a]	-.24[a]	-.21[a]	.17[a]	.19[a]
Study 3						
Parental depression	-.39[a]	-.39[a]	.40[a]	.42[a]	-.28[a]	-.17[b]
Parenting stress	-.18[a]	-.10	.16[a]	.24[a]	-.06	-.06
Conflictual family climate	-.32[a]	-.41[a]	.35[a]	.40[a]	-.20[a]	-.20[a]
Parental role restriction	-.23[a]	-.33[a]	.26[a]	.30[a]	-.11[c]	-.11[c]

Note : [a] p < .001 [b] p < .01 [c] p < .05

4.4.2. Measures

The same criterion measures as in the first study were used. Additionally, a life satisfaction scale and well-being indicator was used.

Well-being was measured by means of one question. "We would like to know how you feel? You can indicate this below by circling the answer (between 1 and 10) that is most applicable. Answering "1" means that you are doing badly and a "10" means that you are doing well".

The *life satisfaction* scales measures the global evaluation of how satisfied one is with life in general. The scale consists of five items with response categories ranging from "1" not at all applicable to "7" very applicable (e.g., "If I could have my life over again, I would change anything"). Alpha is .86 (fathers) and .88 (mothers).

4.4.3. Results

Factorial structure

Using LISREL 8.5 (Jöreskog & Sörbom, 1996) two CFA's were conducted separately for men and women. To evaluate the models, we consider two goodness of fit indices (1) the root mean square error of approximation (RMSEA) and (2) the comparative fit index (CFI). Models with a RMSEA value lower than .05 and CFI values over .95 indicate an acceptable fit between model and data (Billiet & Mc Clendon, 1998; Byrne, 1998; Hu & Bentler, 1999; Mueller, 1996). RMSEA values between .05 and .08, and CFI values of at least .90 are indicative of fair fit (Kline, 1998).

It was hypothesized that three prescribed factors underlie the sixteen manifest items with each item loading significantly on the target factor and having zero-loadings on the non-target factors. The factors were free to correlate and except for two items of the marital satisfaction (ms1 and ms5) scale and two items of the destructive communication scale (dc5 and dc6), the error terms of the items were kept uncorrelated. The completely standardized factor loadings are presented in Table 4.1. Besides one item with a factor loading of .39 all other loadings were above .40. As can be seen in Table 4.3, both the male and the female model show acceptable fit: For men $\chi^2(99) = 333.57$ with RMSEA = .045 and CFI = .982 and for women $\chi^2(99) = 323.65$ with RMSEA = .044 and CFI = .986.

Table 4.3
Goodness of Fit Indices of the CFA on the Marital Satisfaction, Open and Negative Communication Items, for Men and Women, Study 2 and 3

	χ^2	Df	RMSEA	CFI	Comparison χ^2	$\triangle$ df	P
			Study 2 (N = 1187)				
Factorial structure							
Men							
Non invariant model	333.57	99	.045	.982			
Women							
Non invariant model	323.65	99	.044	.986			
			Study 3 (N = 386)				
Both waves participants							
Men							
Non invariant model	835.54	447	.047	.973			
Λ invariant	853.33	460	.045	.973	17.79	13	n.s.
Women							
Non invariant model	897.58	447	.047	.974			
Λ invariant	914.82	460	.041	.974	17.24	13	n.s.

Internal consistency

The DMSCQ-scales were evaluated for internal consistency. For both men and women, Cronbach's alpha showed a value of at least .81 for the marital satisfaction and destructive communication scales (see Table 4.1). The internal consistencies (Cronbach's alpha) of the open communication scale were .69 for men and .70 for women.

Construct validity

Table 4.2 shows the correlations between the DMSCQ-scales and parental depression, parenting stress, conflictual family climate, parental role restriction, life satisfaction and well-being. In accordance with the results from Study 1, the concepts 'parental depression' and 'conflictual family climate' are negatively related to marital satisfaction and open communication but show meaningful positive associations with negative communication. The reverse pattern of associations is found for 'life satisfaction' and 'well-being'. Regarding parenting, it becomes clear that for both men and women 'parenting stress' and 'parental role restriction' are linked with more negative communication and less marital satisfaction. Weak negative correlations exist between open communication and parental role restriction. Parenting stress is negatively related to women's open communication but unrelated to men's open communication.

4.5. STUDY 3

Using a longitudinal measurement model, the objective of this study is to examine the stability of the factor structure across time. This analysis is conducted for the respondents that participated both in 1990 (see Study 1) and in 1995. Internal consistencies of the DMSCQ scales and their correlations with the scales of parental depression, parenting stress, conflictual family climate and parental role restriction are demonstrated.

4.5.1. Procedure and Participants

Of the 646 couples participating in 1990 (Study 1), 386 first married couples also participate in 1995. Their average marital duration is 22 years. Men are on average 47.5 years old and women 45.0 years old.

4.5.2. Measures

The measures used in Study 1 were also used in this study. These concern the scales on parental depression, parenting stress, conflictual family climate and parental role restriction.

4.5.3. Results

Factorial structure

Before testing the stability of the factor model, the factor solution of the previous studies was examined within the sample of subjects who participated at wave 1 and wave 2. The results are given in Table 4.1. As can be seen all factor loadings range between .46 and .87. Goodness of fit indices indicate an acceptable fit for both the male and the female model. RMSEA values are around .05 and CFI's are around .95

Stability of the factor solution over time

In a next step, the stability of the factor solution was examined across time. According to Steenkamp and Baumgartner (1998), and Vandenberg and Lance (2000), two conditions may be fulfilled when assessing this measurement invariance: (1) the same items load on the same underlying factor (configural invariance) and (2) the factor loadings are similar for the two groups (metric invariance). If the purpose is to explore the basic structure of a concept and to demonstrate whether items are similarly conceptualized by two groups or at two different points in time, establishing the same factor structure for these two groups (configural invariance) is sufficient. Although not strictly necessary for this objective, the factor loadings may also be expected to be equal across time (metric invariance). If these criteria are not met, it may be supposed that after a while the (same) group of respondents attached a different meaning to the same set of items.

To test the stability of the factor solution over time, a longitudinal factor model was constructed with marital satisfaction, negative communication and open communication as latent variables at Time 1 and Time 2 and the respective items as their indicators. The same items load on the same underlying factors. Latent variables were allowed to correlate within Time 1 and Time 2 but also over time. Error terms between Time 1 and Time 2 were not correlated. The covariance matrix containing covariances between items at Time 1, Time 2 and between Time 1 and Time 2 was used as the input matrix. Fit indices show that the presumed factor model fits the longitudinal covariance matrix well: For men $\chi^2(447) = 835.54$ with RMSEA = .047 and CFI = .973 and for women $\chi^2(447) = 897.58$ with

RMSEA = .047 and CFI = .974 (see Table 4.3). Moreover, the lambda coefficients are invariant across time. Imposing equality constraints on the factor loadings of T1 and T2, chi-square difference tests demonstrate that with respect to the male and female model, no significant differences are found between T1 and T2. For men $\Delta\chi^2(13) = 17.79$, n.s. and for women $\Delta\chi^2(13) = 17.24$, n.s.

In addition, correlations between concepts at Time 1 and Time 2 were computed. Stability of concepts over time requires a positive correlation between identical factors at Time 1 and Time 2. Table 4.4 presents the correlations between the factors in 1990 (wave 1) and 1995 (wave 2). These correlations have to be higher than correlations of that concept in Time 1 with other concepts in Time 2. The results support this assumption. For men, marital satisfaction (r=.59), negative communication (r=.60) and open communication (r=.38) were (much) more strongly correlated than with any other construct at Time 2. This also applies for marital satisfaction (r=.58), negative communication (r=.61) and open communication (r=.47) among women.

Table 4.4
Pearson Correlations Between the Three Latent Factors of the DMSCQ Across Time
[Women Beneath Diagonal, Men Above Diagonal]

	M. S. '90	O. C. '90	N. C. '90	M. S. '95	O.C. '95	N.C. '95
M.S. '90	--	.30	-.52	.59	.34	-.39
O.C. '90	.44	--	-.22	.25	.38	-.14
N.C. '90	-.52	-.21	--	-.36	-.29	.60
M.S. '95	.58	.29	-.40	--	.40	-.57
O.C. '95	.36	.47	-.26	.42	--	-.28
N.C. '95	-.46	-.20	.61	-.64	-.31	--

Note: M.S. = marital satisfaction, O.C. = open communication, N.C. = negative communication

4.6. DISCUSSION

The Dutch Marital Satisfaction and Communication Questionnaire is designed to assess partners' marital satisfaction and their open and negative communication behavior. The latter two are specifically assessed because of their relevance in understanding marital success. This article addresses three properties of the DMSCQ: (a) the factorial validity of the instrument, (b) the reliability of the identified scales and (c) their construct validity.

With respect to the factorial validity, the first study led us to conclude that the three hypothesized constructs were established but that some items did not successfully discriminate between the different factors. Removing these items resulted in a 16-item version of the DMSCQ representing a solid three-factor structure. This factorial structure is replicated in a new and independent sample (Study 2) and across time (Study 3). Our findings show that marital satisfaction, open communication and negative communication operate in the same way for different samples and for both men and women. Measurement invariance was demonstrated in Study 3 for the longitudinal sample.

Cronbach's alphas demonstrate that the internal consistency of the marital satisfaction and negative communication scales is good. The open communication scale, however, has a somewhat lower reliability, probably due to the smaller number of items. Initially, this scale consisted of six items but was reduced to three items because of the retention criteria.

The three studies reported above, provide support for the construct validity of the DMSCQ. Most results confirmed our hypotheses with respect to the relation between the DMSCQ-subscales and related variables of interest. Evidence was obtained for the hypothesized negative relationship between parental depression and marital outcomes in terms of the three identified scales. The same finding holds with respect to the association with conflictual family climate. The reverse results were obtained regarding life satisfaction and well-being. In line with the spillover effect of satisfaction with different areas of life, individuals who are more satisfied with life in general also tend to be more satisfied with their relationship. Apparently, they also communicate more openly and are less likely to perceive the communication in negative terms. Spouses who feel restricted by their parental role or experience parenting stress tend to be less satisfied with their partnership and to perceive the marital communication as more negative. However, these parents do not necessarily communicate more or less openly. We contend that this lack of association may be due to the unit of analysis. Both the marital satisfaction and negative communication scale refer to the marital relationship whereas the open communication scale is formulated from the perspective of the respondent him/herself. It can be speculated that the parental and marital system are more closely tied up to each other than are the parental system and indicators on the individual level.

In sum, an encouraging effort was made in designing a short, reliable and valid instrument to assess partners' satisfaction and communication in the Dutch-speaking region. Nonetheless, we see three important avenues for future research. First, to increase the reliability of the open communication scale of the DMSCQ, it could be extended with new items. Recent research of Caughlin (2003) on family communication standards may be a source of inspiration for this adaptation. His scale of *openness* also consists of items such as "openly discussing topics like sex" or "freely deal with issues that may be upsetting". Second, the three identified scales of the DMSCQ need to be further validated with observational studies and other assessment methods. Because respondents reported their subjective evaluation of the marital communication processes, standardized procedures to observe marital interaction may indicate the degree to which our measures reflect "real-life" communication. This opinion may be validated for example, by asking partners to fill in the questionnaires for their own communication behavior as well as for one's partner communication. In this way, own and partner's perceptions can be compared. Third, although our instrument was primarily designed for research purposes, it may also be a useful diagnostic tool. To this end, however, more research is needed on the discriminant validity of the DMSCQ.

Despite these limitations and recommendations, our findings suggest that the DMSCQ provides a psychometrically sound tool for assessing relationship satisfaction and communication. Based on theoretical insights in couple's behavior to develop and sustain a satisfying relationship, three related but empirically distinct concepts are measured. The DMSCQ offers an important alternative to researchers who need a brief but valid and reliable measure of marital satisfaction and communication. Moreover, because of the satisfying criterion validity, the instrument it is not only suitable for research purposes but also for the clinical practice.

5. The Relationship Between Communication and Marital Satisfaction: A Cross-Lagged Panel Analysis

5.1. INTRODUCTION

In the past two decades, a considerable body of research has focused on the influence of interaction and communication behavior on marriage and marital quality (Bradbury, Fincham, & Beach, 2000; Matthews, Wickrama, & Conger, 1996). Within this literature, it is widely assumed that marital communication is instrumental for marital quality and even one of the most crucial factors contributing to marital satisfaction (Karney & Bradbury, 1995; Lewis & Spanier, 1979; Noller & Fitzpatrick, 1990; Olson, McCubbin, Barnes, & Hill, 1983). According to Noller and Fitzpatrick (1990, p. 839) "[there is] weight of evidence that marital interaction causes marital satisfaction".

It is most unlikely, though, that only a one-way relationship from communication to marital satisfaction exists. The idea that marital satisfaction may also affect how partners interact with each other is represented in Karney and Bradbury's (1995) vulnerability-stress-adaptation model, but also supported in several observational studies (Gottman, 1994; Gottman & Krokoff, 1989; Noller, 1981).

Little attempt is made, however, to address the relative strength of the two associations in order to clarify whether communication is rather an antecedent or a consequence of marital satisfaction. Instead of cross-sectional studies, a longitudinal design is required to fully capturing this reciprocal relationship. An example is the study of Noller and Feeney (1994) on encoding and decoding behavior of spouses. From their study, it became clear that relationship satisfaction might be a stronger predictor of communication than communication is of later satisfaction. However, because the majority of studies have not aimed to establish the relative strength of the two directions, there is not much evidence for the antecedent-consequent nature of the relationship between communication and marital satisfaction.

According to Karney and Bradbury (1995, p. 25) this lack of evidence regarding the relative contribution of marital satisfaction to communication "leaves open the possibility that marital quality accounts for variation in marital behavior more than marital behavior leads to changes in marital quality". The main topic of our contribution is directed towards this specific issue. Using panel data from 386 couples participating in a Dutch research project, our objective is to provide insight in the nature of this relationship.

Besides the relevance of gaining insight in this dynamic nature, a better understanding of the longitudinal association between marital satisfaction and communication is in particular important because some marital inter-action patterns (e.g., disagreement, anger exchanges) may be harmful for concurrent satisfaction but not for later satisfaction (Gottman & Krokoff, 1989). It is speculated that couples may develop a sense of confidence that they can weather conflict together, positively affecting their satisfaction with marriage. In American and Dutch samples it is demonstrated, for example, that communication behavior such as "getting angry" and "inter-rupting each other" was negatively associated with spouses' current marital experiences (Buunk & Nijskens, 1980; Gottman, 1991; 1993; 1994; Kerkstra, 1985), though, it remains to be seen whether this set of behaviors, hereafter called negative communication, also negatively predicts later satis-faction.

Understanding the longitudinal association between satisfaction and communication is also appealing as regards communication patterns such as "often talking about personal problems" and "often talking about things that happened during the day" for which there is cross-sectional evidence that this behavior is beneficial to partnership (Buunk & Nijskens, 1980; Kerkstra, 1985). In the present study, this communication style is referred to as 'open communication' and can be considered as the compound of two relational maintenance behaviors. The first behavior refers to marital part-ners talking to each other about things that happened during their day. This talk is considered as a type of instrumental and functional talk intended to sustain the relationship (Wood, 1993). Honeycutt and Wiemann (1999) provided support for the positive effect of this "daily event" talk on rela-tionship satisfaction. Another behavior identified as a strategy to sustain the relationship is "openness" (Canary & Stafford, 1992). Canary, Stafford, and Semic (2002) assert that this "openness" strategy, which is defined as discussing the relationship and sharing thoughts and feelings about the relationship, leads to greater satisfaction for marital partners and to the maintenance of the relationship (Weigel & Ballard-Reisch, 1999, 2001).

Behaviors labeled 'good' and 'bad' or 'positive' and 'negative' communication cannot be regarded as absolute but rather as context-specific qualities. The implicit assumption that good communication is open and honest, and hostile communication is indicative of a lack of communication skills, may be an expression of white, Western middle-class values (Coupland, Giles, & Wiemann, 1991). Moreover, not all 'bad' communication styles are equally harmful and not every 'lack' of openness necessarily indicates miscommunication (Brown & Rogers, 1991; Gottman & Krokoff, 1989).

Because the assumed longitudinal and reciprocal relationship between marital satisfaction and both negative and open communication remains elusive, our first research question addresses the degree to which open communication and negative communication can be seen as a predictor or an outcome of marital satisfaction. This question will be examined with help of crossed-lagged panel analysis. Because Meeks, Hendrick, and Hendrick (1998) assert that not only the actual communication *behavior* but also the *experience* of this behavior is important in understanding its effect on marital satisfaction, the perception of negative and open communication and not the overt behavior will be considered in this study. Our theoretical model is presented in Figure 5.1. For reasons of simplicity, two groups of relationships are excluded from the Figure: (1) the effect of control variables and (2) the correlations between husbands and wife's variables at each measurement point.

Figure 5.1
Conceptual Model for Long-Term Association Between Open and Negative Communication and Marital Satisfaction

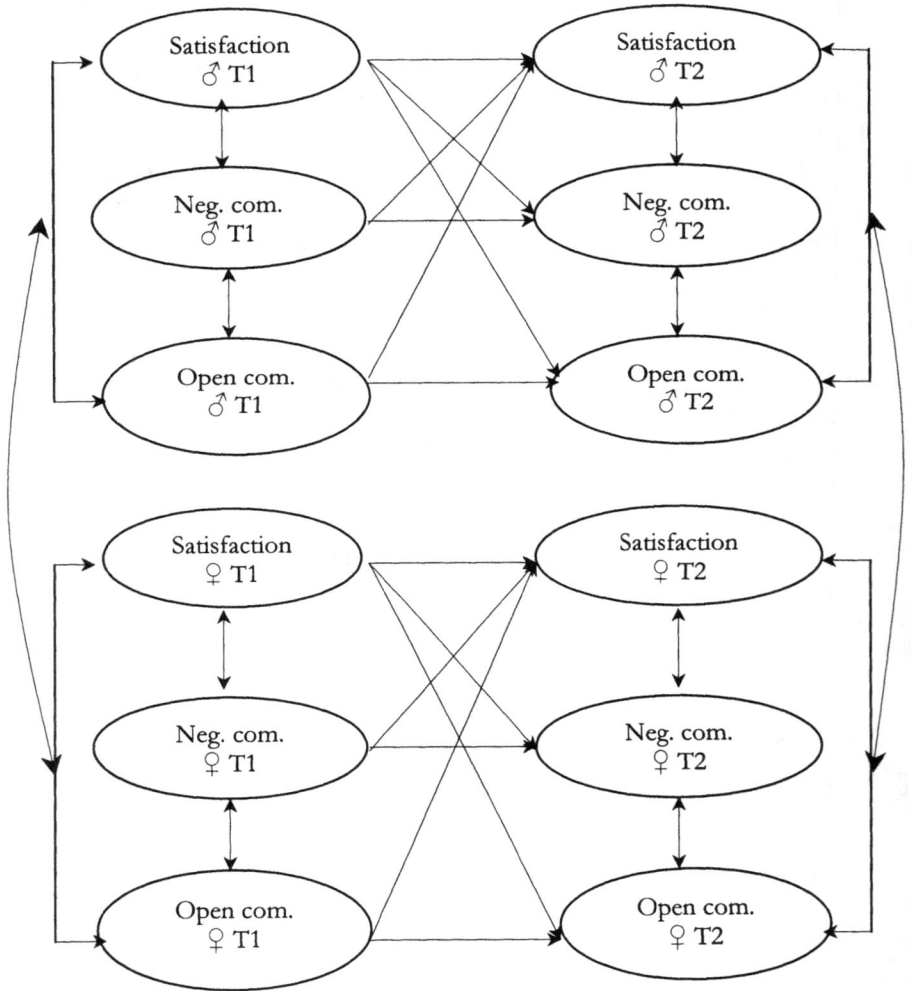

Note: The curved arrow denotes the correlations between husbands and wives' variables

The second research question concerns the sex-specificity of the long-term association between communication and marital satisfaction. In fact, men and women may differ from one another in the degree to which they communicate openly or negatively. This idea is expressed in the so-called *different cultures* perspective (Mulac, Bradac, & Gibbons, 2001). It is a widespread view that marital communication may have different significance for both sexes as women tend to be more relationally-oriented than are their male counterparts (Acitelli, 1992; Goldsmith & Dun, 1997; Thompson & Walker, 1989; Weigel & Ballard-Reisch, 2001; Wood, 1993). Their greater sensitiveness to interpersonal problems and subtleties of communication is reflected in women's role as "relationship architects" (Wood, 1993). This focus on the intimate relationship may stimulate the use of communication behavior that positively contributes to marital partnership. For example it is found that women are more likely to talk about daily events and relationship experiences than men (Canary, Stafford, & Semic, 2002; Rubin, 1983; Weigel & Ballard-Reisch, 2001; Wood, 1993). They also tend to complain more about their partners being too little emotional intimate and too withdrawn (Gottman & Krokoff, 1989; Houck & Daniel, 1994; Rubin, 1983).

However, research evidence for these sex differences is mixed. Some authors found no or small sex differences indicating that men and women are not that different with regard to marital communication or, at least, that these differences might be exaggerated (Canary & Dindia, 1998; Dindia & Allen, 1992; Goldsmith & Dun, 1997; Wright, 1998). Burleson, Kunkel, Samter, and Werking (1996) developed the *same culture* perspective to state that similarities between the sexes far outweigh differences. With respect to Dutch couples, Kerkstra (1985) also showed that men and women did not differ in their perception of the marital communication as negative or open.

Whether or not sex differences are claimed may also be based on one's interpretation of small effects (Allen, 1998). For some researchers they are *important* whereas for others they are *not important enough* to call for differences. Because no conclusive findings are established for the Netherlands, it remains unclear to what degree sex differences in communication can be expected.

Besides, sex differences regarding the direction of the relationship between communication and satisfaction may also be elusive. There is some evidence to assume that, in comparison to men, women tend to experience lower marital satisfaction because of their likely dissatisfaction with marital communication (Fincham & Bradbury, 1987(b); Houck & Daniel, 1994; Jacobson & Moore, 1981; Margolin, Hattem, John, & Yost, 1985). In contrast, the "motivational approach" of marital communication suggests that marital distressed women are more likely to perceive relational communication as more negative than do dissatisfied men (Denton, Burleson, & Sprenkle, 1994). Husbands' satisfaction, however, seems to be more strongly related to their *own* communication behavior than to the *marital* communication of both partners. Research indicates that husbands' communication behavior may improve when they are more satisfied with their relationship. So, men's capacity to communicate might be strongly associated with their experience of the marriage whereas for women this would be not the case (Noller, 1981).

Due to the mixed results with respect to sex differences in marital communication and because of the lack of longitudinal evidence for sex-specific directions of the link between communication and satisfaction, our expectations are tentative. Therefore, our second research question is whether the direction of the relation between satisfaction and communication is the same for both sexes, and whether open communication and negative communication play the same role for both men and women.

5.2. METHOD

5.2.1. Procedure and Sample

The research sample consists of married men and women participating in the longitudinal research project "Child-Rearing and Family in the Netherlands" (Gerris et al., 1992, 1993, 1998). Families were recruited using a multi-stage sampling method. In the first stage, a sample was taken of all Dutch municipalities distinguished by regional zone and degree of urbanization. In the second stage, a sample of children was taken in the selected municipalities. These children were selected in such a way that in each city as many boys as girls and as many children aged 9 to 12 as children aged 13 to 16 were chosen. These children as well as their parents were included in the research group. In 1990, this procedure resulted in a sample of 1829 families. The response ratio was 43 % ($N = 788$). Of the 656 families who agreed in 1990 to participate in the second wave, 627 were contacted and 484 (77%) actually did participate in 1995. More technical details on the database can be found in Gerris et al. (1992; 1993; 1998). The data were gathered by means of structured interviews and questionnaires, completed by both the child and the parents. In order to establish a homogeneous research group, only first marriages in which both men and women have a Dutch nationality were selected. This selection resulted in a research group of 386 couples with children. In 1995, couples had been married for about 22 years. Husbands were 47.5 years, and wives were 45.0 years on average. Men reported higher levels of education than did women. One quarter of the male sample has a university degree, whereas for women this figure is approximately one out of eight. For husbands, 48% reported to have a middle low or low school degree whereas for women this is 61%. Sex differences also exist with regard to employment activities. Whereas only 2% of the men are homemakers or not involved in paid employment, more than one out of three women fall into these categories. Nine out of ten men are employed, but this holds only for six out of ten woman (57%). In comparison to men, women are situated more in the "unskilled jobs" category (13% women versus 2% men) and less in the "higher professions" group (11% women versus 18% men).

5.2.2. Measures

Our three measures of interest (1) marital satisfaction, (2) open communication, and (3) negative communication are based on three scales developed by Kerkstra (1985). The open and negative communication scales are inspired by system- and communication theory and are composed of items derived from the Primary Communication Inventory (Navran, 1967) and the Marital Communication Inventory (Bienvenu, 1970). The marital satisfaction and negative communication scale originally consisted of 9 items each; the open communication scale consisted of 6 items.

The satisfaction and the communication items were validated with the aim to develop concepts that are empirically and conceptually clearly separated from each other. In line with this aim, it was required that the resulting concepts were sufficiently reliable in terms of internal consistency. Using oblique factor-analytic rotation procedure, the relational structure between the concepts was clarified. Items, which met the criterion of a weight of .40 or more on the factor they intended to represent and a weight of .20 or less on the other factors, were retained. This procedure yielded a clear-cut pattern of three concepts whereby each item loaded on only one corresponding factor. This factor solution was obtained for men and women in the first wave and was replicated exactly with the data of the second wave as well as in an independent sample of husbands and wives (see Chapter 4).

Marital satisfaction. To formulate the items of this scale, satisfaction with the relationship and/or the partner was used as the guiding principle (e.g., "Generally, I'm dissatisfied with the relationship with my partner" or "If I could choose again, I would choose the same partner"). The scale consists of seven 7-point Likert items, ranging from 1 = "not at all applicable" to 7 = "very applicable". The scores were added together so that a higher score indicates a more satisfied relationship. In 1990, *alpha* coefficient was .85 for women and .80 for men. In 1995, these values were .87 and .85 respectively.

Negative communication. Respondents were asked to indicate to what degree certain forms of negative communication are characteristic of their marital relationship (e.g., "My partner often blames me when we are quarreling" or "My partner and I interrupt each other a lot when we are talking together"). The scale consists of 7-point Likert items, ranging from 1 = "not at all applicable" to 7 = "very applicable". A higher score on the scale indicates more negative communication. For women the *alpha* reliability coefficient was .76 for 1990, and .80 for 1995. For men this coefficient was .81 and .83.

Open communication. This scale is measured by items indicating the degree to which personal feelings and experiences are shared (e.g., "I often talk to my partner about things we both interested in" or "I often talk to my partner about personal problems"). The scale consists of 7-point Likert items, ranging from 1 = "not at all applicable" to 7 = "very applicable". The *alpha* coefficient for women was .63 in 1990 and .73 in 1995. For men these coefficients were .66 and .68 respectively.

Control variables. Year of birth of the marital partners, marital duration and the educational level of both spouses were included as control variables because they could affect marital satisfaction as well as marital communication (Houck & Daniel, 1994; Noller & Feeney, 1994; White, 1983). Marital duration in 1990 and 1995 was indicated by the year of marriage. *Education* was measured in response to the question "What is your highest educational level?" Nine levels were considered ranging from (1) elementary school to (9) university education.

5.3. RESULTS

Descriptive Analysis

To compare mean scores on the three scales across time, paired-sample t-tests were performed for both men and women. This test indicates that there is a significant difference between the mean satisfaction observed in 1990 and in 1995, respectively $t = 2.49$, p < .05 for men ($M_{90} = 6.13$, $SD = 0.93$; $M_{95} = 6.02$, $SD = 1.00$) and $t = 3.30$, $p < .01$ for women ($M_{90} = 6.09$, $SD = 1.01$; $M_{95} = 5.92$, $SD = 1.09$), showing that the degree to which partners are satisfied with their marriage decreased slightly between 1990 and 1995. This finding is in line with recent studies on the course of marital satisfaction, showing a fairly gradually decline over the marital career (VanLanningham, Johnson, & Amato, 2001).[12] Furthermore, the mean score on the open communication scale for women in 1990 is significantly different from the score in 1995 ($t = -2.07$, p < .05; $M_{90} = 5.53$, $SD = 1.09$; $M_{95} = 5.65$, $SD = 1.09$). The perception of negative communication did not change over time, for women ($M_{90} = 2.69$, $SD = 1.03$; $M_{95} = 2.70$, $SD = 1.05$), or for men ($M_{90} = 2.73$, $SD = 1.09$; $M_{95} = 2.71$, $SD = 1.08$).

A comparison of the mean scores across sex shows that in 1990 as well as in 1995 women had a significantly higher score on open communication ($M_{90} = 5.53$, $SD = 1.09$; $M_{95} = 5.65$, $SD = 1.09$) than did men ($M_{90} = 5.06$, $SD = 1.13$; $M_{95} = 5.16$, $SD = 1.16$), respectively $t = -7.39$, $p < .0001$

---

[12] Until the recent published counterfindings of VanLanningham, Johnson and Amato (2001), the U-shaped pattern of marital satisfaction over the marital career was a long-standing premise (Glenn, 1990). However, the preponderance of evidence with respect to the U-curve is overshadowed by the methodological limitations associated with most previous research such as the use of cross-sectional designs. Using 17-years panel data from a nationally representative sample of married individuals, VanLanningham, Johnson and Amato (2001) conclude that marital happiness declines or flattens after a period of decline throughout the marital career.

and $t = -7.56$, $p < .0001$. The mean satisfaction and negative communication scores were not significantly different between men and women.

Structural Equation Model

Using LISREL 8.30 (Jöreskog & Sörbom, 1989, 1993), a cross-lagged panel analysis with open communication, negative communication and marital satisfaction was conducted jointly for husbands and wives. Cross-lagged panel analysis is a technique that provides more insight into antecedent-consequent relationships between two variables that might mutually influence each other.[13] In a first equation, the effect of A1 and B1 on A2 is estimated, and similarly the effect of A1 and B1 on B2 is estimated in a second equation. The standardized regression coefficients of A1 on B2 and of B1 on A2 can be compared with each other. The 'causal winner' is the relationship with the largest coefficient. Hence, the nature of the mutual relationship is interpreted on the basis of the cross-lagged relationship showing the highest coefficient. The advantage of the cross-lagged approach is that the stability effects between Time 1 and Time 2 are controlled when estimating the cross-lagged effects.

Given that two waves of data are available, we modeled a Two-Wave, Three-Variable model for husbands and wives simultaneously (Finkel, 1995). In this model, each variable at Time 2 is predicted by both its previous value at Time 1 and the other variables of interest. For the purpose of this study, variables at Time 1 only were allowed to affect one's own variables and not those of the partner at Time 2.

---

[13] Actually, this is a question about causality. A condition for causality is that the variable that causes an outcome is temporally prior to the variable that is affected (Scott, 1995). However, there is no consistent consensus on this issue. Some assert that causality happens at such a manner in people's mind that it is no longer observable in the temporal sequences of behavior. For example, there is a strong association between the birth of the first child and women leaving the labor market. Though, some only leave after the birth of the child whereas others already leave before the child arrives. Both behaviors result from anticipations and decisions that are made long before the actual behavior takes place. Therefore, temporal order is not always an indication for causality, demonstrating the vital importance of theory in causal suppositions (Nesselroade & Baltes, 1985; Taris, 2000; Willekens, 2001).

Variables in this analysis are latent concepts measured by manifest scale items. The use of latent variable analysis has the major advantage that biasing effects of measurement errors can be controlled (Campbell & Kenny, 1999). However, an important underlying issue of structural equation modeling is that of statistical power. When the sample size is too small or too many parameters have to be estimated, the statistical stability of the results may be doubtful (Mueller, 1996). In our study, the latter was the case. Using the individual items as indicators for each of the latent variables the number of parameters to be estimated is too large with respect to the sample size ($N = 386$). The number of parameters and the number of observations were in the proportion of 1 to 2, whereas generally criteria of at least 1 to 5 or even 1 to 10 or higher are preferred (Mueller, 1996). A technique to deal with this problem is item parceling. Instead of using the original items as indicators for latent variables, parcels are used. Parcels are combinations of subsets of items underlying a latent variable. Scores on parcels are computed by either summing or taking the mean of a subset of items. Item parceling must be used with care and under certain conditions. Bandalos and Finney (2001) have studied possible problems by using parcels as substitutes for the original items. Their finding is that "unidimensional factor structures of the latent constructs have been well established in other studies and parcels are formed within these factors" (Bandalos & Finney, 2001, p. 288). Given the unidimensionality of the scales (only items loading on their principal factor, no cross loadings) and the validity and reliability of our measurement instrument (see Chapter 4) it is considered sound to use item parceling. Therefore, for each construct, two parcels were computed as the mean score of a subset of items. For marital satisfaction, a parcel of four items and one of three items was made; for negative communication two parcels of each three items were retained, and for open communication a parcel of two items and a parcel consisting of the one remaining item were constructed. Theoretically, all parcels range from 1 to 7.

Using Confirmatory Factor Analysis (LISREL 8.30), the reliability and validity of the three latent constructs and their indicators (parcels) were demonstrated. Table 5.1 presents the standardized factor loadings and alpha coefficients for the three latent constructs for both sexes in 1990 as well as in 1995.

Table 5.1
**Lambda's of the Measurement Model with 6 Manifest Variables and
3 Latent Factors of the DMSCQ, According to Sex and Year**

Factor and indicators	1990		1995	
	Lambda Men	Lambda Women	Lambda Men	Lambda Women
Marit. Sat. (F1)	$\alpha = .82$	$\alpha = .89$	$\alpha = .86$	$\alpha = .88$
ms1	.82	.88	.87	.90
ms2	.84	.91	.87	.88
Neg. Com. (F2)	$\alpha = .81$	$\alpha = .74$	$\alpha = .80$	$\alpha = .78$
nc1	.83	.78	.85	.88
nc2	.81	.76	.78	.74
Open Com. (F3)	$\alpha = .68$	$\alpha = .62$	$\alpha = .71$	$\alpha = .78$
pc1	.85	.78	.87	.90
pc2	.59	.57	.64	.71

Note: Standardized coefficients, $N = 386$.
Marit. Sat. = marital satisfaction, Neg. Com. = negative communication, Open Com. = open communication

For the evaluation of this factor model (and the other models used below), two fit indices were considered: (1) the root mean square error of approximation (RMSEA), and (2) the comparative fit index (CFI). Models with a RMSEA value lower than .05 and a CFI value over .95 indicate an acceptable fit between model and data (Billiet & McClendon, 1998; Byrne, 1998; Hu & Bentler, 1999; Kline, 1998; Mueller, 1996). The model with $df = 186$ showed a χ^2-value of 295.70 with RMSEA = .039 and CFI = .99, indicating a very good fit.

In the next step, the measurement invariance of the three concepts across time and across sex was tested to be sure that it is allowed to compare latent variables across time and between husbands and wives. Measurement invariance on the item level was already established (see Chapter 4). Therefore, it is expected that the parcels also show measurement invariance. To verify this expectation, factor loadings (lambda's) between the manifest parcels and their latent construct at Time 1 were equated with the corresponding loadings at Time 2. The same principle was done with respect to husbands and wives.

This model (with equating the factor loadings of marital satisfaction, of negative communication and of open communication) showed a χ^2-value of 308.52 (df = 195) with RMSEA = .038 and CFI = .99, also indicating a very good fit. The increase in χ^2 was 12.82 (df = 9) with p = .177 showing that a factor model with equal factor loadings on comparable concepts leads to a non-significant increase of χ^2. Our conclusion is that the three concepts are invariant across time and across sex. Hence, for the next analyses, the involved factor loadings (lambdas) were constrained to be equal.

For the cross-lagged analysis, five variables were included as exogenous variables: marital duration, the age of both spouses, as well as their educational level. The covariance matrix of these parcels and the five control variables was used as input matrix for the analysis. Their correlations, means and standard deviations are shown in Table 5.2.

Due to the time span of five years, we did not expect error terms to be correlated over time and thus we did not define these terms. The endogenous variables of husband and wives were allowed to correlate at Time 1 as well as at Time 2. For the initial model, (see Figure 5.1) the control variables did not appear to show any significant relationship with the endogenous variables. For this reason these variables were excluded in the next analyses. Testing the cross-lagged model with the relationships as depicted in Figure 5.1, yields a χ^2-value of 344.96 with df = 218, RMSEA = .038 and CFI = .99, which fits very well. The majority of the cross-lagged effects were not significant. First, none of the female cross-lagged effects reached significance. Second, communication variables at Time 1 were not related to marital satisfaction at Time 2, for women, or for men. Only husbands' marital satisfaction at Time 1 predicted their perception of open communication at Time 2. Without the non-significant cross-lagged relationships, the χ^2-value equals 353.23 with df = 224, RMSEA = .038 and CFI = .99. The decrease in χ^2 equals 8.27, with df = 6 and p = .219, indicating that the omitted cross-lagged effects have a non-significant contribution in the cross-lagged model.

Table 5.2
Correlation Matrix of the Parcels of the Open and Negative Communication, and Marital Satisfaction Scales, and the Control Variables, According to Sex and Year [Women Beneath Diagonal, Men Above Diagonal]

	t1ms1	t1ms2	t1nc1	t1nc2	t1oc1	t1oc2	t2ms1	t2ms2	t2nc1	t2nc2	t2oc1	t2oc2	ym	yb	edu	M	SD
t1ms1	--	.69 ***	-.42 ***	-.48 ***	.22 ***	.22 ***	.51 ***	.52 ***	-.33 ***	-.37 ***	.32 ***	.20 ***	.07	-.01	-.10 *	6.18	0.97
t1ms2	.80 ***	--	-.41 ***	-.46 ***	.23 ***	.24 ***	.52 ***	.58 ***	-.31 ***	-.36 ***	.36 ***	.21 ***	.03	.06	-.11 *	6.07	1.07
t1nc1	-.44 ***	-.46 ***	--	.68 ***	-.16 **	-.13 **	-.31 ***	-.33 ***	.54 ***	.52 ***	-.26 ***	-.11 ***	-.06	-.02	.07	2.80	1.19
t1nc2	-.43 ***	-.46 ***	.59 ***	--	-.19 ***	-.15 **	-.32 ***	-.34 ***	.46 ***	.55 ***	-.33 ***	-.20 ***	-.07	-.02	.03	2.67	1.18
t1oc1	.38 ***	.37 ***	-.18 ***	-.19 ***	--	.51 ***	.20 ***	.21 ***	-.05	-.10 *	.41 ***	.28 ***	-.06	.05	-.05	4.91	1.23
t1oc2	.30 ***	.34 ***	-.08	-.15 **	.45 ***	--	.23 ***	.21 ***	-.09	-.16 **	.22 ***	.27 ***	-.01	.04	-.09	5.30	1.43
t2ms1	.52 ***	.54 ***	-.33 ***	-.32 ***	.28 ***	.17 ***	--	.76 ***	-.56 ***	-.48 ***	.35 ***	.30 ***	.03	.04	-.10 *	6.07	1.00
t2ms2	.50 ***	.54 ***	-.36 ***	-.33 ***	.27 ***	.18 ***	.79 ***	--	-.50 ***	-.46 ***	.38 ***	.30 ***	-.01	-.02	-.09	5.93	1.10
t2nc1	-.39 ***	-.44 ***	.58 ***	.46 ***	-.21 ***	-.07	-.63 ***	-.61 ***	--	.70 ***	-.26 ***	-.15 **	-.10 *	-.06	.01	2.63	1.13
t2nc2	-.38 ***	-.37 ***	.44 ***	.48 ***	-.21 ***	-.08	-.48 ***	-.49 ***	.64 ***	--	-.28 ***	-.15 **	-.05	-.07	-.02	2.79	1.19
t2oc1	.33 ***	.32 ***	-.21 ***	-.21 ***	.48 ***	.28 ***	.38 ***	.38 ***	-.35 ***	-.22 ***	--	.55 ***	-.11 *	-.11 *	.02	5.02	1.25
t2oc2	.28 ***	.30 ***	-.23 ***	-.21 ***	.34 ***	.29 ***	.32 ***	.34 ***	-.25 ***	-.19 ***	.63 ***	--	-.09	-.09	-.01	5.38	1.30
ym	.04	.05	-.13 *	-.13 *	.04	.06	-.02	-.01	-.02	-.03	.03	.02	--	.62 ***	-.02	72.76	3.27
yb	.09	.10	-.06	-.10 *	.11 *	.11 *	-.00	.02	.00	-.02	.09	.06	.72 ***	--	-.12 *	47.52	4.94
edu	-.08	-.10	.02	.02	.02	-.01	.02	-.03	-.02	.00	.05	.02	.03	-.16 **	--	3.87	2.01
M	6.12	6.03	2.72	2.67	5.36	5.85	6.04	5.77	2.59	2.81	5.51	5.93	72.76	50.06	3.24		
SD	1.04	1.11	1.23	1.10	1.23	1.33	1.07	1.24	1.13	1.18	1.19	1.17	3.27	4.26	1.65		

Note. t1 = wave 1, t2 = wave 2, ms = marital satisfaction, oc = open communication, nc = negative communication, ym = year of marriage, yb = year of birth, edu = educational level
*p < .05 ** p < .01 *** p < .001

To examine whether the cross-lagged relationship between marital satisfaction at Time 1 and open communication at Time 2 is different for men and women, a second model was tested. In this model the paths between marital satisfaction at Time 1 and open communication at Time 2 were initially left free. For this model, $\chi^2(223) = 351.98$. For the model with the two paths constrained to equality $\chi^2(224) = 360.26$, a significant increase of χ^2 with 8.28 and df = 1 and p = .004. This equality constraint apparently worsened our model. The restricted model was less successful in accounting for the observed relationships between the latent constructs. In other words, a sex difference exists with respect to the effect of marital satisfaction (Time 1) on open communication (Time 2). For husbands, marital satisfaction was positively related to their perception of open communication five years later, but this finding does not hold for women. The results are presented in Figure 5.2.

As can be seen from Figure 5.2, the correlations at Time 1 and Time 2 demonstrate for both husbands and wives strong negative associations between marital satisfaction and negative communication and significant positive associations between open communication and marital satisfaction. The relation between concurrent marital satisfaction and negative communication perception appears much stronger than their relationship across time. For both sexes, the cross-lagged effects between marital satisfaction and negative communication were not significant. However, our results support the hypothesis that husband's marital satisfaction is predictive of a change in open communication behavior. It appeared that satisfied husbands are more likely to share personal experiences over time and to talk about things that happened during the day. Wives' marital satisfaction was not predictive of their open communication.

Figure 5.2
Cross-Lagged Model for Open and Negative Communication and Marital Satisfaction

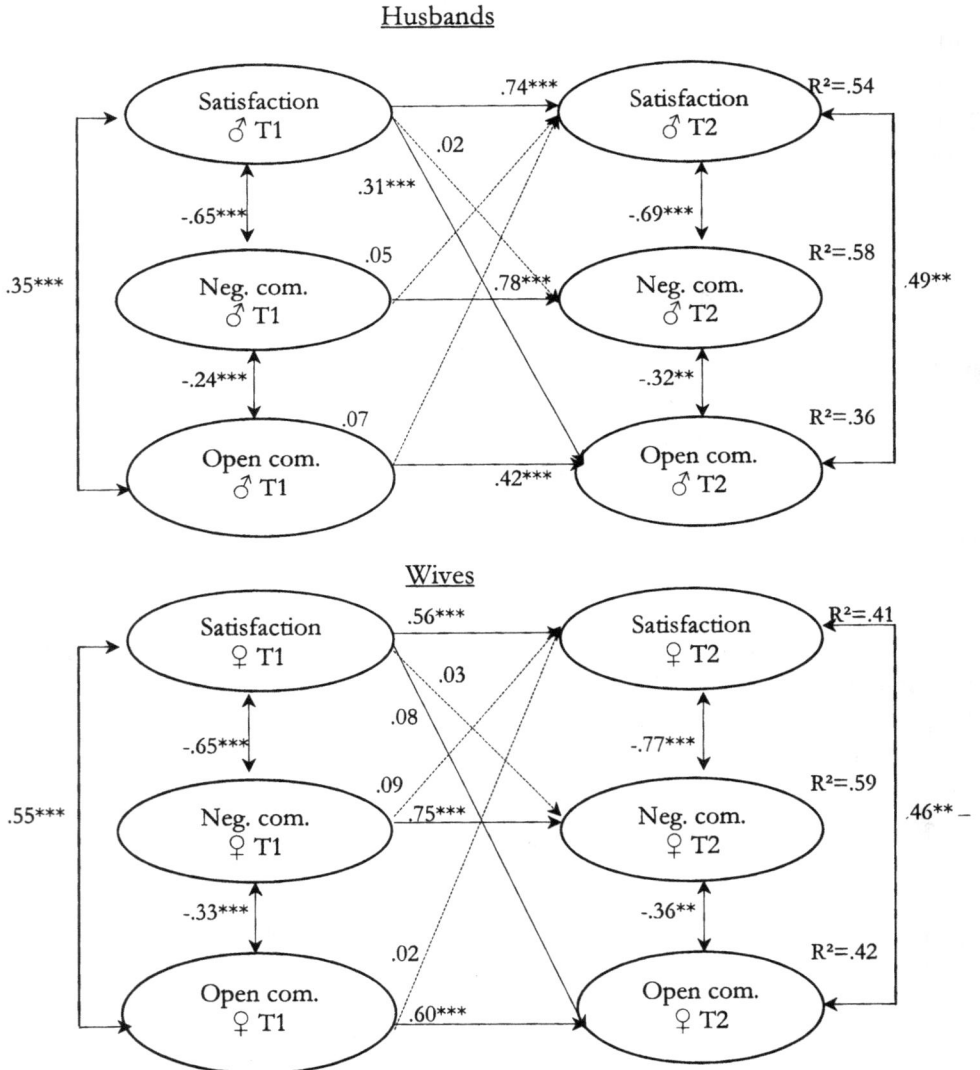

Husbands

Wives

Note: Standardized Parameter Estimates.
*p < .05, **p < .01, ***p < .001

5.4. DISCUSSION

This study was designed to gain insight into the relationship between marital satisfaction and communication. Based on previous literature, it was unclear (1) whether marital satisfaction accounts for variation in marital communication more than communication leads to changes in marital satisfaction and (2) whether the cross-lagged relationships might be sex-specific.

Our major finding is that communication is not predictive of later marital satisfaction. Spouses appear to be no more or less satisfied during a five-years interval when they communicate more openly or less negatively with their partner. This finding holds for both husbands and wives.

More evidence was obtained for the assumption that satisfaction predicts open communication. Moreover, this effect was found to be sex-specific. Marital satisfaction was positively related to husbands' but not wives' open communication. Along with the failure of husbands' open communication to predict later marital satisfaction, it is suggested that satisfaction potentially influences open communication.

When considering negative communication, we found no support for assuming any cross-lagged relationship with marital satisfaction. The non-significance of the cross-lagged effects between marital satisfaction and negative communication may indicate that marital satisfaction is more consistently associated with current negative communication perception than with later or prior assessments. Therefore, no longitudinal evidence was obtained for the motivational approach on the basis of which we expected a negative cross-lagged effect of marital satisfaction on negative communication for women (Denton, Burleson, & Sprenkle, 1994). This finding may account for the fact that the motivational approach is possibly a short-term model or that women's perception of negative communication is a reflection of their marital satisfaction rather than a predictor or outcome (and vice versa).

A striking finding is that satisfied husbands were more likely to share personal experiences with their partner. Thus, men linked their marital experiences with their own communication behavior and not with the communication behavior of their partner. The latter becomes clear from the fact that men's satisfaction was not related with their perception of negative communication, which focuses on the partner communication.

This finding can supplement earlier findings such as those of Noller (1981) and Gottman and Porterfield (1981). They demonstrated that dissatisfied husbands fare poorly in decoding and encoding emotional nonverbal messages of their partners, abilities that appear to be relationship-specific instead of being a general trait.

It is interesting to speculate about why men's supported "capacity" or "willingness" to share personal experiences (open communication) should decrease with declining satisfaction, whereas this finding did not hold for women. At first sight, this result may be remarkable from the assumption that women are more relationally-oriented than men (Acitelli, 1992). If men are not so relationally attuned, why does their marital satisfaction predict their communication over time? An explanation can be found in an earlier finding of Antill (1983) with respect to femininity in relationships. The author provided evidence for the overwhelming importance of femininity on the part of both husband and wife for explaining each other's marital happiness. In our study, it is suggested that in satisfied relationships, men more closely approach a stereotypical feminine communication style. The higher female scores on open communication in our study lend support to this interpretation. That might also be the reason why this trend does not show up in women's marital satisfaction and their perception of open communication nor in men's marital satisfaction and their perception of negative communication because both communication measures focus on women. Indeed, one can expect that women were already characterized by a more relational orientation.

Assuming that the aforementioned explanations are correct, our results may be consistent with the possibility that wives' marital satisfaction may simply reflect their communication behavior, whereas husbands' marital satisfaction may actually affect their communication behavior. Men in satisfied relationships may develop communication behavior that their wives already tend to use to a larger extent. It seems that a marital relationship might benefit not only from partner's pre-existing communication behavior but also from communication behavior developed over the marital life course.

Limitations

Because of some limitations of this study, our findings must be put into perspective. First, the question arises whether the amount of time between the two measurement waves was too lengthy to account for other associations. Longitudinal studies on marital satisfaction and attributions or maintenance behaviors are conducted typically within shorter time intervals (e.g., Fincham & Bradbury, 1987(b); Weigel & Ballard-Reisch, 2001). Because the strength of lagged effects in longitudinal studies depends on the period between two consecutive waves, this is a very difficult issue to deal with (Finkel, 1995). Unfortunately, there is no directive for the optimal lag for marital satisfaction and communication to affect each other. Moreover, to reach stronger conclusions regarding our variables of interest, at least three measurement waves should be used. Therefore, future studies should attempt to confirm our results using different time frames and several waves of data.

A second point worth mentioning is the specific character of the sample. The current project deals with relatively highly educated men and women, who are on average 46 years old and have adolescent children. At the second measurement point, couples were married for about 22 years. Perhaps different cross-lagged relationships between satisfaction and communication could be found when examined in a sample of younger couples or less educated individuals. Moreover, it is possible not only to find different cross-lagged effects but also different sex-specific effects when examining other samples. That is why a definite causal and sex-specific interpretation of our findings is unwarranted at this stage. Because no established longitudinal findings are at our disposal, future research is needed to confirm our results over time.

Conclusion

Despite these limitations, our results are relevant. From a therapeutic point of view, it is helpful to know that changing marital communication by itself may not be as important for improving marital satisfaction as previously thought. As Holmes (2000) emphasizes, 'good' communication cannot eradicate, for example, incompatibility between the spouses. Therefore, a therapeutic goal orientated towards the marital process or communication might appear ineffective if it is opposed to spouse's interest. Theoretically, the study makes a valuable contribution to our understanding of relationship satisfaction and communication because of the longitudinal approach in combination with a focus on sex. Parott (2000) asserts that emotions, and thus satisfaction, can involve changes in thinking or behavior and, therefore, can affect social interaction and relationships. To be (dis)satisfied with one's partner and relationship might play a considerable role in men's communication behavior within marriage. For women, the perception of her own and her partner's communication behavior may be a reflection of her marital satisfaction rather than a predictor or outcome. These findings are relevant because the role of communication in marriage has moved from the periphery to the centre (Fitzpatrick, 1988). This 'changed role' of communication is a result of the prominent position of the emotional function of partnership in society's view of marriage on the one hand, and contemporary society's absence of fixed and clear external rules for partnership on the other hand.

Three directions for future research in this specific topic are recommended. First, the antecedent-consequent relationships between marital satisfaction and marital communication need to be corroborated in different spousal samples. Second, the sex-specific nature of these cross-lagged relationships has to be investigated. Third, and more profound, is the analysis of how marital satisfaction is built up over time. In other words, when communication is not an important building block in established marriages, is this also true in newlywed couples? And, which other factors contribute to marital satisfaction in each phase of marital relationships?

6. Effects of Spousal Economic and Cultural Characteristics on Marital Satisfaction

6.1. INTRODUCTION

Do women's economic resources have a harmful effect on spousal marital satisfaction and are there cultural conditions moderating this effect? These questions are explored in the present study. The main purpose is to examine the influence of husbands' and wives' socioeconomic position and cultural orientation on their satisfaction with marriage. Since both are inherently connected, attention is particularly paid to the interaction between economic and cultural factors. In fact, the increase in women's educational level and labor force participation that the past 40 years witnessed, are not only economical but also cultural in nature (De Graaf & Vermeulen, 1997; Lye & Biblarz, 1993; Rogers & Amato, 2000; South, 2001). The shift in women's social roles is accompanied by other social transformations, among which are changing gender role attitudes. We are moving towards an androgynous egalitarianism emphasizing the similarities rather than the differences in sex roles (Davis, 1984; Thornton, Alwin, & Camburn, 1983). Moreover, individualization processes cause individuals to think less traditionally about family life, no longer attaching primary importance to marital life and raising children (Peters & Gerris, 1995). In the present study, it is argued that these cultural changes need to be taken into account when examining the relationship between women's economic position and spousal marital satisfaction. Disregarding the cultural aspect, as is often the case in studies examining the effect of spousal economic resources on marriage, might partially account for inconsistent findings regarding economic variables and marital satisfaction.

Besides, previous studies have been primarily done in the United States. Accordingly, relatively little is known about this subject in Western Europe and particularly in the Netherlands. Recent findings on the covariates of divorce among Dutch couples suggest that the effect of wives' employment is not the same for all marriages and women (Kalmijn, De Graaf, & Poortman, 2004). Whether outside employment gets translated into marital instability depends on wives' emancipatory values. It was demonstrated that women's employment increases the chance of divorce for traditional but not for more liberal women. Therefore, it is reasonable to also consider this hypothesis with respect to Dutch couples' marital satisfaction.

Moreover, because prior studies on the association between marital satisfaction and economic and cultural aspects mostly relied upon cross-sectional designs, we cannot tell if *changes* in these variables are also associated with *changes* in spousal marital satisfaction. This issue invites further investigation.

Using panel data of Dutch first-married couples, our aim is to incorporate cultural variables in tandem with economic proxies in order to examine their separate and joint effects on marital satisfaction. This question is addressed cross-sectionally as well as longitudinally.

6.2. THEORETICAL AND EMPIRICAL BACKGROUND

The importance of differentiated sex roles for a stable marital system is a longstanding and influential tradition in the social science literature. Talcott Parsons already emphasized this idea in the postwar period and later on Becker elaborated the same theme in his economic theory of marriage. The converging view is that marital satisfaction is higher to the extent that wives have fewer labor market resources and husbands have more resources (Ono, 1998).

Economic approaches, such as rational choice and social exchange theories, emphasize the efficiency and productivity of a sex-segregated arrangement. According to Becker (1981), the major gain to marriage lies in spousal mutual dependence arising out of their specialized functions as breadwinner and homemaker. Therefore, dual earner couples may develop a less rewarding marriage as both sexes become less specialized and less powerful in a domain that is important for the other. This non-specialization and imbalance of the marital relationship may result in lower satisfaction with marriage (Brennan, Barnett, & Gareis, 2001; Scanzoni, 1979).

Psychosocial approaches rather emphasize the change in options and needs that couples are confronted with when wives dispose of more resources. Proponents assert that the greater availability of women's resources may reduce the costs of leaving a distressed marriage (Davis, 1984). More economically independent wives might be less motivated to work out their marital problems whereas their husbands may feel less restricted or guilty to leave a relationship in which their wives are able to support themselves (Kalmijn, De Graaf & Poortman, 2004; Peatsch, Bala, Bertrand & Glennon, 2004).

The above ideas are commonly translated in the so-called wife's *independence hypothesis* and husband's *income hypothesis* (Ono, 1998). The former states that women's labor market resources are likely to put marriage under stress whereas the latter hypothesis reflects the opposite for men. Husbands' income hypothesis assumes higher gains for marriage to the degree that husbands have more economic resources. Both arguments have received widespread attention among sociologists as well as economists in explaining recent family trends (see Oppenheimer, 1997; 2001).

However, research yields inconsistent results with respect to the effect of women's resources on marital experiences. Even though studies in the sixties (Axelson, 1963; Orden & Bradburn, 1969) confirmed the poorer marital satisfaction of couples where the wife is employed, more recent studies provide mixed support (see Oppenheimer, 1997). Some studies fail to demonstrate a relationship (Glenn & Weaver, 1978) whereas others obtain evidence that wives' labor market participation reduces husbands' but not their own marital satisfaction (Booth, Johnson, Whyte, & Edwards, 1984; Greenstein, 1990; Kessler & McRae, 1982). The latter may hold because wives' employment is not only driven by financial reasons but also serves other goals such as personal development and improved social status for women. When considering wives' occupation or earnings in specific, Vannoy & Philliber (1992) failed to demonstrate a significant association with husbands or wives' marital satisfaction. Using panel data, Rogers (1999) found no support for the idea that a change in wives income is related to changes in marital discord.

However, wife's independence hypothesis needs to be considered in light of men's breadwinner status. As long as this status is unchallenged by wives' employment, men's marital satisfaction is higher than in case their breadwinner's position is threatened (Crowley, 1998). Hence, relative earning power rather than women's employment as such appears to be the differentiating factor. Moreover, other findings do not support the disruptive effect of wives incomes on marriage. A recent study of Gupta, Smock, and Manning (2004) on the correlates of non-residential fatherhood in the U.S. demonstrate that the probability of non-residence decreased to the degree that both fathers' and mothers' incomes increased, suggesting the stabilizing effects of women's income on family life.

Other evidence contrary to the independence hypothesis concerns wife's educational level. Higher levels of education may be associated with better relationship skills and hence higher marital satisfaction. Indeed, Locksley (1982) found that higher educated wives are happier with their marriage than those who are less educated. Kurdek (1993) reported similar results for his 5-year longitudinal sample of newlywed couples. Whyte (1990), in contrast, showed that women's education was unrelated to marital satisfaction. However, in this respect it is interesting to note that in the Netherlands the likelihood of divorce is higher among better rather than among lower educated women, questioning the validity of the American hypothesis for the Dutch context (Kalmijn, de Graaf, & Poortman, 2004). It remains to be seen whether this finding is also true with respect to marital satisfaction.

These mixed findings lead us to conclude that the wife's independence hypothesis is contentious. More consistent support is found for the male income hypothesis (Ono, 1998; Whyte, 1990). Vannoy and Philliber (1992) demonstrate that employed wives are more satisfied with their marriage when their husbands are higher educated. However, if women are not employed, their marital satisfaction appears to be unrelated to men's education. Both findings are consistent with the interpretation that educated husbands may be better prepared for developing an egalitarian marriage. Although not entirely indicative, studies on marital instability also demonstrate that husbands' poorer economic position in terms of income and education is linked to a higher risk of marital dissolution (Ono, 1998).

Economic factors might be accompanied by subjective appraisals, which may also affect the marital relationship (Mugenda, Hira, & Fanslow, 1990). A review of White and Rogers (2000) suggests that subjective evaluations of one's economic position are more strongly related to marital outcomes than measures such as income and employment. Conger et al. (1990) reported similar results and concluded that subjective assessments of one's economic situation are important determinants of marital satisfaction, rather than the material component of income or status. In a similar vein, Mugenda et al. (1990) identified satisfaction with the financial status as an important mechanism through which socioeconomic factors relate to quality of life.

Missing from the above studies, however, is the consideration of cultural conditions. The inconsistent support provided for the independence hypothesis may be due to the lack of attention paid to circumstances under which spousal resources are more or less beneficial for marital satisfaction. One of these conditions may be cultural in nature. Indeed, the values that spouses hold towards sex roles and family life, for example, are a cultural reflection of the shift in women's and men's social roles. However, values in a sociological sense of indicating culturally defined standards serving as broad guidelines for social living, are seldom allowed in economic approaches (Macionis, 1997; Moors, 2001). Nonetheless, studies indicate the relevance of these values. Vannoy and Philliber (1992), for example, even identify gender role identities and role expectations as a primary explanation for marital experiences.

Considering cultural conditions may put economic effects on marriage in a proper perspective, the more so since previous work has been shown that the effect of gender attitudes on marital satisfaction is gender-specific. Women with a nontraditional view on gender roles tend to experience lower marital satisfaction whereas for men the reverse finding is true (Amato & Booth, 1995; Lye & Biblarz, 1993). Husbands' egalitarian attitudes might be advantageous for couples because those husbands tend do more household labor and are more supportive for their employed wives (Ferree, 1991; Suitor, 1991; Vannoy-Hiller & Philliber, 1989). Peters and Gerris (1995) also demonstrated that the marital relationship of spouses being strongly orientated on traditional family values such as being married and living for your family, is more satisfying.

Despite the fact that economic and cultural explanations go hand in hand, they are not always perfectly correlated. Although it may be more acceptable for egalitarian than for traditional or familial spouses that wives work outside, traditional women may also work outside because of financial reasons while nontraditional women decide to stay home because of the difficult combination of employment and family care (Kalmijn, De Graaf,

& Poortman, 2004). Hence, there are reasons to assume that cultural and economic characteristics interact in their effect on marital satisfaction.

Studies on this interaction hypothesis with respect to marital satisfaction are exceptional. Nonetheless, one study dealing with this issue tended to find moderating effects. Vannoy and Philliber (1992) demonstrate that husbands' gender role attitudes are more important for marital satisfaction when the wife is employed than when she is not. These authors did not examine, however, to what degree wives' employment has different effects when holding more or less traditional attitudes. Hence, their finding justifies further investigation on the interaction between cultural characteristics and economic aspects in their association with marital satisfaction. This interaction assumption is also supported in research on marital stability. Divorce studies suggest that the negative effects of women's economic resources are conditional on cultural values with more negative or no effects for women holding traditional gender ideologies (Greenstein, 1990; Kalmijn, De Graaf & Poortman, 2004).

However, no attempt is made to examine the interaction between women's labor market resources and spouses' familialism. Familialism refers to the degree to which the private sphere of family and marital life is considered important (Peters & Gerris, 1995). In general, this orientation is associated with traditionalism and economic inequality. However, in the Netherlands the connection between familialism and traditionalism has become weaker during the nineties, indicating that the Dutch cultural context of familialism has lost most of its traditional nature (Peters & Gerris, 1995). In this way, the question arises whether the effect of women's labor market resources on marital satisfaction might be contingent upon spouses' familial orientation.

Besides their interaction, we are also interested in the effects of economic and cultural factors across time. However, economic and cultural explanations are seldom addressed jointly in a longitudinal design. Nonetheless, marital satisfaction can be better understood when it is compared with earlier and later satisfaction. In this way, the issue is directed towards the factors that contribute to an increase or decrease in marital satisfaction over time. Because previous work mostly relied upon cross-sectional designs it remains unclear to what degree economic and cultural variables as well as their change predict later marital satisfaction when considered jointly. This issue needs further exploration.

6.3. PRESENT STUDY AND HYPOTHESES

As became clear from the above review, previous findings regarding spousal economic resources and marital satisfaction did not provide straightforward conclusions. We argued that the failure to include the cultural dimension in this discussion might explain some of the contrasting findings. Cultural variables not only need to be taken into account when evaluating the effect of spousal economic position on the marital satisfaction experienced, they also need to be linked to cultural variables to examine the circumstances in which the association between economic indicators and marital satisfaction may become more or less positive. Therefore, this study addresses the above issue by examining how economic and cultural indicators – separately and jointly – are related to spousal marital satisfaction. It is firstly hypothesized that cultural variables have an independent effect beyond the economic variables on the satisfaction reported by husbands and wives. Second, we reassess the association between women's economic resources and spousal marital satisfaction by considering this relationship as contingent upon spouses' cultural orientations. We examine this topic using a Dutch sample of married couples that were followed during a five-years interval (2 measurement points). Our analyses are conducted separately for men and women.

A first model (Model 1) tests the independence hypothesis for women and the income hypothesis for men. It can be expected that couples in which the wife has more economic resources experience lower marital satisfaction than couples in which the wife has fewer economic resources. Conversely, we hypothesize that couples in which the husband has more economic resources experience higher marital satisfaction than couples in which the husband has fewer economic resources.

A second model (Model 2) examines the first model supplemented with husbands and wives' satisfaction with their income to spend. We test the hypothesis that spouses, who are more satisfied with their financial situation, are also more likely to be satisfied with their relationship.

Third, we test the additional effect of cultural orientations (Model 3). Spouses' attitudes towards both sex roles and traditional family values will be considered. In general, it is hypothesized that nontraditional role attitudes are negatively associated with spousal marital satisfaction. More specifically, we anticipate that this hypothesis holds primarily for women's attitudes whereas men's liberal attitudes may positively affect spousal marital satisfaction. Regarding familialism, however, it can be expected that both husbands and wives are more satisfied with their marriage when endorsing family values. Based on the study of Vannoy and Philliber (1992) we expect that cultural variables will have a significant effect on spouses' marital satisfaction independent of their economic resources.

Fourth, the interaction hypothesis is examined by linking wives' economic characteristics with the cultural variables of *both* husbands and wives (Model 4). Whether wives are employed or not is considered in function of both spouses' orientations towards traditional family values and sex roles. The same is done using wives' educational level as indicator of their economic position. Husbands' economic characteristics are not related to spouses' cultural orientations because this is not our main point of attention. To capture the employment status (employed or not) of the couple, we also included the interaction term between wives and husbands' employment.

Because research has shown that family income (Conger et al., 1990), parental divorce (Amato, 1996) and young age at marriage (Holman, 2001) are negatively related to marital satisfaction, the following control variables will be included in the analysis: age of the spouses, number of years married, parental divorce, net family income and number of children.

6.4. STUDY DESIGN

We report on three studies. Using hierarchical regression analysis, we examine in a first study the additional effects of cultural characteristics to economic characteristics in understanding husbands and wives' marital satisfaction. Subsequently we test whether the interaction between economic and cultural characteristics add supplementary value to this model. It is also examined whether female employment is less disruptive for spousal marital satisfaction in case husbands are unemployed. We use the first wave data of a national panel study of couples.

In a second study we replicate the hierarchical models in a subset of the larger sample used in Study 1. Specifically, we perform our analyses on those couples that remain married through the two waves. The potential selective character of the panel attrition may result in different results within the two samples at the first measurement point. The findings from this second study must inform us about the specificity of the both-waves participants. This information must put the results of the third study in the proper perspective.

In the third study, we assess spousal marital satisfaction five years after the first measurement. It is analyzed whether changes in economic and cultural variables relate to changes in marital satisfaction. Comparing these results with those of the first and the second study must inform us about the variables that are specifically associated with concurrent and later marital satisfaction.

6.5. METHOD

6.5.1. Procedure and Sample

The research sample consists of married men and women participating in the longitudinal research project "Child-Rearing and family in the Netherlands". In 1990 and 1995 the same family members (mother, father and target child) provided information about similar sets of measures. Families were recruited using a multi-stage sampling method. In a first stage, a sample was taken of all Dutch municipalities distinguished by regional zone and degree of urbanization. In a second stage, a sample of children was taken in the selected municipalities. The children were selected in such a way that in each city as many boys as girls and as many children aged 9 to 12 as children aged 13 to 16 were chosen. In 1990 this procedure resulted in a sample of 1829 families. The response ratio was 43% ($N = 788$). As pursued, the sample was representative regarding regional zone and degree of urbanization. Of the 656 families who agreed in 1990 to participate in the second wave, 627 were contacted and 484 (77%) actually did participate in 1995. This sample proved to be still representative for regional zone but not for degree of urbanization. More technical details on the database can be found in Gerris et al. (1992; 1993; 1998). The data were gathered by means of structured interviews and questionnaires.

Because the original sample includes married couples - both first and higher order marriages - as well as one-parent households and households with children of whom the parents are not married, we restrict our research sample to first marriages because of the potentially different social processes involved when considering higher-order marriages. This selection resulted in a research group of 646 couples in the first wave and 386 couples in the second wave. At the first measurement point, the couples are averagely married for 17 years. Husbands age 42 years and wives are on average 40 years old. 95% of the husbands in the sample are employed whereas this only holds for 47% of women. The majority of the employed women work part-time. Hence, the couples included in our study primarily represent single earner- and main-earner households. Median monthly family income is between 1250 and 1625 €. About a quarter of the male sample enjoyed higher vocational or university education, while for women this figure was approximately one out of eight.

Using logistic regression, we examined the selective character of the panel attrition between the first and the second wave. The inclusion in "both waves" versus "first wave" was regressed on all variables of interest in this study. Two variables significantly predicted the likelihood of being included in one of the two groups (χ^2 (19) = 28.94, p = .07): husbands' sex role attitudes and their income satisfaction. Husbands who participate at both waves are more satisfied with the net family income ($p < .05$) and slightly more traditional in their sex role attitudes ($p = .055$).

6.5.2. Measures

Education was measured in response to the question "What is your highest educational level?" Nine levels were considered ranging from 1 = "elementary school" to 9 = "university education".

Employment status of husbands and wives was dichotomized with 0 = not employed and 1 = employed.

Income position is indicated by the net family income, measured in Dutch guilders. One guilder is approximately 0.45 Euro. Seven income groups were distinguished: 1 = "1100-1600", 2 = "1600-1800", 3 = "1800-2100", 4 = "2100-2500", 5 = "2500-3250", 6 = "3250-4500" and 7 = "more than 4500".

Income satisfaction is indicated by the response to the question "Are you satisfied with the income you can spend freely?". This is a 5-point item scale rated from 1 = "more than enough" to 5 = "much too little".

Attitude towards sex roles measures the degree to which the respondent reports to value a traditional division of roles and tasks between males and females in household, career, child-rearing and education. This orientation is measured with a scale consisting of 6 items. The response scale is a 5-point Likert scale ranging from 1 = "totally agree" to 5 = "totally disagree" (e.g., "A woman is better suited to raise small children than a man"). After recoding, higher scores indicate higher valuation of this orientation. Cronbach's alpha is .78 for men and .83 for women.

The *Traditional family values* scale measures the degree to which the respondent reports to value traditional characteristics of the family as a living form. It is a 4-item scale with 1= "extremely important" to 5= "unimportant" (e.g., "To live for your family"). After recoding, higher scores indicate higher valuation of these family values. Internal consistency for this scale is .76 for men and .77 for women.

The construction of the "Attitudes towards sex roles" and "Traditional family values"-scales is reported in Gerris et al. (1992, 1993).

Marital satisfaction is measured by the Marital Satisfaction scale as described and validated in Chapter 4. For formulating the items, satisfaction with the relationship and/or the partner was used as the guiding principle (e.g., "Generally, I'm dissatisfied with the relationship with my partner" or "If I could choose again, I would choose the same partner"). The scale consists of seven 7-point Likert items, ranging from 1 = "not at all applicable" to 7 = "very applicable". For women the alpha reliability coefficient is .85 and .87 for 1990 and 1995 respectively. For men this coefficient is .80 and .85.

Control variables: Because they could affect marital satisfaction as well as our independent variables of interest, age of the marital partners (year of birth), number of years married (year of marriage), number of children and parental divorce were included as control variables. The year in which the couple married indicates marital duration in 1990 and 1995. Marital duration and age together represent a proxy for emotional maturity, which may be crucial for developing satisfying relationships.

6.6. RESULTS

Before running the hierarchical regression analyses, correlations of the variables of interest are displayed in Table 6.1. Figures are presented for the sample at Time 1.

Using paired t-tests, differences across time and sex are examined. The between-sex results for the initial sample indicate that men are significantly more educated than women ($t = 8.85$, $p < .001$). Results demonstrate that both spouses are equally satisfied with the financial situation of the family. Regarding gender role attitudes, it appears that husbands advocate a more traditional orientation than women ($t = 10.13$, $p < .001$), which might be due to the advantaged position of men in a sex-segregated role pattern (van Yperen, 1990). Women, however, score higher on traditional family values ($t = -4.78$, $p < .001$), lending support to the stronger relational and familial orientation of women. Considering spousal marital satisfaction, a paired-sample t-test indicates that women and men are equally satisfied at the first measurement point.

Within-sex differences across time reveal that both men ($t = 2.13$, $p < .05$) and women ($t = 3.30$, $p < .001$) become less satisfied during the period of the study. T-tests demonstrate that spousal orientation towards sex roles (Men, $t = 2.37$, $p < .05$; Women, $t = 4.75$, $p < .001$) and family values (Men, $t = 3.34$, $p < .001$; Women, $t = 3.31$, $p < .001$) becomes less traditional. A comparison of the mean satisfaction with the family income shows that both men ($t = -4.00$, $p < .001$) and women ($t = -2.71$, $p < .01$) had become less satisfied during the period under study.

Table 6.1
Correlation Matrix of Spousal Economic and Cultural Variables and Marital Satisfaction at Time 1, Men [Above Diagonal] and Women [Below Diagonal]

	1 Marital satisfaction	2 Year of marriage	3 Number of children	4 Parental divorce	5 Education	6 Year birth	7 Income	8 Income dissatisfaction	9 Familialism	10 Sex role traditional.	11 Employment
1	/	.05	.01	-.00	-.14*	.02	-.07	.02	.24***	.05	-.01
2	.07	/	-.13***	.02	.01	.63***	-.04	-.02	-.03	-.10**	.11**
3	.04	-.13***	/	-.03	.06	-.15***	.03	-.01	.05	.11**	.02
4	.02	-.01	-.02	/	-.06	-.09*	.00	-.00	-.01	-.11**	-.06
5	-.08*	.04	-.02	-.05	/	-.11*	.57***	-.24***	-.17***	-.21***	.11**
6	.12**	.69***	-.15***	-.01	-.08*	/	-.06	-.02	-.01	-.11**	.20***
7	.01	-.04	.03	-.00	.40***	-.06	/	-.45***	-.13***	-.29***	.20***
8	-.11**	.00	.06	.02	-.22***	-.01	-.46***	/	.03	.11**	-.19***
9	.27***	-.06	.13***	.02	-.15***	-.02	-.13***	.03	/	.21***	-.06
10	.00	-.13***	.08*	.05	-.29***	-.10**	-.23***	.09*	.20***	/	-.06
11	.00	.05	-.14***	-.05	.20***	.04	.27***	-.15***	-.04	-.25***	/

Note: *p < .05 ** p < .01 *** p < .001, Employment, 1=yes, 2=no.

The correlational analysis presented in Table 6.1, clearly demonstrates the interrelation between economic and cultural factors. For both sexes, negative associations are found between education and familialism as well as between education and sex role traditionalism. The same conclusion can be drawn using income instead of education. From Table 6.1 it also become clear that familialism and sex role traditionalism are positively correlated, suggesting that familialism in our sample reflects a rather traditional orientation. This would contrast the earlier statements made in the introduction that familialism increasingly looses its 'traditional' character in the Netherlands.

Study 1

Using the data of the first measurement wave, separate hierarchical regression analyses were conducted for men and women. In order to reduce the problem of multicollinearity, raw scores on all the variables of interest were mean-centered (Jacard, Turussi , & Wan, 1990). Because in none of the models, control variables had a significant effect, their results will not be presented in the Tables.

For both husbands and wives we found that despite the significant effect of female education, the model including both spouses' economic characteristics was not significant. Adding men and women's satisfaction with their income free to spend to our model, it becomes clear from Table 6.2 that husbands' satisfaction is negatively related to both spouses' educational level but not associated with spousal financial satisfaction. This result contrasts the findings for the female model. Wives are more satisfied with their marriage to the degree that they are lower educated and more satisfied with the financial situation. Women's employment does not seem to make any difference for the marital satisfaction experienced by the spouses.

Table 6.2
Regression of Marital Satisfaction on Economic and Cultural Variables, (Un)Standardized Coefficients, Study 1

	Men			Women	
	Model 2	Model 3	Model 2	Model 3	Model 4
Socioeconomic variables					
Education, H	-.12 *	-.10 †	-.01	-.01	-.00
	(-.06)	(-.05)	(-.00)	(-.01)	(-.00)
Education, W	-.10 *	-.10 *	-.11 *	-.11 *	-.10 *
	(-.06)	(-.06)	(-.07)	(-.07)	(-.07)
Employment, H	.01	.04	.07	.08	.06
	(.05)	(.18)	(.35)	(.42)	(.32)
Employment, W	-.03	-.04	.00	-.02	-.02
	(-.05)	(-.08)	(.00)	(-.04)	(-.05)
Family income	.03	.05	-.01	.01	.00
	(.02)	(.04)	(-.01)	(.01)	(.00)
Income dissatisfaction, H	.02	.03	.06	.01	.00
	(.02)	(.04)	(.07)	(.02)	(.00)
Income dissatisfaction, W	-.05	-.06	-.15 *	-.11	-.10
	(-.05)	(-.07)	(-.17)	(-.12)	(-.12)
Role and family orientations					
Role traditionalism, H		-.07		-.12 *	-.12 *
		(-.09)		(-.18)	(-.18)
Role traditionalism, W		-.03		-.01	-.01
		(-.05)		(-.01)	(-.01)
Familialism, H		.20 ***		.07	.06
		(.27)		(.10)	(.09)
Familialism, W		.18 ***		.27 ***	.27 ***
		(.25)		(.42)	(.42)
Employment, W* Familialism, H					.09 *
					(.24)
Employment, W* Employment, H					.10 *
					(1.06)
F	1.53	4.52 ***	1.93 *	4.82 ***	4.90 ***
N	584	563	586	564	564
R²	.03	.12	.04	.13	.15

Note: † p < .10 *p < .05 ** p < .01 *** p < .001

Adding cultural characteristics to the economic model, our results show that men are more satisfied when their wives are lower educated. This finding supports the independence hypothesis. Moreover, it appears that men report higher satisfaction when they and their wives both endorse family values such as "being married" and "to live for your family" (also labeled familialism). Comparing this model to the previous model, we see that the effect of husbands' education is less significant, showing that the negative effect of husbands' educational level is partially based on the fact that those men endorse less traditional family values. More or less conservative attitudes towards sex roles do not seem to differentiate between more or less satisfied husbands.

Women's satisfaction, however, was found to be dependent on their husbands' sex role attitudes. The more traditional husbands are oriented towards these roles, the more likely wives report to be dissatisfied with their marriage. Besides, women also appear to be more dissatisfied with their marriage the higher their educational level is and the less importance they attach to traditional family values. Comparing this model to the prior economic model, the effect of women's income dissatisfaction is no longer significant. Apparently, this is due to association between income satisfaction and husbands' sex role attitudes. Indeed, the less conservative men are, the more women are satisfied with the financial situation of the family.

In a final step, we evaluated the significance of the interaction effects. For the male model, it appears that none of the interaction terms meaningfully add to a model already comprising economic and cultural characteristics. For the female model, in contrast, the interactions between women's employment and their husbands' employment as well as between women's employment and their husbands' traditional family orientation explain significant more variance than a model including only the main effects. The effect of women's employment on their own marital satisfaction is much more positive when their husbands are employed as well. Moreover, women's employment has more positive effects on wives' marital satisfaction to the extent that husbands are stronger orientated towards familialism. More specifically, our analysis indicates that for every unit that husbands' familialism changes, the slope of women's marital satisfaction on women's employment increases by 0.24 units. Comparing this model to the model without interaction terms, we see that adding the interaction effects do not reduce the effect of the other variables. In Figure 6.1 the interaction effect between wives' employment and husbands' traditional family values is visually presented.[14]

Figure 6.1
Visual Presentation of the Interaction Effect Between Female Employment and Husbands' Familialism on Wives' Marital Satisfaction

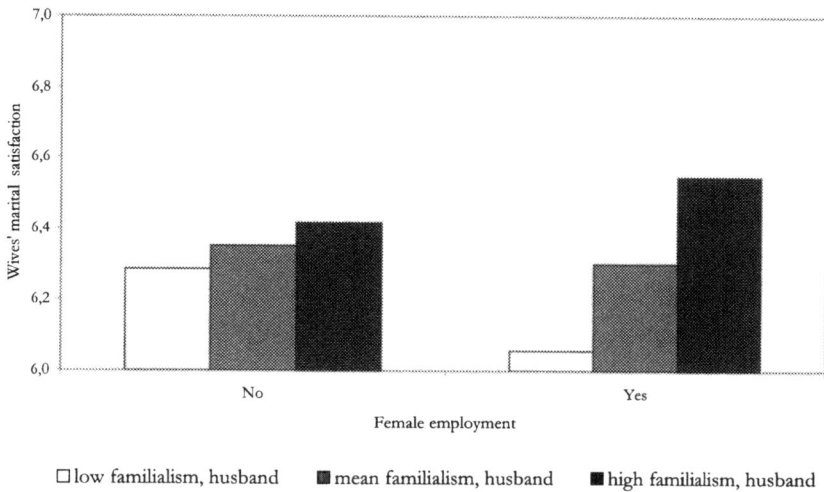

Study 2

In this study, we aim to replicate the theoretical model of Study 1 in a smaller sub-sample of husbands and wives of whom information was gathered at a second measurement point as well. We attempt to examine the stability of our results and to evaluate the degree to which potential deviating findings are due to the selective panel attrition or rather to the smaller sample size in which effects become less easily significant. This information is necessarily to evaluate the results from the third study. If it appears that the results of the sub-sample at Time 1 are similar to those of the larger

---

[14] A 'low' score on familialism is defined as one standard deviation below the mean and a 'high' score on familialism is defined as one standard deviation above the mean.

sample at Time 1, than our conclusions about marital satisfaction change may not be biased because of the selective panel attrition.

As in Study 1, the economic model was not found significant despite the negative effect of women's educational level on spouses' marital satisfaction (see Table 6.3). Including women and men's financial satisfaction, the models were not significant either. However, for both men and women it can be seen that the same variables that were significant in Study 1 are also significant at .10 level in this study. Moreover, parameter estimates do not show great differences and have the same directions in both studies.

Adding the cultural variables to the model, both the male and the female model are acceptable. For men, the same conclusion as that of the first study can be drawn. The more husbands and wives adopt traditional family values, the higher the marital satisfaction reported by men.

In accordance with the results of Study 1, we found meaningful associations between wives' marital satisfaction and their educational level, their husbands' sex role attitudes and their own traditional family orientation. Besides, Table 6.4 also shows a significant correlation with husbands' family orientation. To the extent that both spouses endorse traditional values such as "being married" and "living for your family", the more satisfied women are with their marriage.

Comparable to Study 1, the defined interaction terms were not related to husbands' satisfaction. However, the two interaction effects that were significant for women in the initial sample were also found to be meaningful in this study. Indeed, the effect of women's employment on their own marital satisfaction is more positive to the extent that their husbands endorse more traditional family values. Moreover, their employment is also more positive when husbands themselves are employed. The latter effect was significant at the .10 level.

It can therefore be concluded that the smaller sub-sample, which was followed at two points in time, is a relatively good reflection of the initial larger sample. The lower significance of the effects might be probably due to the smaller sample size.

Table 6.3
Regression of Marital Satisfaction on Economic and Cultural Variables, (Un)Standardized Coefficients, Study 2

	Men		Women		
	Model 2	Model 3	Model 2	Model 3	Model 4
Socioeconomic variables					
Education, H	-.12 †	-.10	-.05	-.03	-.03
	(-.05)	(-.04)	(-.02)	(-.02)	(-.01)
Education, W	-.11 †	-.11 †	-.11 †	-.13 †	-.13 *
	(-.06)	(-.06)	(-.07)	(-.08)	(-.08)
Employment, H	.02	.03	.04	.06	.06
	(.10)	(.16)	(.21)	(.32)	(.18)
Employment, W	-.03	-.03	-.04	-.05	-.05
	(-.05)	(-.05)	(-.08)	(-.10)	(-.10)
Family income	.06	.06	.05	.05	.05
	(.04)	(.04)	(.04)	(.04)	(.03)
Income dissatisfaction, H	.04	.02	.11	.01	.01
	(.04)	(.02)	(.12)	(.02)	(.01)
Income dissatisfaction, W	-.04	-.03	-.17 †	-.07	-.07
	(-.04)	(-.03)	(-.18)	(-.08)	(-.09)
Role and family orientations					
Role traditionalism, H		-.09		-.14 *	-.14 *
		(-.12)		(-.21)	(-.21)
Role traditionalism, W		-.01		-.03	-.03
		(-.02)		(-.05)	(-.05)
Familialism, H		.19 ***		.11 *	.11 *
		(.23)		(.14)	(.14)
Familialism, W		.20 ***		.29 ***	.29 ***
		(.27)		(.43)	(.43)
Employment, W* Familialism, H					.10 *
					(.26)
Employment, W* Employment, H					.09 †
					(.94)
F	1.14	3.02 ***	1.16	3.43 ***	3.41 ***
R²	.04	.13	.04	.15	.16
N	360	353	359	352	352

Note: † p < .10 *p < .05 ** p < .01 *** p < .001

Study 3

In this study we are interested in the question whether changes in economic and cultural variables, result in an increase or decrease in subsequent marital satisfaction (Time 2). Therefore, satisfaction scores at Time 2 are regressed on the change in independent variables between Time 1 and Time 2. Changes in interaction variables were not taken into account because of the difficult and complex interpretation.

To measure changes in variables a difference score between Time 2 and Time 1 was computed. Rogossa (1995, p. 11) asserts that, "with only two observations the difference score [...] is a natural estimate of the amount of true change, [...] regardless of the form of the growth curve". He showed that the difference score is quite reliable under a wide range of moderate true score correlations.[15] However, because the magnitude and direction of change across time largely depends on the initial score, it is recommended to control for the initial scores that make up the difference score (Rogossa, 1995; Taris, 2000).[16] With respect to the employment status of men and women, the change between T1 and T2 is indicated by dummy variables. The reference category is 'spouses who are not employed at both T1 and T2'. Because the initial score of women's employment (1 = yes, 0 = no) is already included in the definition of the dummy variable indicating

---

[15] The use of a difference score as indicator for the degree of change is subject to much criticism (Taris, 2000). Particularly, the difference between two scores would be less reliable than the initial scores on the variables of which it is composed (Plewis, 1985). The higher the correlation between two measurements of the same variable, the less reliable the difference should be. Rogossa (1995), however, opposes to this critic and demonstrates that the difference score does extremely well when true change exists. In most examples used to show the low reliability of the difference score it appears that "[...] all individuals are growing at nearly the same rate which translates into almost no individual differences in true change [...], and therefore [...]the difference score cannot be expected to detect them" (Rogossa, 1995, p. 12).

[16] If this score is very low or very high, it is not likely that respondents move towards even lower or even higher scores. This is referred to as the *floor*-effect, respectively *ceiling*-effect (Rogossa, 1995; Taris, 2000). Moreover, these "extreme" respondents may also be more sensitive for stimuli to increase, respectively decrease their score. Thus, respondents with high scores tend to report lower scores in a follow-up round and vice versa. This is called the "regression effect" or "regression to the mean".

the (un)changed employment status between T1 and T2, the dummy variable at T1 for women's employment is not included in the model.

The idea of controlling for the initial score is applied to the assessment of change in the dependent variable as well. Hence, change in marital satisfaction is predicted controlling for marital satisfaction at Time 1 (Taris, 2000).

We pass through the same stages as in the previous studies. The control (not presented) and economic variables at Time 1 as well as the change in these variables between Time 1 and Time 2 are entered in the first step of the analysis. Spouse's marital satisfaction score at Time 1 is also included in this first step. In the second step, spousal financial satisfaction and the shift in financial satisfaction are added to the model. In the third step, the model is complemented with the cultural variables of Time 1 as well as their change between Time 1 and Time 2. The results of our analysis are presented in Table 6.4.

Let us first consider husbands' satisfaction with marriage. As Table 6.4 shows, couple's economic resources, in terms of net family income, negatively predict husbands' marital satisfaction five years later. Moreover, our results indicate that husbands' emphasis on traditional family values is positively associated with their subsequent marital satisfaction. Men, who become more traditionally oriented towards family values over time, also become more satisfied with their marriage.

Considering wives' marital outcomes, our analysis show that a change in wives' satisfaction is related to their husbands' experience of parental divorce. It was found that wives become more dissatisfied with their marriage over time in case the parents of their husbands ever separated.

Besides, our analysis demonstrates that wives' employment affects their marital satisfaction across time. In comparison to women who are unemployed at both measurement points, it appears that women who are employed at T1 but unemployed at T2 report lower marital satisfaction. Hence, the loss of work negatively affects women's perception of marriage.

Rather than being affected by the family income (see husbands' marital satisfaction), wives become less satisfied with their marriage when they are less satisfied with the family income and when this dissatisfaction becomes worse during time.

Table 6.4
Regression of Marital Satisfaction at Time 2 on the Difference Effects of Spousal Economic and Cultural Variables, (Un)Standardized Coefficients

	Men			Women		
	Model 1	Model 2	Model 3	Model 1	Model 2	Model 3
Marital satisfaction (T1)	.59 ***	.56 ***	.50 ***	.62 ***	.56 ***	.50 ***
	(.63)	(.61)	(.54)	(.66)	(.60)	(.54)
Background variables						
Parental divorce, H	.02	-.00	.03	-.13 **	-.13 **	-.13 **
	(.05)	(-.01)	(.07)	(-.36)	(-.40)	(-.37)
Parental divorce, W	.05	.05	.04	-.04	-.04	-.03
	(.13)	(.15)	(.13)	(-.12)	(-.13)	(-.09)
Socioeconomic variables						
Education, H	.12	.14 *	.13	.03 .	.06	.03
	(.06)	(.07)	(.07)	(.02)	(.03)	(.02)
Education, W	.07	.08	.05	.04	.03	.00
	(.04)	(.05)	(.03)	(.03)	(.02)	(.00)
Family income (T1)	-.18 *	-.29 **	-.24 *	-.00	-.14	-.17
	(-.13)	(-.22)	(-.18)	(-.00)	(-.12)	(-.14)
Wife employed at both T1 and T2	.11	.13	.12	-.03	-.02	-.05
	(.22)	(.25)	(.24)	(-.07)	(-.04)	(-.11)
Wife employed at T1 and not T2	.06	.10	.09	-.13 *	-.12 *	-.12 *
	(.19)	(.36)	(.32)	(-.47)	(-.47)	(-.46)
Wife employed at T2 but not at T1	.08	.06	.05	.01	-.02	-.03
	(.19)	(.17)	(.13)	(.01)	(-.06)	(-.07)
Husband employed at both T1 and T2	-.00	-.03	-.08	-.08	-.05	-.15
	(-.01)	(-.08)	(-.27)	(-.27)	(-.19)	(-.54)
Husband employed at T1 and not T2	-.07	-.09	-.13	-.12	-.09	-.16
	(-.26)	(-.33)	(-.46)	(-.48)	(-.38)	(-.68)
Husband employed at T2 but not at T1	.05	.04	.01	.04	.02	-.00
	(.88)	(.57)	(.12)	(.83)	(.32)	(-.02)
Difference in family income	-.03	-.09	-.06	.01	-.03	-.03
	(-.03)	(-.08)	(-.06)	(.01)	(-.04)	(-.03)
Income dissatisfaction, W (T1)		-.05	-.02		-.25 **	-.25 **
		(-.05)	(-.03)		(-.31)	(-.31)
Income dissatisfaction, H (T1)		-.07	-.06		.06	.00
		(-.07)	(-.07)		(.08)	(.00)
Difference in income dissatisfaction, W		-.01	-.01		-.18 **	-.20 **
		(-.01)	(-.01)		(-.21)	(-.24)
Difference in income dissatisfaction, H		-.05	-.07		-.03	-.04
		(-.05)	(-.07)		(-.04)	(-.04)

	Men			Women		
	Model 1	Model 2	Model 3	Model 1	Model 2	Model 3

Table 6.4 (continued)

Role and family orientations

Role traditionalism, H (T1)			-.04			-.19 **
			(-.05)			(-.31)
Role traditionalism, W (T1)			-.04			-.03
			(-.07)			(-.05)
Familialism, H (T1)			.21 **			.08
			(.26)			(.12)
Familialism, W (T1)			.03			.18 **
			(.04)			(.30)
Difference in role traditionalism, H			.08			.05
			(.12)			(.09)
Difference in role traditionalism, W			.05			-.04
			(.08)			(-.07)
Difference in familialism, H			.15 *			.03
			(.20)			(.04)
Difference in familialism, W			.11 †			.19 **
			(.15)			(.29)
F	8.40 ***	6.09 ***	4.97 ***	10.66 ***	7.26 ***	6.81 ***
R^2	.35	.36	.40	.41	.40	.48
N	298	263	252	299	263	252

Note: Familialism refers to a traditional family orientation
*p < .05 ** p < .01 *** p < .001

Including cultural variables to the model (Model 3), Table 6.4 shows that husbands' traditional orientation towards sex roles at T1 causes women to be less satisfied with marriage throughout time. Moreover, if women attach great importance to traditional family values and put greater stress on these values during the five-years time interval, their marital satisfaction significantly increases.

6.7. CONCLUSION AND DISCUSSION

The aim of this study was to assess the relative influence of economic and cultural characteristics in understanding spousal marital satisfaction. This question was addressed cross-sectionally as well as longitudinally.

With respect to economic variables, our study demonstrates that wives' educational level significantly affects spousal marital satisfaction.

Both husbands and wives tend to be less satisfied with their marriage when women are better educated. This effect is not overruled when taking into account that higher educated wives are more likely to adopt less traditional attitudes towards sex roles and family values. Hence, our results lend support to the independence hypothesis stating that women's labor market resources are not beneficial for marriage. However, our findings contrast with empirical (American) literature in which it is demonstrated that better educated women are more satisfied because of their greater interpersonal skills. Although they cannot be used interchangeably, it is striking to note that a recent study on divorce in the Netherlands also shows that Dutch women's education significantly increases their divorce risk (Kalmijn, de Graaf, & Poortman, 2004). Why do Dutch higher educated women report lower marital satisfaction and apparently have a higher divorce risk? Although the inclusion of attitudes towards sex roles and family values did not change the significance of women's education, it might be assumed that in some way the broader cultural and more emancipatory orientation of these women explains our findings.

However, in the long-term analysis wives' employment and not their educational level appeared to be a significant determinant. It was found that compared to those who where unemployed both at T1 and T2, wives report lower subsequent marital satisfaction when becoming unemployed between T1 and T2. However, no significant differences exist between women who were employed at both measurement points and those who were not, suggesting that loosing one's job and not employment as such, yields negative consequences for women's well-being in marriage. The explanation for this negative effect might be sought in the adaptation to a new unpaid labor situation and the negative consequences with which it is associated (e.g. less social contacts, no personal income etc.).

Our study also shows that men experience a greater decrease in marital satisfaction when belonging to a higher income family. This contrasts with the idea that it is more difficult within lower social strata for adequately performing marital roles (Lewis & Spanier, 1979; Ono, 1998). The explanation for our finding is not clear-cut. One indication may be found in the correlational analysis. It appears that wives belonging to higher income families are better educated and hold more nontraditional sex role and family orientations. The latter, in particular, negatively affect spousal marital satisfaction. Hence, the broader cultural orientation of women in higher income families, not fully captured in this study, might explain the negative effect.

In contrast to husbands' marital satisfaction over time, it appears, that wives' change in satisfaction is stronger related to their contentment with the income than with the income as such. We found that the more women are satisfied with couple's financial situation and to the extent that this financial satisfaction increases over time, women report higher marital satisfaction. It is interesting to investigate in future research why men's marital satisfaction over time is more closely tied up to the absolute family income whereas women's marital satisfaction is more associated with relative income. Indeed, for women, the impact of income seems to depend on (changeable) standards and/or social comparison levels.

Nonetheless, based on the cross-sectional as well as the longitudinal analyses, evidence was obtained for the relevance of economic variables in understanding spousal marital satisfaction. Particularly with respect to changes in marital satisfaction, economic characteristics may not be overlooked.

In addition, our study clearly shows the importance of spousal cultural orientations with respect to sex roles and family values. As regards family values, for men, it appears that the more both spouses stress the importance of "being married" or "to live for your family", the higher their marital satisfaction reported. For women, though, not their husbands but only their own appraisal of these family values results in higher satisfaction. This could be explained by the motivation of these spouses to invest in family life. Kalmijn and Jansen (2000) have found that people with traditional family values more often engage in activities that make them dependent on a family. These investments may be rewarding for both spouses. The finding that one's family orientation primarily affects one's own marital satisfaction (and not that of the other spouse) may point toward cognitive dissonance. Indeed, it is more congruent for traditional spouses to be happy with their marriage and to idealize their partnership because their marital relationship has great salience in their identity hierarchy (Stryker, 1980). The converse may also hold. Because they are happily married for a relatively long time, spouses changed attitudes towards a more traditional family orientation. People may learn to value characteristics that are appropriate to their conditions of life. Moreover, one can suggest that traditional orientations still offer a rewarding security because expectations are clearly defined (Lye & Biblarz, 1993).

Nevertheless, regarding sex role attitudes, the latter reasoning does not hold. In the cross-sectional analyses, we found that a less traditional sex role attitude advocated by husbands has a positive effect on their wives' marital satisfaction. Women's role attitudes, however, are not meaningful related neither to their husbands' nor to their own marital satisfaction. These findings lead us to suggest that women's expectations for more gender equality do not put current marriage under pressure. Rather the alternative idea is supported. If men with less traditional attitudes towards sex roles positively affect their wives' satisfaction and are equally satisfied than men with more traditional attitudes, it may be suggested that men may relieve the stress in marriage by supporting gender equal attitudes. This hardly comes as a surprise as changes in men's lives towards more gender egalitarianism essentially refer to a pro-family attitude. These findings are in line with the conclusions of Amato and Booth (1995). These authors demonstrated that husbands themselves become more satisfied with their marriages when their views on gender roles become less traditional.

An important finding of our study is that cultural orientations also moderate the effect of women's employment on marital satisfaction. More specifically, employed women feel more satisfied with their marriage when their husband put stronger emphasis on traditional family values. Or to put it differently, husbands' traditional family orientation provides a context that is more compatible with women's outside employment. This might be due to the earlier mentioned family investment motivation of these husbands.

The importance of cultural orientations is further strengthened when considering marital satisfaction over time. Spouse's increase in marital satisfaction is related to his/her family orientation as well as the strengthening of this orientation during the five years under study. Moreover, husbands' egalitarian sex role attitudes also enhance their wives' subsequent marital satisfaction. Thus men's cultural flexibility with respect to gender roles is not only a significant factor in contemporary wives' satisfaction but also in wives' marital satisfaction over time. However, no interaction effects were found between spousal attitudes towards sex roles and women's labor market resources, indicating that the above-mentioned importance of husbands' role attitudes do not vary according to their wives' employment status.

While the present research has focused on the consequences of economic and cultural variables on marital satisfaction, it is important to note that marital satisfaction may also exert an influence on spousal cultural orientations and economic position. Cross-lagged models are appropriate means to handle this sort of questions but at present not frequently applied. Exception is Amato and Booth (1995) who demonstrated that sex role attitudes influence marital satisfaction rather than the other way around.

Some limitations of this study require comment. First, this study is limited by the constraints of the sample. We are dealing with established first marriages with children. As a result, the sample is composed of individuals who have chosen for at least two traditional characteristics of family life: marriage and children. Therefore, we evaluated whether the spouses included in our sample deviate from the Dutch population in their orientation towards traditional family values. Based on longitudinal data of the national project 'Sociaal-culturele ontwikkelingen in Nederland [Sociocultural Developments in the Netherlands]' (SOCON), it appears that our research sample even scored lower on the traditional family values-scale than the respondents of the SOCON study (Peters & Felling, 2000). Hence, we can reasonably assume that our sample is not strongly biased on their orientation towards familialism. Second, the average marital duration at the start of the panel study is 17 years, which means that our research group represents 'marital survivors'. It is recommended to replicate our findings in a sample of couples without children as well as couples married for longer and shorter time periods. A following limitation concerns the two measurement points. As we have only two time observations, we can provide some information about change over time, but the design surely has its limitations. Therefore, replications of the study over at least three measurement points are advisable in order to gain deeper insight in social change. Fourth, it should be noted that in spite of their relevance, economic and cultural variables explained a small amount of the variance in concurrent marital satisfaction. Other characteristics, such as couples' interaction behavior, may be more important in gaining insight into spousal satisfaction in a later marital stage. Fifth, additional economic and cultural proxies need to be included. For example, income differences between men and women, dimensions of economic pressure as well as values of self-actualization have to be distinguished in future research. Sixth, shorter or longer time intervals between successive measurement points might yield different economic and cultural covariates. More longitudinal research on this specific theme is needed to depict time-specific covariates. Seventh, we demonstrated as far as possible that the sample used at the two measurement points does not show great differences with the total sample of the first measurement point with respect to the subject under study. Nonetheless, it was shown that husbands who participate at both waves are more satisfied with the net family income and slightly more traditional in their sex role attitudes. The former may account for the fact that husbands' income satisfaction is not a strong differentiating factor. Given the consistent importance of the latter variable in the female analyses, it might be assumed that the slight difference between the two samples has not strongly biased our results.

Attention to these constraints in coming studies must enable family researchers to draw more specific conclusions about the relative significance of economic and cultural variables in comprehending marital satisfaction (over time).

7. Social Position, Gender Role Identity and Marital Satisfaction

7.1. Introduction

Bestsellers such as "Men are from Mars, women are from Venus" (Gray, 1992) and "Why men don't listen and women can't read maps" (Pease, 1999) are only two examples of popular literature that supports the widely held idea that men and women are different. The assumed 'stable' sex disparities in this literature, strongly contrast the widely held view of gender theorists that gender is a social product that individuals (re)produce in the context of daily life (Walker, 1999; West & Zimmerman, 1987). The meaning of 'being masculine' and 'being feminine' not only depends on broad transformations in the larger society such as changing attitudes towards sex roles, but also on more proximal contexts in which men and women act such as higher and lower social strata.

In the current juncture characterized by blurring sex roles, some speculate that the stereotypical ways of being man or woman are becoming counterproductive (McDowell, 2001). Women increasingly enter the male area of paid labor whereas men are increasingly expected to be more nurturant and involved with their families (Duncombe & Marsden, 1993; Yogev & Brett, 1985). Consequently, expressiveness, which reflects stereotypical feminine qualities such as kindness and understanding, as well as instrumentality, which reflects stereotypical masculine qualities such as agency, independence and self-confidence, may both become qualities that men and women use in meeting new social circumstances (Vannoy-Hiller & Philliber, 1989). However, research by Perry-Jenkins and Folk (1994) suggests that differences might appear between social groups in the degree of acceptance of new sex role qualities as well as in the linkages between these qualities and marital outcomes. A similar line of reasoning holds with respect to family stage. Couples tend to become more traditional in their role behavior after the birth of children, suggesting that sex role stereotypes and role expectations are affecting couples differently (Thompson & Walker, 1989).

The present study relates to this issue. Specifically, it is examined whether and to what degree expressiveness and instrumentality, hereafter also referred to as gender role identity, are important qualities in understanding spouses' marital satisfaction at different marital stages as well as in different socioeconomic contexts. It is argued that marriages may not equally benefit from stereotypical sex role qualities early in the relationship and later on. Moreover, since gender and class strongly interact, the importance of expressiveness and instrumentality in explaining husbands' and wives' emotional life may differ according their income and educational level.

7.2. EMPIRICAL BACKGROUND

Several studies suggest that expressiveness rather than instrumentality is beneficial for partners' marital satisfaction (Antill, 1983; Kurdek & Schmitt, 1986; Lamke, Sollie, Durbin, & Fitzpatrick, 1994; Peterson, Baucom, Elliott, & Farr, 1989). Although initially designated *femininity*, the new label *expressiveness* is more linked to the fact that the representing qualities refer to personal qualities that both sexes can incorporate in one's self, rather than reflecting a much broader phenomenon of stereotypical femininity (Spence, 1984; 1993). Moreover, the label better fits the idea that female traits are also important for men. Lamke, Sollie, Durbin, and Fitzpatrick (1994) for example, found support for a positive effect of husbands' femininity on their marital quality but found no effects for women. In contrast, Antill (1983) has demonstrated that both husbands and wives appear to be happiest when they define themselves in expressive terms, and when they are paired with highly feminine partners. Ever since the publication of Antill (1983) it is widely assumed that expressiveness is beneficial for partnership. Recent research suggests that two processes are responsible for this association (Garrido & Acitelli, 1999; Miller, Caughlin, & Huston, 2003). On the one hand, expressiveness leads spouses to engage in more affectionate behavior; on the other hand, it results in a more idealized image of one's partner.

However, the conclusion that husbands and wives' expressiveness may be the most important ingredient in marital happiness may be unwarrantedly. Some studies found support for the idea that masculinity, and specifically wives' masculinity, is positively related to spouses' marital quality (Aube & Norcliffe, 1995; Parmelee, 1987; Peterson et al., 1989). This result might be explained by the fact that characteristics such as independence and assertiveness are highly valued in an achievement-oriented society. Spouses who endorse these traits may develop positive self-concepts and consequently higher well being and satisfaction (Aube & Norcliffe, 1995).

However, the above claims require further investigation, first and foremost because the majority of literature is American. Therefore, the question arises to what extent these findings can be replicated within a Dutch sample of couples. This question is particularly relevant since Hofstede (1998) has identified the United States as a masculine and the Netherlands as a feminine nation. Masculinity stands for a society with a stereotypical orientation on men being assertive and success-orientated and with women being tender and concerned with the quality of life. In feminine countries, however, both men and women are supposed to have the latter qualities. At the individual level, this would imply that 'being feminine' for a man is less undesirable than in masculine countries. Brinkgreve (1989) indeed asserts that in the Netherlands qualities such as care, and commitment are no longer reserved for women but are increasingly expected to be virtues also acquired by men. Given the identified 'emotionalisation' in partnership and the gender specificity in this respect (see Chapter 1), it can be expected that femininity, particularly on part of the husband, also positively contributes to spousal marital satisfaction in the Netherlands and to women's satisfaction in particular.

Second, more attention needs to be paid to the specific demands and expectations that couples may encounter in different stages of their partnership. Previous research has already speculated that the importance of instrumentality and expressiveness might not play a similar role early in the relationship or in a later stage (Antill, 1983; Parmelee, 1987). Antill (1983) has shown that wife's feminine characteristics tend to be more important early in the relationship, whereas husband's feminine characteristics appear to be more important later. In the early stage of the relationship husbands' satisfaction seem to depend on their wives filling in the traditional female role (Antill, 1983). In a later stage, especially when more children may be present, wives' marital satisfaction should become more dependent on their husbands' ability and willingness to perform female nurturance tasks. This argumentation contrasts the findings of Parmelee (1987). She speculated that wives' instrumentality rather than expressiveness is important early in the relationship because in this stage interaction patterns have still to be negotiated whereas responsibilities are minimal. Wives' expressiveness should become more important later. Particularly with the arrival of children, which is often associated with a move towards more traditional sex roles, wives' expressiveness may be essential. However, these speculations have not been systematically tested and might suggest that spouses not only have to adapt to new partnership expectations but also to expectations associated with specific family life stages. In this study this issue is examined. Specifically, we deal with couples having adolescent children. During this marital stage, husbands and wives are confronted with demands for increased autonomy from their children. When these demands are reciprocated by more expressive or instrumental oriented parents, different outcomes might be expected, for instance, with respect to marital satisfaction. Responding to autonomy claims with expressiveness might result in less pressure and conflict and thus in more satisfaction, as opposed to more instrumentalistic responses (Kreppner, 2000). Although the importance of displaying supportiveness and affection during the adolescent years, Holmbeck, Paikoff, and Brooks-Gunn (1995) also denote the benefits of maintaining consistent effective discipline and control, which may be more strongly tied up with instrumental qualities. Hence, it is not clear to what degree marital partners benefit from instrumental and expressive qualities in this specific stage.

A third issue worth investigating in this respect relates to the context-specificity of our subject under study. Implicit in most literature on gender role identity and marital satisfaction is the assumption that this relationship is invariant across social groups. However, there are reasons for speculating otherwise. Expressiveness and instrumentality are both qualities that may be socially steered. Assuming this, the meaning and standards of being a man or woman is not uniformly adhered to in distinct social levels. Precisely because the female and male identity is acted out in different social contexts, these contexts may not only reproduce the 'gendered' social structure to a different degree but may also differently condition the *effect* of this reproduction (Stryker, 1992; West & Zimmerman, 1987). In this way, gender could be fragmented into multiple masculinities and femininities (Pyke, 1996).

Considering *between*-class variation, it is suggested that lower-class husbands compensate their subordinated status in relation to higher-class men, by exerting power in the private sphere (Pyke, 1996; Rubin, 1976). Therefore, relying on stereotypical gender arrangements enables lower-class husbands to (re)produce their masculinity (Huston & Geis, 1993; Komarowsky, 1964; Mirowsky & Ross, 1987; Rubin, 1976). Women in these families are supposed to deal with the expressive side whereas men are expected to take responsibility for the instrumental side and to devalue emotional sensitivity (Weber, 1998). In contrast, higher-class spouses are less likely to be tied to traditional prescribed traits of men and women (Huston & Geis, 1993). Because of their higher material or educational capital, they are less hampered in the endorsement of nontraditional options (Laermans, 1993). According to Pyke (1996), however, the observed differences between higher and lower social strata mainly refer to a discourse and not to a daily routine. It may be even true that in practice lower-class husbands act more egalitarian than middle and upper-class men. The latter are often released from feminine tasks because of the impor-tance, or even hegemony, of the male career. Despite much effort devoted to examining the influence of instrumentality and expressiveness on marital quality, previous studies paid no systematic attention to their specific effects in higher and lower social strata.

In this study, we distinguish between higher and lower social strata in terms of the family income and both partners' educational level. Doing so, a distinction is made between the cultural and the material aspects of social class. According to the reasons outlined above, it is hypothesized that lower income couples and lower educated spouses will be more satisfied with their marriage when husbands adhere to stereotypical instrumental qualities and women to expressive qualities.

Fourth, we do not only pay attention to spouses' social position in terms of income and education, but also more specifically to women's position in terms of their participation at the labor market. Since expres-siveness and instrumentality are both qualities that are strongly associated with stereotypical male and female roles, they might produce different marital outcomes in case wives are employed or not. Essentially, employed women enter a male sphere in which they may also need to adopt male qualities. According to McDowell (2001), women's attachment to the labor market has never been as significant for their personal identities as in the current decades. Therefore, it is reasonable to assume that the importance of instrumental and expressive qualities for spouses' marital experiences might depend on whether women are employed or not. On the one hand, it can be hypothesized that employed wives are supposed to ascribe to the required instrumental qualities. Consequently, marital partners might experience women's instrumentality as less negatively in case of labor market participation (Vannoy-Hiller & Philliber, 1989). On the other hand, however, it can be expected that precisely because of the accomplishment of non-stereotypical roles, women need to be reaffirmed in their femininity by strongly adhering to traditional gender expectations. Hochschild and Machung (1989) describe a similar phenomenon known as *balancing*. Women working outside the home and earning more than their partner, curiously enough, do more at home than other women, and more than their husband. A comparable conclusion was reached by Tichenor (1999) demonstrating that wives occupying a higher status than their husbands, bear the large burden of domestic labor. It is speculated that those wives develop a new – socially induced – sense of guilt for which they try to compensate through overemphasizing their femininity (Hochschild & Machung, 1989; Matthijs & Van den Troost, 1998). Thus, the effect of instrumental and expressive qualities does not seem to depend only on women's employment but also on the social position of their husbands. In one respect, it might be therefore hypothesized that in higher social strata it is more likely that spouses share the expectation that women seek personal fulfillment through performing public roles and adopt qualities required for this performance. In another respect, there are reasons to believe that precisely in higher social strata some wives consider the blurring of roles as a threat for their femininity and therefore overemphasize their feminine identity or their husbands' masculine identity. Hence, it remains contentiously whether women benefit more from expressive or from instrumental qualities when they are (un)employed.

It should be stressed, however, that the positive effect of husbands' expressiveness on spousal satisfaction might not depend on women's employment (Vannoy & Philliber, 1992). The ability of men to take on a supportive role is beneficial in both traditional and nontraditional situations.

7.3. PRESENT STUDY AND HYPOTHESES

The main goal of this study is to provide insight into the conditionality of the association between marital satisfaction, instrumentality and expressiveness in a sample of married couples with children. Our purpose can be divided into four research aims. First, we examine to what degree the inclusion of instrumental and expressive traits into one's self concept is associated with one's own and one's partner marital satisfaction. We expect that husbands and wives are more satisfied when their partners are more expressive (H1). Moreover, it can be anticipated that husbands' expressiveness is more closely tied up to women's than to men's marital satisfaction (H2).

A second purpose is to study the relationship between instrumentality and expressiveness, and marital satisfaction in different relationship stages and more specifically according to the age of the children. Given the fact that the target child of the couples included in our study are adolescents aged between 14 and 21 years, we hypothesize that expressiveness is more important the younger the child is (H3). However, it can also be expected that instrumentality is more important the younger the child is (H4).

Third, we are interested in the influence of expressiveness and instrumentality on marital satisfaction across various socioeconomic circumstances. We distinguish different conditions by considering couple's income, spousal educational level and women's employment. It is expected that spouses from lower social classes are more satisfied to the extent that they are more characterized by stereotypical traits than are spouses from higher social classes (H5). The term social class will hereafter refer to both the income level of the household and the educational level of the spouses.

Fourth, with respect to the effect of stereotypical traits on spouses' marital satisfaction when wives are employed, no conclusive findings are at our disposal. Anticipation becomes even more difficult when dealing with Dutch couples. Yet, the Netherlands takes on a peculiar position regarding women's employment. In comparison to other Western countries, a high proportion of women working part-time characterizes Dutch women's employment. For the objective of our study, two hypotheses seem to be plausible. For one, emphasizing stereotypical female traits will have more positive effects on spousal satisfaction in higher than in lower social classes when wives are employed (H6). By doing so, women accentuate their female identity. For another, however, it might be expected that lower class spouses, and men in particular, tend to stress the stereotypical male identity to keep in accordance with traditional sex segregated ideals, even when women are employed (H7). Figure 7.1 visualizes the general research model of this study. The four interaction terms included refer to the interaction between each spouse's gender role identity and social position.

Figure 7.1
Conceptual Model for Gender Role Identity and Marital Satisfaction

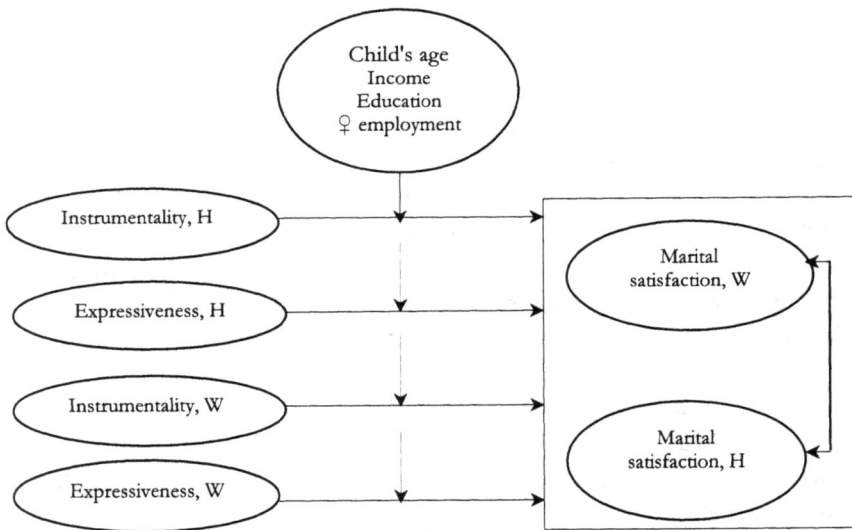

This study extends prior research on gender role identity and marital satisfaction in two important ways. First, gender differences are documented by analyzing husbands and wives belonging to the same couple instead of examining independent men and women. Second, analyses are conducted within distinct social contexts to determine if different processes link gender role identity with spousal evaluation of marriage for different social groups.

7.4. METHOD

7.4.1. Procedure and Sample

The research sample consists of married men and women participating in the longitudinal research project "Child-Rearing and Family in the Netherlands". Families were recruited using a multi-stage sampling method. In a first stage, a sample was taken of all Dutch municipalities distinguished by regional zone and degree of urbanization. In a second stage, a sample of children aged 9 to 16 years was taken in the selected municipalities. The children as well as their parents were included in the research group. Of the 788 families participating in 1990, 484 (61%) did participate in 1995. More technical details on the database can be found in Chapter 3 and in Gerris et al. (1992; 1993; 1998). The data were gathered by means of structured interviews and questionnaires. The first wave of the study was not included in our analysis as gender role identity variables were only measured in the second wave. Only first marriages in which both men and women have a Dutch nationality were selected. Of this group in the year 1995, 386 couples could be potentially taken into account for our analysis.

Couples had been married for about 22 years. Husbands were 47.5 years and wives were 45.0 years on average. Men reported higher levels of education than did women. One quarter of the male sample has a university degree, whereas for women this figure is approximately one out of eight. For husbands, 48% reported to have a middle low or low school degree whereas for women this is 61%. Sex differences also exist with regard to employment activities. Whereas only 2% of the men are homemakers or not involved in paid employment, more than one out of three women fall into these categories. Nine out of ten men are employed, but this holds only for six out of ten women (57%). In comparison to men, women are situated more in the "unskilled jobs" category (13% women versus 2% men) and less in the "higher professions" group (11% women versus 18% men).

To examine whether the couples, used in our study, are representative for the couples that participated in the first measurement wave, we conducted a logistic regression. The dependent variable is a dummy coded variable representing whether the couple participated only once or both times. The independent variables included are all the variables of interest for this study, except from spousal gender role identity, which was only measured at the second wave. The χ^2 test for the total model was not significant indicating that the included variables do not account for significant differences. Therefore, we assume that the research sample reflects the initial group with respect to age of the spouses, educational and income level of the family, women's employment and spousal satisfaction.

7.4.2. Measures

Education was measured in response to the question "What is your highest educational level?" Nine levels were considered ranging from 1 = "elementary school" to 9 = "university education".

Family income was measured in response to the question "What is the monthly net family income (in guilders)?" Seven income groups were distinguished: 1 = "1100-1600", 2 = "1600-1800", 3 = "1800-2100", 4 = "2100-2500", 5 = "2500-3250", 6 = "3250-4500" and 7 = "more than 4500". One guilder is approximately 0.45 Euro.

Instrumental and expressive traits were measured by two scales derived from the Personal Attributes Questionnaire of Spence & Helmreich (1978). The scale of instrumentality contains items about instrumental and independent characteristics, which are more likely to be endorsed by males than females. The expressiveness scale consists of seven items about expressive, communal characteristics of which it is believed that women possess them in greater abundance than males. The questionnaire consists of bipolar items with 5 boxes between the two poles. The respondents have to indicate which characteristic is more applicable to them by putting their mark near the pole representing the characteristic. If they think that both characteristics are somewhat applicable to them, they put their mark in the box in the middle. The validity of both scales is described in Gerris et al. (1998). Because some items did not significantly load on one but two dimensions, they were removed from the scale. Hence, the retaining scale items represent a limited indication of the initial 'expressiveness' and 'instrumentality' items. The instrumentality scale in particular covers items rather indicating emotional stability or imperturbability. In accordance with Garrido and Acitelli (1991), the scales could also represent interdependency versus independency. However, to preserve the link with the literature on expressiveness and instrumentality and to situate our study in this tradition, we will hereafter use the original labels while keeping the just mentioned qualification in mind. Cronbach's alpha coefficient for the instrumentality scale is .75 for men and .76 for women. For the expressiveness scale these figures are .71 and .70 respectively.

Marital satisfaction refers to the satisfaction with the partner and the relationship in general. This measure is based on the marital satisfaction scale developed by Kerkstra (1985). Only the items measuring general marital satisfaction were included. Using factor analysis a scale of 7 items was retained. The same factor solution was obtained for men and women and was exactly replicated with the data of the second wave. The validation analysis is elaborated in Chapter 4. For formulating the items of this scale, satisfaction with the relationship and/or the partner was used as the guiding principle (e.g., "Generally, I'm dissatisfied with the relationship with my partner" or "If I could choose again, I would choose the same partner"). The scale consists of seven 7-point Likert items, ranging from 1 = "not at all applicable" to 7 = "very applicable". The replies were added together so that a higher score indicates a more satisfied relationship. In 1995, alpha coefficient was .87 for women and .85 for men. I.

Control variables: Authors have been shown that individuals modify their identities and self-perceptions as a function of their life situation and stage of family life (Feldman, Biringen & Nash, 1981; Tamir & Antonucci, 1981). Therefore, marital duration was controlled for in all our analyses. Moreover, individuals' age and their educational level, the family's net income level as well as whether women are employed or not, were included in all models.

7.5. RESULTS

Descriptive analysis and correlations among measures

Means and standard deviations as well as correlations are shown in Table 7.1. The results show moderate but positive correlations between individuals' scores on instrumentality and expressiveness. Spouses who define themselves in terms of stereotypical qualities are more likely to also ascribe qualities of the opposite sex to themselves.

In contrast, social conditions such as the family income or one's educational level are not related to spouses' adoption of expressive or instrumental traits.

Considering husbands and wives' marital satisfaction, the correlational analysis demonstrates that husbands' expressiveness is positively correlated with both spouses' marital satisfaction. Neither husbands' instrumentality, nor wives' instrumentality and expressive traits are associated with spousal marital satisfaction.

Sex differences on the gender role identity variables were examined with paired t-tests. Results of the between-spouse correlations indicate that in comparison with one's spouse, wives score significantly higher on expressiveness ($t = -8.12$, $p < .0001$) whereas husbands score higher on instrumentality ($t = 10.27$, $p < .0001$).

Mean scores on the marital satisfaction scale were 6.0 for husbands and 5.9 for wives. A paired t-test indicate that this difference is not significant ($t = 1.51$, $p = 0.14$). Thus, wives and husbands are equally satisfied with their marital relationship.

Table 7.1
Correlation Matrix of Gender Variables, Women's Employment, Household Income, Educational Level and Marital Satisfaction [Husbands Below Diagonal, Wives Above Diagonal]

	1	2	3	4	5	6	7	8	M	SD
1 Income	/	.37 ***	.15 **	.09	.02	.09	-.05	.07	6.70	1.28
2 Education	.46 ***	/	.11 *	-.01	.06	.01	-.07	.00	3.24	1.65
3 Employ, W	.15 **	.00	/	-.01	.03	.02	.01	.03	0.57	0.50
4 Inst, H	.09	-.01	-.01	/	.18 ***	.03	.04	-.03	3.68	0.58
5 Expr, H	.02	.04	.03	.18 ***	/	.02	.09	.20 ***	3.44	0.56
6 Inst, W	.09	-.00	.02	.03	.02	/	.14 *	.06	3.23	0.63
7 Expr, W	-.05	-.05	.01	.04	.09	.14 **	/	.06	3.77	0.53
8 Marital sat.	-.08	-.08	.08	.02	.13 *	-.06	.07	/	5.92	1.10
M	6.70	3.89	0.57	3.68	3.44	3.23	3.77	6.02		
SD	1.28	2.02	0.50	0.58	0.56	0.63	0.53	0.99		

* p < .05 ** p < .01 *** p < .001

Note. Income = net family income; Employ, W = employment, wife (1 = yes, 0 = no); Inst, H = instrumentality, husband; Inst, W = instrumentality, wife; Expr, H = expressiveness, husband; Expr, W = expressiveness, wife; Marital sat. = marital satisfaction

Multiple regression analyses

Our research questions were addressed using regression and multi-group analysis in LISREL 8.5 (Jöreskog & Sorböm, 1996). LISREL is used to exploit the important feature of dealing with dyadic data rather than because of its progressiveness in addressing measurement reliability and validity (Kenny & Cook, 1999). The possibility to equal husbands' and wives' coefficients and to subsequently test whether this equality constraint is acceptable or not, is a major advantage of using LISREL for dependent data.

Despite the fact that most variables in our analysis are latent variables measured by manifest scale items, we used the summated scale scores as manifest indicators. Using the individual items as indicators for each of the latent variables the number of parameters to be estimated is too large with respect to the sample size ($N = 386$), casting doubt on the stability of the results (Mueller, 1996). Therefore, we defined all variables of interest as observed variables in LISREL, strongly reducing the numbers of parameters to be estimated.

Before testing our models, we created two-way interaction terms in SAS by computing the product between gender role identity and indicators of socioeconomic position or family life stage. Note that we mean-centered our variables of interest to minimize multicollinearity problems. It is acknowledged that considerable estimation problems can arise when multicollinearity is introduced into a regression equation with interaction effects (Aiken & West, 1991; Jaccard, Turussi, & Wan, 1990). Because multicollinearity in regression analysis with higher order terms is primarily due to scaling, centering variables can strongly lessen this problem.

All formulated hypotheses that concern three-way interaction terms were tested using multi-group analysis. It concerns the hypotheses referring to both spouses' educational levels as well as the hypotheses relating women's employment to spousal socioeconomic position. Therefore, we applied a median split approach to divide the third variable of the interaction term in two categories. Within each of those categories, we conducted regression analyses with two-way interaction terms, which were created in SAS as indicated above. For the hypotheses implying two-way interaction terms, we preferred the use of this two-way product term above a multi-group approach because of the loss of information when splitting up metric variables in groups.

Table 7.2
The Effect of Gender Role Identity on Marital Satisfaction Without and With the Inclusion of Two-Way Interactions with Age of the Child and Household Income (Unstandardized Effects and Associated T-Values, for Men and Women)

Model without interaction effects

Women's satisfaction	b	$t^{(a)}$	Men's satisfaction	b	t
Inst, H	-.13	-1.13	Inst, H	.10	0.98
Inst, W	.14	1.51	Inst, W	-.07	-0.77
Expr, H	.40	3.69	Expr, H	.21	2.20
Expr, W	.14	1.52	Expr, W	.14	1.52

$R^2 = .07$ $R^2 = .05$
Correlation (Eta1, Eta2) = .44 (b) $\chi^2(27) = 17.27$ p = 0.92   RMSEA = .00   CFI = 1.00

Interaction effects with age of the child

Women's satisfaction	b	t	Men's satisfaction	b	t
Inst, H	-.13	-1.18	Inst, H	.09	0.93
Inst, W	.13	1.37	Inst, W	-.08	-0.96
Expr, H	.39	3.68	Expr, H	.20	2.16
Expr, W	.16	1.72	Expr, W	.16	1.72
Year birth, C	.00	-0.04	Year birth, C	-.02	-0.85
Year birth, C * Inst, H	.09	2.22	Year birth, C * Inst, H	.09	2.22
Year birth, C * Expr, H	-.06	-1.68	Year birth, C * Expr, H	-.06	-1.68
Year birth, C * Inst, W	.02	0.60	Year birth, C * Inst, W	.02	0.60
Year birth, C * Expr, W	.07	1.59	Year birth, C * Expr, W	.07	1.59

$R^2 = .09$ $R^2 = .08$
Correlation (Eta1, Eta2) = .42 $\chi^2(83) = 56.27$ p = 0.99   RMSEA = .00   CFI = 1.00

Interaction effects with income

Women's satisfaction	b	t	Men's satisfaction	b	t
Inst, H	-.13	-1.19	Inst, H	.11	1.08
Inst, W	.17	1.79	Inst, W	-.06	-0.71
Expr, H	.39	3.64	Expr, H	.18	1.90
Expr, W	.15	1.60	Expr, W	.15	1.60
Income	.08	1.40	Income	-.07	-1.41
Income * Inst, H	.01	0.18	Income * Inst, H	.01	0.18
Income * Expr, H	.02	0.29	Income * Expr, H	.02	0.29
Income * Inst, W	.11	1.96	Income * Inst, W	.11	1.96
Income * Expr, W	.10	1.17	Income * Expr, W	-.17	-2.24

$R^2 = .08$ $R^2 = .07$
Correlation (Eta1, Eta2) = .42 $\chi^2(63) = 41.87$ p = 0.98   RMSEA = .00   CFI = 1.00

Note: Inst, H = instrumentality, husband; Inst, W = instrumentality, wife; Expr, H = expressiveness, husband; Expr, W = expressiveness, wife; Year birth, C = year of birth, child
[a] t = 2.58 (p < .01); t = 1.96 (p < .05); t = 1.64 (p < .10)
[b] Correlation (Eta1, Eta2) = Correlation between husbands and wives' marital satisfaction

The process of testing our models in LISREL involves several steps. In a first step, a baseline model without equality constraints was tested. This model included the variables of interest and the control variables. The set of exogenous variables as well as the set of endogenous variables are allowed to correlate. In a second step, non-significant correlations between exogenous variables were fixed to zero. In subsequent steps, it is tested whether significant gamma path coefficients can be equated between husbands and wives or between the distinguished groups. Chi-square difference tests between constrained and non-constrained models indicate if the constraining of these paths result in a (non)significant increase of the chi-square. If imposing an equality constraint does not result in a significant increase of chi-square value, it can be concluded that the coefficients do not significantly differ from each other. For the sake of brevity, we only present the final models in the Tables. The results of the control variables are not included in the presentation.

Before testing the moderating nature of one's social position, the main effects of spousal instrumentality and expressiveness on their marital satisfaction was examined in a first model. As can be seen in Table 7.2, for husbands as well as wives it appears that male's expressiveness is positively associated with spousal marital satisfaction. This association, though, is stronger for women than for men, lending support to the second hypothesis. The effect of wives' expressiveness, however, was not found significant ($t = 1.52$, $p > .10$). Consequently, it can be concluded that the first hypothesis is supported for husbands' expressiveness but not for wives' expressiveness.

Regression model with interaction between gender role identity and age of the child

Our third hypothesis assumes that expressiveness may have a more positive effect on spousal marital satisfaction when children are in their early adolescence. The results are given in Table 7.2 and indicate that husbands' instrumental qualities such as being "self-confident" and "consciousness" have a more positive effect on both spouses' satisfaction the younger is the child. For every year that year of birth changes, the slope of marital satisfaction on husbands' instrumentality increases by 0.09 units. Because the age of the children included in our study (indicated by year of birth) ranges from 14 to 21 years, this result implies that husbands' instrumentality is more beneficial for marriage when children are in their early adolescence phase and is less important when children become older, supporting the fourth hypothesis. At a lower significance level ($t = -1.68$, p $<$ .10) it also becomes apparent that besides the positive main effect of husbands' expressiveness, the latter appears to be less positive for spousal satisfaction in the period of early adolescence. Our third hypothesis, stating that expressiveness may yield more positive effects when children are younger, cannot be supported.

Besides these interaction effects, the analysis shows that husbands' expressiveness and at a weaker significance level also wives' expressiveness ($t = 1.72$, $p <$ .10) has a positive main effect on both spouses' satisfaction.

Regression model with interaction between gender role identity and spouses' income position

Testing the fifth hypothesis, we assume that spousal income position mitigates the effect of expressiveness and instrumentality on marital satisfaction. Therefore, a model with four two-way interactions was fitted (RMSEA = .00 and CFI=1.00). The results are given in Table 7.2. As in the previous models, husbands' expressiveness has a positive effect on both spouses' marital satisfaction and this association is stronger for wives than for husbands.

Furthermore, two interaction effects were significant. First, our results demonstrate that husbands report lower satisfaction to the extent that the family income is higher and wives define themselves in expressive qualities. Specifically, it appears that for every unit that income changes, the slope of husbands' marital satisfaction on wives' expressiveness decreases by 0.17 units. Second, both husbands and wives, are more satisfied to the degree the family income is higher and wives define themselves in instrumental qualities. These results lend support to Hypothesis 5, assuming that the effect of endorsing stereotypical qualities is more beneficial for lower class couples.

Table 7.3

The Effect of Gender Role Identity on Marital Satisfaction With Two-Way Interactions Between Wives' Educational Level and Gender Role Identity, Multi-Group Analysis Between Higher and Lower Educated Husbands (Unstandardized Effects and Associated T-Values, for Men and Women)

	Lower educated husbands					
Women's satisfaction	b	t [a]	Men's satisfaction	b	t
Inst, H	-.10	-0.96	Inst, H	.11	1.22
Inst, W	.28	2.42	Inst, W	-.06	-0.80
Expr, H	.26	3.35	Expr, H	.26	3.35
Expr, W	.21	2.57	Expr, W	.21	2.57
Educ, W	.12	1.82	Educ, W	.11	1.96
Educ, W * Inst, H	-.07	-1.51	Educ, W * Inst, H	-.07	-1.55
Educ, W * Expr, H	.03	0.51	Educ, W * Expr, H	.03	0.51
Educ, W * Inst, W	.07	1.75	Educ, W * Inst, W	.07	1.75
Educ, W * Expr, W	-.01	-0.19	Educ, W * Expr, W	-.01	-0.19

$R^2 = .08$ $R^2 = .17$

Correlation (Eta1, Eta2) = .43 [b]

	Higher educated husbands					
Women's satisfaction	b	t	Men's satisfaction	b	t
Inst, H	-.10	-0.96	Inst, H	.11	1.22
Inst, W	.00	-0.03	Inst, W	-.06	-0.80
Expr, H	.26	3.35	Expr, H	.26	3.35
Expr, W	.21	2.57	Expr, W	.21	2.57
Educ, W	-.10	-1.89	Educ, W	-.09	-2.02
Educ, W * Inst, H	-.07	-1.51	Educ, W * Inst, H	-.07	-1.51
Educ, W * Expr, H	.03	0.51	Educ, W * Expr, H	.03	0.51
Educ, W * Inst, W	.07	1.75	Educ, W * Inst, W	.07	1.75
Educ, W * Expr, W	-.01	-0.19	Educ, W * Expr, W	-.01	-0.19

$R^2 = .10$ $R^2 = .08$

Correlation (Eta1, Eta2) = .38

Model: $\chi^2(136) = 118.35$ p = 0.86   RMSEA = .00   CFI = 1.00

Note: Inst, H=instrumentality, husband; Inst, W=instrumentality, wife; Expr, H = expressiveness, husband; Expr, W=expressiveness, wife; Educ, W=education, wife
[a] t = 2.58 (p < .01); t = 1.96 (p < .05); t = 1.64 (p < .10)
[b] Correlation (Eta1, Eta2) = Correlation between husbands and wives' marital satisfaction

Regression model with interaction between gender role identity and spouses' educational level

The fifth hypothesis is also tested using educational level as an indication of higher and lower social class. As indicated above, testing the moderating effect of spouses' educational level on the association between gender role identity and satisfaction requires a three-way interaction term. To capture this complex relationship, we gave preference to the use of a two-way interaction term within the categories of the third variable. Therefore, we split up our sample. The interaction between wives' educational level and spousal expressiveness and instrumentality is examined in a sub-sample of higher respectively lower educated men. The median split of educational level corresponds to husbands who enjoyed at least higher secondary education and those who finished lower secondary education or less.

Two main effects were found significant in the higher as well as the lower educated sub-sample and for both husbands and wives. It was demonstrated once more that husbands' expressiveness and also wives' expressiveness are positively associated with marital satisfaction. This effect appeared to be just as strong in the higher as in the lower educated group of husbands. Besides, in the latter subgroup, wives' instrumentality also appeared to have a positive effect on women's satisfaction. The more women are "self-confident" and "not excitable in crises" the higher their reported satisfaction.

None of the interactions are meaningful related to spousal marital satisfaction, except for one interaction effect that was found significant at the .10 level ($t = 1.75$). For both husbands and wives in the lower and the higher educated sub-sample it appears that wives' instrumentality has a more positive effect on spousal satisfaction the higher women are educated.

Table 7.4
The Effect of Gender Role Identity on Marital Satisfaction With Two-Way Interactions Between Wives' Employment and Gender Role Identity, Multi-Group Analysis Between Higher and Lower Income Couples (Unstandardized Effects and Associated T-Values, for Men and Women)

Lower income couples					
Women's satisfaction	b	t [a]	**Men's satisfaction**	b	t
Inst, H	.04	0.45	Inst, H	.04	0.45
Inst, W	.00	0.03	Inst, W	.00	0.03
Expr, H	.29	3.58	Expr, H	.29	3.58
Expr, W	.06	0.68	Expr, W	.33	2.64
Employ, w	-.04	-0.22	Employ, w	.11	0.74
Employ, w * Inst, H	.44	1.82	Employ, w * Inst, H	.44	1.82
Employ, w * Expr, H	-.11	-0.66	Employ, w * Expr, H	-.11	-0.66
Employ, w * Inst, W	-.05	-0.39	Employ, w * Inst, W	-.05	-0.39
Employ, w * Expr, W	-.32	-1.29	Employ, w * Expr, W	-.32	-1.29

$R^2 = .06$ $R^2 = .15$

Correlation (Eta1, Eta2) = .42 [b]

Higher income couples					
Women's satisfaction	b	t	**Men's satisfaction**	b	t
Inst, H	.04	0.45	Inst, H	.04	0.45
Inst, W	.00	0.03	Inst, W	.00	0.03
Expr, H	.29	3.58	Expr, H	.29	3.58
Expr, W	.06	0.68	Expr, W	.06	0.68
Employ, w	.15	0.98	Employ, w	.12	0.84
Employ, w * Inst, H	-.37	-1.73	Employ, w * Inst, H	-.37	-1.73
Employ, w * Expr, H	-.11	-0.66	Employ, w * Expr, H	-.11	-0.66
Employ, w * Inst, W	-.05	-0.39	Employ, w * Inst, W	-.05	-0.39
Employ, w * Expr, W	.11	0.48	Employ, w * Expr, W	.11	0.48

$R^2 = .06$ $R^2 = .07$

Correlation (Eta1, Eta2) = .41

Model: $\chi^2(123)=107.55$ p = 0.84   RMSEA = .00   CFI = 1.00

Note. Inst, H = instrumentality, husband; Inst, W = instrumentality, wife; Expr, H = expressiveness, husband; Expr, W = expressiveness, wife; Employ, w = employment, wife
[a] t = 2.58 (p < .01); t = 1.96 (p < .05); t = 1.64 (p < .10)
[b] Correlation (Eta1, Eta2) = Correlation between husbands' and wives' marital satisfaction

Regression model with interaction between gender role identity and female employment according to spouses' socioeconomic position

To test the sixth and seventh hypothesis stating that the effect of spousal gender role identity on marital satisfaction depends on women's employment in higher and lower social strata, we performed two multi-group analyses. In a first model we examined the interaction between gender role identity and female employment (1 = yes, 0 = no) on husbands' and wives marital satisfaction in a sample of lower respectively higher income couples. A similar multi-group analysis was conducted in a sample of lower and higher educated husbands. Both multi-group models showed an excellent fit with RMSEA values of .00 and CFI values of 1.00.

Considering the multi-group analysis in higher and lower income couples our results show that in the latter, husbands' endorsement of instrumental qualities has a stronger positive effect on both spouses' marital satisfaction when the wife is employed ($t = 1.82$). The reverse, however, holds for higher income couples. In these couples, husbands' endorsement of instrumental qualities has a more negative effect on both spouses' marital satisfaction when the wife is employed ($t = -1.73$).

Table 7.5
The Effect of Gender Role Identity on Marital Satisfaction With Two-Way Interactions Between Wives' Employment and Gender Role Identity, Multi-Group Analysis Between Higher and Lower Educated Husbands (Unstandardized Effects and Associated T-Values, for Men and Women)

Lower educated husbands					
Women's satisfaction	b	t [a]	**Men's satisfaction**	b	t
Inst, H	-.07	-0.70	Inst, H	.13	1.51
Inst, W	.03	0.48	Inst, W	.03	0.48
Expr, H	.30	3.84	Expr, H	.30	3.84
Expr, W	.18	2.28	Expr, W	.18	2.28
Employ, w	-.10	-0.59	Employ, w	.21	1.54
Employ, w * Inst, H	.42	1.92	Employ, w * Inst, H	.42	1.92
Employ, w * Expr, H	-.13	-0.84	Employ, w * Expr, H	-.13	-0.84
Employ, w * Inst, W	-.07	-0.50	Employ, w * Inst, W	-.07	-0.50
Employ, w * Expr, W	-.15	-0.94	Employ, w * Expr, W	-.15	-0.94

$R^2 = .07$ $\qquad\qquad\qquad\qquad\qquad\qquad$ $R^2 = .17$

Correlation (Eta1, Eta2) = .40 [b]

Higher educated husbands					
Women's satisfaction	b	t	**Men's satisfaction**	b	t
Inst, H	-.07	-0.70	Inst, H	.13	1.51
Inst, W	.03	0.48	Inst, W	.03	0.48
Expr, H	.30	3.84	Expr, H	.30	3.84
Expr, W	.18	2.28	Expr, W	.18	2.28
Employ, w	.18	1.10	Employ, w	.05	0.32
Employ, w * Inst, H	-.48	-2.13	Employ, w * Inst, H	-.48	-2.13
Employ, w * Expr, H	-.13	-0.84	Employ, w * Expr, H	-.13	-0.84
Employ, w * Inst, W	-.07	-0.50	Employ, w * Inst, W	-.07	-0.50
Employ, w * Expr, W	-.15	-0.94	Employ, w * Expr, W	-.15	-0.94

$R^2 = .11$ $\qquad\qquad\qquad\qquad\qquad\qquad$ $R^2 = .09$

Correlation (Eta1, Eta2) = .38

Model: $\chi^2(154) = 142.56$ $\qquad$ p = 0.74 $\qquad$ RMSEA = .00 $\qquad$ CFI = 1.00

Note: Inst, H = instrumentality, husband; Inst, W = instrumentality, wife; Expr, H = expressiveness, husband; Expr, W = expressiveness, wife; Employ, w = employment, wife
[a] t = 2.58 (p < .01); t = 1.96 (p < .05); t = 1.64 (p < .10)
[b] Correlation (Eta1, Eta2) = Correlation between husbands and wives' marital satisfaction

Considering the same analysis in a sample of lower and higher educated husbands, quite similar findings were obtained. Spouses in the higher educated sample appear to be less satisfied when wives are employed and husbands endorse instrumental qualities ($t = -2.13$) whereas the reverse conclusion can be drawn for the lower educated sample ($t = 1.92$). Hence, our findings lend support to Hypothesis 7, stating that emphasizing husbands' instrumentality in lower social classes where wives are employed, contributes to spousal marital satisfaction.

Besides the just described interaction effects, the positive main effect of husbands' expressiveness as well as wives' expressiveness on spousal satisfaction was demonstrated once again.

The interaction effects between women's employment and husbands' instrumentality within higher and lower educated groups of husbands are visualized for women's marital satisfaction in Figure 7.2. All interaction effects described above are summarized in Table 7.6.

Figure 7.2
Visual Presentation of the Interaction Effect Between Female Employment and Husbands' Instrumentality on Wives' Marital Satisfaction in Lower and Higher Educated Groups of Husbands

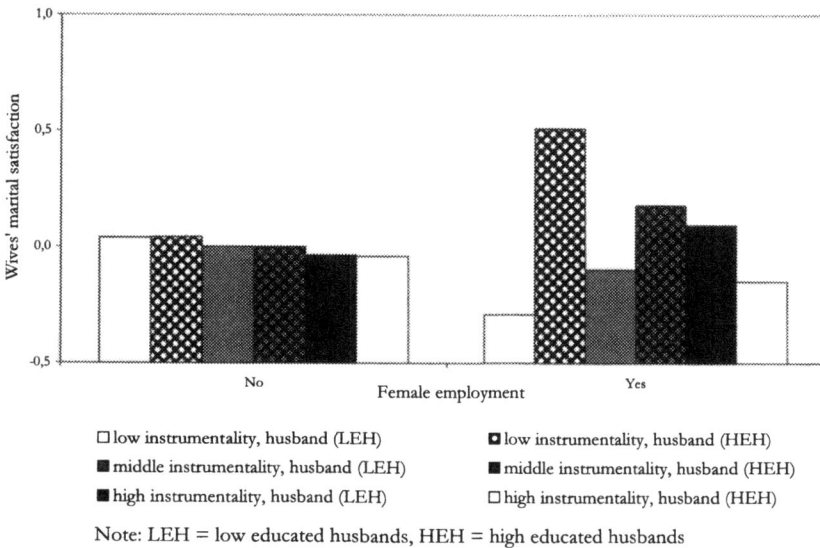

□ low instrumentality, husband (LEH)   ▣ low instrumentality, husband (HEH)
■ middle instrumentality, husband (LEH)   ■ middle instrumentality, husband (HEH)
■ high instrumentality, husband (LEH)   □ high instrumentality, husband (HEH)

Note: LEH = low educated husbands, HEH = high educated husbands

7.6. DISCUSSION

The aim of this study was twofold. Using couple data, it was firstly examined how expressiveness and instrumentality is associated with spousal marital satisfaction. Second, we studied whether and how this association is moderated by couple's marital stage, family income, spousal educational level and women's employment. This question was addressed in a Dutch sample of established couples with children.

Table 7.6

Summary of the Significant Interaction Effects Between Gender Role Identity and Wives' Employment, Couple's Income and Spousal Educational Level on Marital Satisfaction

	Children younger (min. 14 years)	Higher income levels	High educational level of the couple
Wives' satisfaction	Husbands' instrumentality (+) Husbands' expressiveness (-)[a]	Wives' instrumentality (+)	Wives' instrumentality (+)[a]
Husbands' satisfaction	Husbands' instrumentality (+) Husbands' expressiveness (-)[a]	Wives' instrumentality (+) Wives' expressiveness (-)	Wives' instrumentality (+)[a]

	Wives' employment	
Wives' satisfaction	**Lower income level** Husbands' instrumentality (+)[a]	**Lower educational level, husband** Husbands' instrumentality (+)
	Higher income level Husbands' instrumentality (-)[a]	**Higher educational level, husband** Husbands' instrumentality (-)
Husbands' satisfaction	**Lower income level** Husbands' instrumentality (+)[a]	**Lower educational level, husband** Husbands' instrumentality (+)
	Higher income level Husbands' instrumentality (-)[a]	**Higher educational level, husband** Husbands' instrumentality (-)

Note: The direction of the effect of expressiveness or instrumentality is noted between brackets.
[a] $p < .10$

160

Throughout all the analyses conducted within the realm of this study, evidence was obtained for a positive effect of husbands' expressiveness on both spouses' marital satisfaction. This finding is in line with the generally supported idea that femininity, and expressiveness in particular, is beneficial for one's partnership (Antill, 1983). However, by including husbands and wives from one dyad into the same analysis, we demonstrated that the positive association between husbands' expressiveness and marital satisfaction is stronger for women's marital evaluation than for men's.

Despite the unequivocal importance of husbands' expressiveness, our results also indicate that this quality might be less paramount in the stage when one's children are young adolescents (about 14 years old). In this specific marital phase, partnership seems to benefit from husbands being instrumental rather than from husbands being expressive. Although the effect of wives' expressiveness was not significant, one can observe a tendency for spouses to report higher satisfaction when wives are more interpersonal oriented (expressive) in this stage. As children become older, and thus less demand is placed on the couple, these associations and trends become less strong. Apparently, in the phase of early adolescence men and women are better off when adopting traditional prescribed qualities, the latter holding particularly for men. In a similar vein, previous research has been shown that couples easily slip back into traditional gender role behavior at the arrival of children (Burke & Cast, 1997). How can we explain our finding? Perhaps, the family climate is more cohesive and adaptable when fathers assert their influence by means of their controlling qualities. Olson et al. (1983) demonstrated that balanced levels of cohesion and adaptability are indispensable for coping with the demands and stresses of the adolescent stage. As Holmbeck, Paikoff, and Brooks-Gunn (1995) suggest, control and effective discipline are essential components in realizing this cohesion and adaptation. At the same time, mothers seem to be more important sources of support and more responsive for the desires for adolescents than are fathers (Vandemeulebroecke, et al., 2000), explaining the observed tendency that wives' expressiveness may become more important in this stage. These speculations, however, require further investigation.

Our analysis yielded an interesting pattern of findings regarding the sex-specificity as well as the context-specificity of one's gender role identity on spousal marital satisfaction. We discern two groups of analyses: one that controls for women's employment and one that includes interactions between gender role identity and women's employment. Within each group, analyses are conducted using partners' educational level or family income as an indicator for social class.

When controlling for women's employment, it becomes clear that husbands as well as wives in lower income groups are less satisfied when women endorse non-stereotypical male qualities. This finding supports the idea that lower strata more strongly adhere to stereotypical sex qualities (Huston & Geis, 1993). In a sense, lower income husbands may affirm their status position in the private sphere by disfavoring *masculine-typed (instrumentality)* women and preferring women who are typified as stereotypically feminine. The latter becomes clear from the significant interaction effect between wives' expressiveness and income on husbands' satisfaction. However, it is not apparent whether lower class men selected their wives on these characteristics or whether these characteristics developed during marriage.

Considering cultural (education) instead of economic capital as an indicator of higher and lower social class, it is found once more that wives' instrumentality, be it at a .10 significance level, is a differentiating factor in spousal satisfaction when controlling for women's employment. Specifically, it is demonstrated that the effect of women endorsing instrumental qualities is more positive on women's satisfaction to the extent that they are higher educated. This association, however, was supported for couples in which husbands are higher as well as lower educated. In other words, to the extent that women gain more cultural capital, both marital partners seem to be more satisfied when wives adopt male stereotypical qualities. This result partially supports the idea that the effect of endorsing non-stereotypical qualities is more accepted within higher social strata. However, the question remains why lower educated husbands also report higher marital satisfaction when their higher educated wives adopt instrumental characteristics? Or, education has a broad emancipatory effect that clashes with male's instrumentality as role affirmative; or, lower educated husbands are not so much threatened by their wives' educational capital but rather by their economical capital.

The latter speculation emanates from two considerations. First, the Netherlands occupy a peculiar position with regard to women's employment (Niphuis-Nell & de Beer, 1997). In comparison to other Western countries, the Dutch labor market is characterized by a high rate of female part-time employment, accounting for the fact that Dutch men derive status from their position as main providers. It is important to note, however, that until the nineties the Netherlands lagged far behind the other Western countries with respect to female employment. As a result, Dutch men are only recently, and certainly at the time of our study, confronted with this new female status, which might come over as a threat or at least as a new situation to deal with. This situation has two opposite side-effects. For one, the traditional male status as (single) wage earner becomes now also a female 'status'; for another, new norms of material comfort and welfare increasingly require an additional income, particularly for lower classes. Moreover, being a single provider may put serious pressure on husbands (Oppenheimer, 1994; 1997). These mixed considerations might explain the positive trend of women's employment on husbands' marital satisfaction in lower classes and at the same time the accentuation of husbands' instrumental qualities under these circumstances.

A second thought accounting for the particular significance of women's employment in lower classes becomes clear in Table 7.3. This Table presents the model that controlled for women's employment, showing that for both higher and lower educated husbands, the interaction between women's education and husbands' instrumentality tends to be negative, be it not significant. This effect, though, reverses for the group of lower educated husbands when considering the interaction between women's employment and husbands' instrumentality, indicating that the distinct meaning of female educational and economical capital is vital in this group. In contrast, within the group of higher educated husbands, a negative effect between husbands' instrumentality and women's enhanced status remains whether or not one considers educational or economical capital. Similar evidence, yet at a lower significance level ($p < .10$), is obtained when considering interaction terms with women's employment in higher and lower income groups.

Hence, husbands' instrumentality and not wives' instrumentality or expressiveness seems to be essential in differentiating between more and less satisfied spouses in marriages where wives are employed. In lower social layers, husbands' instrumentality is beneficial for spousal evaluation of marriage whereas in higher strata it has a negative effect on spousal marital satisfaction. These results may reflect the different nature and meaning attached to women's employment in distinct social layers. Probably, because women's employment in higher strata is more understood in terms of personal needs than as a financial necessity, stereotypically typed men are incompatible with the demands of 'non-stereotypical' women (Pyke, 1996). This line of reasoning is further supported by some post-hoc variance analyses we conducted. First, it appears that in higher social layers women are not only employed in higher occupations but they also work more hours than do women in lower social layers. Second, the former also report higher work-related stress. This may point to the greater salience of work for women in higher strata. Because of the importance of the work role, women devote more hours to this task but may also experience more stress because of their greater involvement. Hence, in higher social layers spouses might be better able to deal with women's employment when husbands do *not* endorse stereotypical male qualities, which are more orientated on independency and less on interdependency. These independency-oriented and stereotypical qualities of men do not seem to be congruent with the requirements associated with wives participating in the labor market. In lower strata, however, this status-enhancing act of women is managed, or perhaps even countered, by a stronger emphasis on husbands' stereotypical qualities. Notably, the lower economic status of employed women in these strata might not represent a serious challenge for touching upon male stereotypical qualities, but rather leads to an accentuation of it. Perhaps, the privileged status of lower strata men may be threatened or undermined by the consequences of women's employment for the internal functioning of the family. Indeed, the results from our post-hoc analyses demonstrate that within higher educated groups (but not in higher income groups), men spend significantly more time at childrearing tasks than in the lower educated groups. The reverse, though, holds for women. In higher educated layers, women take up less childrearing tasks than do their female counterparts from the lower educated groups. This might illustrate the different adaptations utilized by distinct educational groups to meet the demands of work and family life (Gottfried et al., 1995).

The reason why this distinctiveness was not found in higher and lower income groups might explain why the interaction between women's employment and husbands' instrumentality is more significant in the analysis using educational groups (Table 7.5) than in the one using income groups (Table 7.4). These interpretations, however, are tentative and unwarranted at this stage and therefore need further examination. In particular, attention should be paid to the interrelations between spousal gender role identities, women's income position and the way spouses evaluate the benefits and detriments resulting from wives' labor market participation.

Taken our findings together, though, our results show that in higher social class couples with women working outside the home, satisfied marriages become possible when husbands develop a less stereotypical male identity whereas in lower social layers they need to accentuate their traditional sex role qualities. In higher social layers, a strengthened economic position of women results in renouncing the 'traditional man' whereas in the lower layers it leads to an accentuation of it. Thus, in both social groups it appears that women's economic position is linked with men's stereotypical qualities and not with women's. This finding may point toward the idea, voiced by Amato & Booth (1995), and Vannoy and Philliber (1992), stating that husbands may relieve the potential negative consequences associated with women's employment. Our analysis demonstrates that this phenomenon is typical, though, for higher social strata. In lower layers, both husbands and wives are better off when taking the 'traditional' lines. By emphasizing stereotypical aspects of masculinity, spouses in lower strata may confirm husbands' status position also in case when wives work outside. Note that social class instead of sex accounts for the variety in marital experiences as a result of spousal identities.

It becomes clear that, beyond the overall positive effect of husbands' expressiveness, spousal marital experiences in distinct social strata are not related to female qualities but rather result from the weighing up of stereotypical male qualities, either endorsed by men or by women. Considering the items of the instrumentality scale, one can notice that they primarily refer to feelings of independence or imperturbability. According to Marusic (1998) "stable" individuals are characterized by less vulnerability and more assertiveness. Orlofsky and Stake (1981) assert that these qualities are a source of psychological strength, resulting in a healthy self-confidence in one's abilities. This study shows that the endorsement of these qualities, conditional upon social strata and women's employment, seems to make the difference between more and less satisfied spouses.

It is worth emphasizing that apart from the context-specific effects of instrumentality, husband's expressiveness is paramount in understanding husbands and wives' satisfaction. The more men endorse traits such as "being kind", "expressing tender feelings" and "not hiding emotions", the more satisfied are both marital partners. This holds for lower as well as higher social layers and for couples in which wives are employed or not. Connecting with others may be a new element in the old image of masculinity (Blazina, 2003). If these traits are characteristic of the so-called "new man", it can be asserted that not only wives but also husbands benefit from these qualities.

Some limitations of our study must put our results in the proper perspective. First, the scales of instrumentality and expressive traits are only a limited indication of one's masculinity or femininity. For example, we did not investigate gender behaviors or gender interests. Literature has shown that a different pattern of findings might appear when considering these different phenomena (Aubé & Koestner, 1992). Therefore, a more differentiated measurement of gender identity may be a fruitful way to gain a deeper understanding of the interplay of gender and social class for marital experiences. Second, instrumentality and expressiveness are measured as self-concepts. Data collected from one's partner or from the social network of the couple may yield a different pattern of results. Third, in two models the interaction effects just failed to reach a significance level of .05 (husbands' educational level * wives' educational level * instrumentality, wife and women's employment * income * husbands' instrumentality). However, because both effects point into the same direction as the results of the competing models, we tentatively interpreted these effects. It is recommended to further examine the significance of these associations in larger samples. Fourth, we deal with couples averagely married for 22 years with at least one child between 14 and 21 years old. Thus, our findings regarding the marital stage are limited to the period under study. Examining the subject in a sample of couples married for shorter as well as longer periods will broaden our insight in the phenomenon. Fifth, as we did not use a longitudinal design, it remains possible that the direction of causality among our variables may turn out to be the opposite of what is hypothesized with marital satisfaction leading spouses to adopt a specific gender role identity. Satisfied partners might infer their degree of 'interdependency' from their satisfied feelings. Panel studies are needed to more fully explore this relationship over the marital life course as well as along different social strata. Sixth, except for husbands' satisfaction in lower social layers, the variance explained in our models is relatively limited, indicating that gender role identity is not a major determinant of spousal marital satisfaction. It is likely, however, that expressiveness and instrumentality become more important when considering them in relation to marital satisfaction through means of spousal interaction. Seventh, husbands and wives' occupation was not included in this study. Besides education and income, consideration of spousal occupations in general, and job dimensions such as autonomy and control in specific, may further deepen our insight in the processes suggested in this research (Perry-Jenkins & Folk, 1994).

Nevertheless, our study documents that social conditions are important when dealing with instrumentality and expressiveness. It is demonstrated that instrumentality and expressiveness are elements of one's personality or identity structure with a distinct relevance in different marital stages and social classes. As a consequence, husband's expressiveness is not the only constructive ingredient for marital satisfaction. Stereotypical male qualities are also a point of particular interest. Hence, marital reality is more complex than Antill's (1983) "femininity model" may suggest. Thus far our knowledge of this issue along different social levels and throughout the marital life course remains limited and in need of further exploration.

8. Associations Between Gender Characteristics and Marital Outcomes. A Test of Identity Theory in Established Marriages

8.1. INTRODUCTION

The present study considers whether gender characteristics are related with marital outcomes in the specific way predicted by *identity theory*. According to identity theory, gender and its associated meanings represent an important part of individuals' self-identity. *Identity theorists* (Burke & Reitzes, 1991; Stryker, 1980) assert that the identities and gendered meanings of being masculine or feminine motivate actions that result in the social confirmation of the male respective female identity, and therefore can be considered as a key element in understanding spousal behavior and affect in marriage. This view extends theories, which assume that actors respond to others based on membership in certain status categories, such as one's biological sex (see Burke, 1980; Stets & Burke, 1996). In this respect, men as higher status individuals should display more negative communication whereas women as the lower status category should use more positive and open communication. According to identity theory, however, it is not only the fact of being male or female in a biological sense but also the meanings that individuals attribute to themselves as masculine or feminine (i.e., gender role identity) that determine individuals' interaction behavior. Because *being male* is linked with dominance, independence and competitiveness whereas *being female* is related to affiliation and cooperation, this theory presumes that negative and positive communication behavior is more likely to be used when subscribing to a masculine and feminine identity respectively (Ridgeway & Smith-Lovin, 1999; Stets, 1995; 1997; Stets & Burke, 2000). In this way, the identity theoretical assumption that actors' identities guide their conduct is compatible with the "doing gender" approach (Kroska, 1997).

Gender role identity versus other gender-related characteristics and marital communication

By focusing on someone's attribution of stereotypical feminine (expressive) and masculine (instrumental) traits, identity theory still uses a limited conceptualization of gender identity. Neither attitudes towards sex roles nor engaging in stereotypical sex role behavior such as domestic labor are explicitly included in the concept of gender identity. This conceptualization contrasts the principles underlying a *multifactorial theory of gender*. In this perspective and in a gender perspective in general, it is believed that individual behaviors and roles have gendered meanings as well (Ferree, 1990; West & Zimmerman, 1987). Therefore, one's gender identity is composed of several gender-related characteristics such as gender prefer-ences, gender attitudes and gender behaviors. These characteristics, though, are not self-evidently incorporated in one's self in a consistent manner but rather organized in multiple and loosely connected ways (Aube & Koestner, 1992; Aube & Norcliffe, 1995; Huston & Geis, 1993; Katsurada & Sugihara, 2002; Koestner & Aube, 1995; Orlofsky & O'Heron, 1987; Spence, 1984; 1993; Twenge, 1999). To define one's self as masculine or feminine does not necessarily mean that one also endorses specific sex role attitudes or behaves in a masculine or feminine way. This so-called multi-factorial perspective to gender not only attacks the traditional thinking on gender as a bipolar construct, that identity theorists assume as well, but also questions theories built on the notion that gender behaviors, gender attitudes and gender identity are closely related (Bem, 1985).

Nonetheless, the framework of identity theory offers a theoretical tool to assume that stereotypical role behavior and sex role attitudes are similarly related to marital communication than is one's gender identity. Indeed, identity theorists assert that identities serve as a compass to steer individu-als' behavior and attitudes in a mass of social meanings (Burke & Reitzes, 1991; Stryker, 1980). Identities act as a sort of reference frame in which to interpret one's actions and attitudes. In their turn, these behaviors and attitudes reinforce and support one's identity (Burke & Reitzes, 1981; 1991; Stryker, 1980). For example, a man may affirm his instrumental self-identity by *not* doing the laundry but by repairing the car while his wife may do exactly the opposite to confirm her expressive identity.

However, not every person experiences specific behavior and attitudes to be as relevant and important in reaffirming one's identity (Burke &

Reitzes, 1981). Some women, for example, may not consider doing the laundry as essential for their female identity. Moreover, also other dimensions of meanings, which are associated with other roles or identities, might apply. We are not only men or women, but also relatives, employees, and so on.

Therefore, one's gender identity, sex role attitudes and sex role behavior do not need to be necessarily consistent. According to Spence (1993), men are more consistent than women are in this respect. Conventional sex role attitudes and behavior that give men superior status are part of their overall assessment of how masculine they are. Women, in contrast, are less likely to perceive conventional aspects of gender ideology as a relevant part of their self-image as feminine. This might be due to the more negative consequences men experience when deviating from gender stereotypes (O'Heron & Orlofsky, 1990). Thus, it might be hypothesized that on the one hand, men display more congruence between different gender aspects; and on the other hand that the latter have more consistent effects on men's marital outcomes than on women's (Aube & Norcliffe, 1995; Twenge, 1999).

Inconsistencies notwithstanding, identity theorists assert that identities are the basis for one's attitudes and related behaviors and thus they assume that identities can predict behavior more accurately than do attitudes (Kroska, 1997). Therefore, adherents of identity theory expect that identities, and thus gender identity, guide marital communication over and above the effects of other gender-related characteristics such as sex role attitudes or sex role behavior.

Identity theory and marital satisfaction

Identity theory cannot only be extended to a broader range of gender characteristics but also to the marital outcome that is studied. Besides the attention paid by identity theorists to the link between gender identity and marital communication, one could pursue a similar line of reasoning with respect to marital satisfaction. In a behavioral perspective, for example, it is assumed that masculine and feminine characteristics influence marital satisfaction through the behaviors that spouses display toward each other and more specifically through their marital communication (Miller, Caughlin & Huston, 2003). Moreover, previous research has demonstrated positive associations between marital satisfaction and open communication and negative correlations between marital satisfaction and negative communication (Kerkstra, 1985). Hence, understanding the link between gender identity and communication on the one hand and between communication and satisfaction on the other hand, may also specify how gender characteristics become associated with marital satisfaction.

This speculation, however, must be put in the proper perspective, as marital satisfaction is an affective evaluation of the marital relationship and hence a more general and broader marital outcome than is communication. Besides an evaluation of the marital communication, marital satisfaction also includes evaluations of other elements deemed important to the partner. Therefore, gender characteristics that are (not) meaningful related to communication should not be necessarily (un)associated with marital satisfaction.

According to a multifactorial approach to gender, this link is indeed not obvious. Inherently associated with the multifactorial nature of gender is precisely the idea that the same gender characteristic might be differently related to distinct relationship outcomes such as satisfaction or communication (Koestner & Aube, 1995). Previous empirical work in this area provides support for this assumption. For example, evidence is obtained for the idea that men's expressiveness is positively related to spousal marital satisfaction (Antill, 1983; Kurdek & Schmitt, 1986; Lamke, Sollie, Durbin & Fitzpatrick, 1994; Peterson, Baucom, Elliott, & Farr, 1989) but unrelated to spouses' negative communication styles (Huston & Geis, 1993). For women, expressiveness may be unrelated to their marital satisfaction but tends to reduce a negative interaction style towards their husbands (Aube & Norcliffe, 1995). Hence, identical gender characteristics may be differently related to husbands and wives' marital outcomes.

The inconsistencies of gender effects become also apparent from the finding that different characteristics, which both reflect stereotypical femininity (or masculinity) lead to different marital experiences. Despite men's higher marital satisfaction when adopting feminine traits, they tend to report lower satisfaction when displaying feminine role behavior such as doing housework (Aube & Norcliffe, 1995; Broman, 1988; Parmelee, 1987; Shelton & John, 1996). For women, feminine role behavior seems to positively predict marital satisfaction as well as higher levels of sharing during interactions. Thus, whereas some aspects of femininity may encourage positive marital experiences, others seem to have the reverse effect.

The different manifestations of feminine-related characteristics within marriage are intriguing because of the social appraisal of feminine qualities in contemporary partnership (cf. Chapter 1). It looks as if a distinction needs to be made between the actual performances of traditional - and socially lower valued - feminine role behavior and the social emphasis on mere feminine qualities. As to this distinction, three important qualifications need to borne in mind. First, the present study examines Dutch married couples with children. Characteristic for Dutch wives is their low labor market participation in terms of worked hours. Hence, Dutch women take the large burden of family work and considerably 'do gender'. Second, studies examining the consequences of the division of household labor, suggest that the link between household tasks and marital outcomes must be sought in the perception of 'fairness' rather than in the absolute amount of housework (Perry-Jenkins & Folk, 1994; Yogev & Brett, 1985). This assessment of fairness does not strongly relate to the actual share of housework but is rather based on elements such as the different value attached to family chores, role expectations, and one's relational identity (Garrido & Acitelli, 1999; Perry-Jenkins & Folk, 1994). Third, the majority of literature on family work does not distinguish between household tasks and childrearing tasks (Coltrane, 2000). The latter, however, might be a more important source of marital satisfaction than household chores since expectations about father involvement have risen. As Knijn (1997) asserts, a hierarchy of care might be operating within marriages with caring for children more socially valued than the performance of household tasks, and therefore probably also more positively associated with spousal evaluation of marriage than household labor (Knijn, 1997).

Towards a new research agenda

All in all, the above findings illustrate the complex associations that exist between gender characteristics and marital features. Although several of these associations received empirical support, there are still some gaps in our understanding. First, the majority of studies addressed gender in relation to global marital outcomes such as marital quality or marital satisfaction. With the exception of expressive and instrumental traits, we know relatively little about how gender attitudes and gender role behavior are associated with more specific marital behavior such as communication (Aube & Norcliffe, 1995). Nevertheless, the latter may be particularly relevant in understanding the processes responsible for the relation between gender and marital satisfaction.

Second, the bulk of research dealt with gender and marital experiences in younger or newlywed couples (e.g., Antill, 1983; Aube & Norcliffe, 1995; Lamke et al., 1994; Parmelee, 1987). This focus means that little is known about the influence of gender-related characteristics on different marital behaviors in established marriages. Some speculate, for example, that husbands' feminine characteristics become more important in later stages of the relationship, especially when more children may be present (Antill, 1983). In the early stages, husbands' satisfaction should depend on their wives filling in the traditional female role whereas later on, wives' marital satisfaction should become more dependent on their husbands' ability and willingness to perform nurturance tasks. This study examines the gender theme in a sample of couples averagely married for 22 years.

Third, previous work only paid limited attention to the possibility that the complex relations between gender and marriage are different according to spouses' social position. There is no doubt, however, that gender intersects other social divisions such as class (Jackson & Scott, 2002). As Dillaway and Broman (2001) denote, each intersection of structural location, such as class and sex, has the ability to shape marital experiences and behavior. It has been found, for example, that traditional gender traits, attitudes and behavior may be more strongly endorsed in lower social strata (Komarowsky, 1964; Prince-Gibson & Schwartz, 1998; Rubin, 1976) whereas unconventional gender orientations are more prevalent in higher social strata (Huston & Geis, 1993; Straver, van der heiden, & van der vliet, 1994). Perry-Jenkins and Folk (1994) contend that working-class wives' adherence to traditional attitudes affirming the provider role for men, attach great importance to do 'the women's work' whereas in middle-class couples this behavior may result in conflict (Burris, 1991). It might therefore be hypothesized that gender identity in the broad sense is more consistently enacted within lower than in higher social classes.

It must be stressed, however, that despite the expectation that traditional gender identities are more consistently affirmed in lower social classes, great importance is attached to feminine qualities in developing egalitarian partnership in higher social classes. At an aggregate level, Arrindell (1998) demonstrates that a feminine mentality is more easily maintained within a wealthier environment. Hence, it might be tentatively anticipated that within higher income groups, husbands especially live up more strongly to a female identity. Thus, despite the expectation that identity theory may hold particularly in lower income groups, it can also be hypothesized that the female identity is stronger enacted by men in higher income groups.

8.2. PRESENT STUDY

In the present study, different linkages between gender characteristics and marital outcomes in established marriages are examined by measuring both constructs in multiple ways. In order to test whether associations between gender and marital outcomes are consistent with identity theory or with a multifactorial gender approach, besides instrumental (masculine) and expressive (feminine) traits as self-concepts, also attitudes towards stereotypical gender roles, and behavioral reports on domestic household tasks and childrearing tasks of husbands and wives are assessed. Three marital outcome variables are used: marital satisfaction, open communication, and negative communication.

First, it is tested whether expressiveness and instrumentality are characteristics for wives and husbands respectively. According to strict identity theoretical positions, wives and husbands would be identified with merely one trait.

Second, it is tested whether instrumentality predicts negative communication and whether the same results are obtained in case of stereotypical gender role attitudes, and lower scores on behavioral reports of household and childrearing tasks. In a similar vein, it will be tested whether expressiveness, less stereotypical gender role attitudes and higher scores on behavioral reports of household and childrearing tasks predict open communication.

Third, it is examined whether instrumentality, lower scores on household and childrearing behavior and a stereotypical gender role attitude negatively predicts marital satisfaction. Similarly, it will be examined whether expressiveness, higher scores on household and childrearing behavior, and a more egalitarian gender role attitude positively relates to spousal marital satisfaction. As to behavioral reports of household and childrearing tasks, it is expected that childrearing behavior yields more positive results than household behavior.

Fourth, based on identity theory it is hypothesized that instrumentality and expressiveness influence marital outcomes independent of the effects of sex role attitudes and gender role behavior.

Fifth, based on previous research it can be anticipated that gender characteristics and their effects on marriage are more consistently for men than for women.

The final question is whether family's income position (i.e., at the household level) mitigates the associations between gender characteristics and marital outcomes. It is expected that more traditional gender – marital outcome patterns will prevail in lower income couples. Additionally, it is hypothesized that men from higher income couples more strongly confirm a feminine identity than husbands from lower income groups.

Our analyses are conducted using structural equation modeling in LISREL, which allows for testing husband-wife jointly.

8.3. METHOD

8.3.1. Participants

The research sample consists of married men and women participating in the longitudinal research project "Child-rearing and family in the Netherlands". In 1990 and 1995 the same family members (mother, father and target child) provided information about similar sets of measures. Families were recruited using a multi-stage sampling method. In a first stage, a sample was taken of all Dutch municipalities distinguished by regional zone and degree of urbanization. In a second stage, a sample of children was taken in the selected municipalities. The children were selected in such a way that in each city as many boys as girls and as many children aged 9 to 12 as children aged 13 to 16 were chosen. In 1990 this procedure resulted in a sample of 1829 families. The response ratio was 43% ($N=788$) and as required, the sample was representative regarding regional zone and degree of urbanization. Of the 656 families who agreed in 1990 to participate in the second wave, 627 were contacted and 484 (77%) actually did participate in 1995. This sample proved to be still representative for regional zone but not for degree of urbanization. More technical details on the database can be found in Chapter 3 and in Gerris et al. (1992; 1993; 1998). The data were gathered by means of structured interviews and questionnaires.

Because the original sample includes married couples - both first and higher order marriages - as well as one-parent households, we restrict our research sample to first marriages because of the potentially different social processes involved when considering higher-order marriages. This selection resulted in a research group of 646 couples of which 386 couples were still married after five years and were prepared to participate in the second wave. At the second measurement point, the average marital duration is 22 years.

Using logistic regression, we examined the selective character of the panel attrition between the first and the second wave. The inclusion in "both waves" versus "first wave" was regressed on the variables of interest in this study, except from household and childrearing tasks as well as expressiveness and instrumentality, which were only inquired in the second data wave. Results demonstrate that there were no significant differences between both groups with respect to the *independent* variables. However, in comparison to those who participated twice, women who dropped between the first and second measurement point reported more negative marital outcomes in terms of marital satisfaction, negative and open communication. The satisfaction of women, who participated once, averages 5.13 in contrast to the mean satisfaction of 6.09 for women who remained in the panel. Despite the smaller difference, a similar conclusion may be drawn for women's open and negative communication. For those taken part both times their scores were 5.53 and 2.69 respectively whereas women who dropped from the panel scored 5.49 and 2.79.

The men in our sample are on average 47 years old and women average 45 years of age. Men reported higher levels of education than did women. One quarter of the male sample has a university degree, whereas for women this figure is approximately one out of eight. For husbands, 48% reported to have a middle low (lower secondary education) or low school degree; for women this is 61%. The majority of the couples in the present study can be characterized as traditional couples in terms of paid labor. About nine out of then husbands are employed whereas only 57% of the wives participate at the labor market.

8.3.2. Measures

Income position is indicated by the net family income, measured in Dutch guilders. One guilder is approximately 0.45 Euro. Seven income groups were distinguished: 1 = "1100-1600", 2 = "1600-1800", 3 = "1800-2100", 4 = "2100-2500", 5 = "2500-3250", 6 = "3250-4500" and 7 = "more than 4500".

Instrumental and expressive traits were measured by two scales derived from the Personal Attributes Questionnaire of Spence & Helmreich (1978). The scale of instrumentality contains items about instrumental and independent characteristics, which are more likely to be endorsed by males than females. The expressiveness scale consists of seven items about expressive, communal characteristics of which it is believed that women possess them in greater abundance than males. The questionnaire consists of bipolar items with 5 boxes between the two poles. The respondents have to indicate which characteristic is more applicable to them by putting their mark near the pole representing the characteristic. If they think that both characteristics are somewhat applicable to them, they put their mark in the box in the middle. The validity of both scales is described in Gerris et al. (1998). Because some items did not significantly load on one but two dimensions, they were removed from the scale and hence, the remaining items do not cover all information included in the original scales. However, as indicated in the previous chapter, we use the original labels 'expressiveness' and 'instrumentality' to identify the scales, allowing us to situate our study within the scientific tradition on femininity and masculinity. Cronbach's alpha for the instrumentality scale is .75 for men and .76 for women. For the expressiveness scale these figures are .71 and .70 respectively.

Sex role attitudes. The scale "Orientation toward traditional sex roles" measures the degree to which the respondent reports to value a traditional division of roles and tasks between males and females in household, career, child rearing and education. This orientation is measured with a scale consisting of 6 items. The response scale is a 5-point Likert scale ranging from 1 = "totally agree" to 5 = "totally disagree". After recoding, higher scores indicate higher valuation of this orientation. The internal consistency of this scale is .78 for men and .83 for women.

Sex role behavior. Two domains of family tasks were selected: household tasks, and child-rearing/child care tasks. The respondent was asked whether he/she thinks that he/she performs this task more often or less often than the other members of the family. The answer scale consisted of 7 points, ranging from 1 = "in our family I always carry out this job" to 7 = "in our family I never carry out this job". After recoding, higher scores indicate that the individual performs a task more often than the other family members. For men, Cronbach's alpha is .67 for the childrearing scale and .82 for the household scale. For women these figures are .76 and .78 respectively.

Marital satisfaction refers to the satisfaction with the partner and the relationship in general. It is measured by the marital satisfaction scale described in Chapter 4. In order to formulate the items, satisfaction with the relationship and/or the partner was used as the guiding principle (e.g., "Generally, I'm dissatisfied with the relationship with my partner" or "If I could choose again, I would choose the same partner"). The scale consists of 7-point Likert items, ranging from 1 = "not at all applicable" to 7 = "very applicable". The replies are added together so that a higher score indicates a more satisfied relationship. For women the alpha reliability coefficient is .87. For men this coefficient is .85.

Negative communication. The negative communication scale, discussed in Chapter 4, maps out the negative communication styles of the *couple*. Respondents were asked to indicate to what degree certain forms of negative communication are characteristic of their marital relationship (e.g., "My partner often blames me when we are quarreling" or "My partner and I interrupt each other a lot when we are talking together"). The focus is on the subjective perception of the respondent and not on individual communication skills. The perception of own behavior and partner's behavior is included, but the focus is on partner behavior. The negative communication scale consists of six items (7-point Likert items, ranging from 1 = "not at all applicable" to 7 = "very applicable"). A higher score on the scale indicates more negative communication. For women, alpha reliability coefficient is .80 whereas for men this coefficient is .83.

Open communication. The open communication scale maps out the open communicational style of the *respondent* and couple. For more information on this scale, see Chapter 4. Previous studies confirmed the positive effect of the selected items on marital satisfaction (Buunk & Nijskens, 1980; Kerkstra, 1985) Respondents were asked to indicate to what degree personal feelings and experiences were shared (e.g., "I often talk to my partner about things we are both interested in" or "I often talk to my partner about personal problems"). The focus is on the subjective perception of the respondent and not on individual communication skills. Items refer to verbal behavior. The open communication scale consists of three items (7-point Likert items, ranging from 1 = "not at all applicable" to 7 = "very applicable"). Higher score on the scale indicates more positive or open communication. The alpha coefficient is .73 for women and .68 for men.

Control variables: Because they could affect the dependent as well as the independent variables of interest, marital duration, women's employment (dichotomized into employed versus non-employed, regardless of how many hours women work), educational level and age of the spouses were included as control variable.

8.4. RESULTS

We began by examining the correlations between the distinct gender-related characteristics included in our study. Next, to test the assumptions of identity theory, we estimate regression models in LISREL using multiple indicators for gender as well as marital outcomes.

Multidimensional nature of gender

Table 8.1 presents the mean scores and correlations of the gender characteristics of interest. Considering the mean scores of husbands and wives, paired t-tests show that men report significantly higher scores on instrumentality (t = -8.12, p < .001) and sex role traditionalism (t = 5.24, p < .001) whereas women score higher on expressiveness (t = 10.27, p < .001), the performance of household (t = -41.04, p < .001) and childrearing tasks (t = -14.34, p < .001).

For both husbands and wives, positive correlations exist between one's instrumentality and expressiveness. This finding contrasts the assumption of gender identity theory that both concepts are negatively associated.

Our findings do not demonstrate strong associations between traditionalism towards sex roles, expressiveness and instrumentality. Traditional women are no less instrumental or more expressive than those with non-traditional sex role attitudes. Traditional men, however, are less likely than their more egalitarian male counterparts to define themselves as expressive.

With respect to gender role behavior, Table 8.1 shows complementary findings for men and women. Men who define themselves more expressively are more likely to perform childrearing tasks whereas expressive wives seem less likely to perform childrearing and household labor. There is no evidence that instrumental husbands or wives are less apt to perform childrearing and household tasks than less instrumental spouses.

Husbands' with a traditional attitude toward sex roles are less involved in household tasks than egalitarian husbands, but do not participate more or less in the upbringing of their children.

Table 8.1
Correlation Matrix of Gender-Related Characteristics, Men [below diagonal] and Women [above diagonal]

		1	2	3	4	5	Mean	Sd
1	Instrumentality	/	.14 **	-.07	-.07	.01	3.23	0.63
2	Expressiveness	.18 ***	/	.01	-.11 *	-.10 *	3.77	0.53
3	Traditional role	-.08	-.13 *	/	.16 **	.07	1.92	0.68
4	Household	-.05	.07	-.15 **	/	.31 ***	5.85	0.77
5	Childrearing	.06	.20 ***	.01	.25 ***	/	4.76	0.79
	Mean	3.68	3.44	2.16	2.53	3.84		
	Sd	0.58	0.56	0.71	0.89	0.68		

* p < .05 ** p < .01 *** p < .001
Note: N = 386, Traditional role = sex role traditionalism, Household = perception of performing household labor more than other members, Childrearing = perception of performing childrearing tasks more than other members

The effect of gender-related characteristics on marital outcomes

Paired t-tests firstly indicate that women (M_{95} = 5.65, SD = 1.09) have a significantly higher score on open communication than men (M_{95} = 5.16, SD = 1.16) (t = -7.56, p < .0001). The negative communication scores are not significantly different between men and women, implying that men are no more or less likely than women to blame their partners, to interrupt or get angry.

Testing the assumptions of identity theory, three separate multiple regression models were conducted for the three marital outcome measures. Each model includes different sets of gender-related characteristics: (1) expressiveness and instrumentality, (2) sex roles traditionalism and (3) performance of household and child-rearing tasks. Six control variables were included in each model: husband's and wife's age, marital duration, husband's and wife's educational level, and women's employment (1 = yes, 0 = no). Net family income was included as well to test for the interactions between income and the gender characteristics of interest.

Since husbands and wives in our sample are married with each other, they represent dependent observations. Therefore, we ran the regression analyses in LISREL, allowing us to consider the data of husbands and wives simultaneously in one model and to test for significant differences (Kenny & Cook, 1999). Variables were defined as observed variables with an error variance equal to zero and an item loading equal to one. Consequently, we did not exploit the advantage of LISREL to model measurement errors because our focus is directed to wife-husband differences regarding the interrelationships between gender characteristics and marital outcomes. The proceeding of this task involves two major steps. In a first step, the regression model is fitted in LISREL for husbands and wives simultaneously. The set of exogenous variables as well as the set of endogenous variables are allowed to correlate. In a second step, non-significant correlations between exogenous variables were fixed to zero. In the following steps, paths from the gender characteristic of interest to the marital outcome under study are successively constrained to be equal between husbands and wives. Chi-square difference tests between the unconstrained and the constrained models indicate which paths significantly differ between the marital partners. Only the final models are presented in this chapter.

To investigate whether gender aspects are differently related to marital outcomes in higher and lower income couples, the product term between net family income and the gender characteristic(s) under study were included in the model. To solve the problem of multicollinearity when using interaction terms, we first mean-centered all the variables and then computed the cross-products using the mean-centered variables (Jaccard, Turrisi, & Wan, 1990). Comparable to the procedure indicated above, it was tested which interaction terms could be constrained to equality between husbands and wives.

In the following, each set of gender characteristics are discussed in relation with the three marital outcomes. The regression coefficients are presented in the Tables. The effects of the control variables are not shown in the Tables because our main interest is directed towards the gender characteristics themselves.

Expressiveness, instrumentality and marital outcomes

Table 8.2 presents the regression coefficients from the models examining the effect of expressiveness and instrumentality on spousal marital outcomes.

First, our results show that expressive husbands communicate less negatively and more openly than do non-expressive husbands. The latter effect appears to be stronger for men belonging to higher income couples. The former effect becomes clear in wives' perception of negative communication because this latter measure focuses on one's partner communication rather than on one's own communication behavior.

Second, expressiveness of the husband is also associated with higher marital satisfaction of both spouses. Yet, this association is stronger for women's satisfaction than for men's satisfaction.

Third, husbands' expressiveness does not only affect their own open communication behavior but also that of their wives. The same holds when considering wives' expressiveness. The more women endorse expressive qualities, the more open they communicate with their partner and the more open their partners communicate with them.

Fourth, wives' expressiveness is differently associated with their husbands' marital satisfaction in higher and lower income couples. The higher the family income is, the more negative is the effect of wives' expressive qualities on their husbands' marital satisfaction.

Fifth, it also appears that the higher the income level is, the more positive is the effect of women's instrumental traits on both spouses' satisfaction with marriage.

Table 8.2
Effects of Expressiveness and Instrumentality on Spousal Marital Outcomes, Unstandardized Effects and Associated T-Values

Women's satisfaction	b	t	Men's satisfaction	b	t
Inst, H	-.13	-1.19	Inst, H	.11	1.08
Inst, W	.17	1.79	Inst, W	-.06	-0.71
Expr, H	.39	3.64	Expr, H	.18	1.90
Expr, W	.15	1.60	Expr, W	.15	1.60
Income	.08	1.40	Income	-.07	-1.41
Income * Inst, H	.01	0.18	Income * Inst, H	.01	0.18
Income * Expr, H	.02	0.29	Income * Expr, H	.02	0.29
Income * Inst, W	.11	1.96	Income * Inst, W	.11	1.96
Income * Expr, W	.10	1.17	Income * Expr, W	-.17	-2.24

$R^2 = .08$

Correlation (Eta1, Eta2) = .42 $\chi^2(63) = 41.87$ p = 0.98   RMSEA = .00   CFI = 1.00

$R^2 = .07$

Women's neg. com.	b	t	Men' s neg. com.	b	t
Inst, H	-.05	-0.50	Inst, H	-.05	-0.50
Inst, W	-.21	-2.64	Inst, W	-.21	-2.64
Expr, H	-.25	-2.73	Expr, H	-.25	-2.73
Expr, W	-.12	-1.24	Expr, W	-.12	-1.24
Income	-.03	-0.45	Income	-.01	-0.09
Income * Inst, H	-.08	-0.89	Income * Inst, H	.00	-0.02
Income * Expr, H	.03	0.32	Income * Expr, H	-.07	-0.82
Income * Inst, W	-.03	-0.39	Income * Inst, W	-.12	-1.65
Income * Expr, W	.03	0.31	Income * Expr, W	.07	0.75

$R^2 = .07$

Correlation (Eta1, Eta2) = .44 $\chi^2(32) = 29.23$ p = 0.66   RMSEA = .00   CFI = 1.00

$R^2 = .06$

Women's open com.	b	t	Men' s open com.	b	t
Inst, H	.12	1.41	Inst, H	.12	1.41
Inst, W	.04	0.50	Inst, W	.04	0.50
Expr, H	.36	4.30	Expr, H	.36	4.30
Expr, W	.19	2.13	Expr, W	.19	2.13
Income	.08	1.85	Income	.08	1.85
Income * Inst, H	-.03	-0.46	Income * Inst, H	-.03	-0.46
Income * Expr, H	-.03	-0.36	Income * Expr, H	.30	3.29
Income * Inst, W	.00	-0.04	Income * Inst, W	.00	-0.04
Income * Expr, W	-.03	-0.45	Income * Expr, W	-.03	-0.45

$R^2 = .11$

Correlation (Eta1, Eta2) = .22 $\chi^2(40) = 39.64$ p = 0.49   RMSEA = .00   CFI = 1.00

$R^2 = .11$

Note: Inst, H = instrumentality, husband; Inst, W = instrumentality, wife; Expr, H = expressiveness, husband; Expr, W = expressiveness, wife

[a] t = 2.58 (p < .01); t = 1.96 (p < .05); t = 1.64 (p < .10)

[b] Correlation (Eta1, Eta2) = Correlation between husbands' and wives' marital outcome variables

Sixth in contrast to identity theory, the more instrumental traits wives ascribe to themselves, the less negative is their communication. At a weaker significance level, our results additionally show that this effect is stronger the higher is the income.

Sex role traditionalism and marital outcomes

The regression analyses reported in Table 8.3 reveal that wives nor husbands appear to be more or less satisfied when they or their partners endorse (non)traditional attitudes towards sex roles. Only at a weak significance level ($t = -1.64$), the analysis shows the negative influence of husbands' sex role traditionalism on both spouses' marital satisfaction.

However, it appears that traditional women communicate more negatively than more egalitarian women. This finding becomes clear in their husbands' perception of negative communication. Besides, traditionally orientated women have also a more negative perception of the marital communication and this effect appears to be even stronger in higher income couples. At a lower significance level ($t = 1.78$, $p < .10$) support is also found for husbands to communicate more negative when holding traditional attitudes towards sex roles.

In line with identity theory, husbands who embrace attitudes representing a superior status for men, communicate less openly. This finding does not hold for women. However, wives communicate less openly when married with a husband endorsing traditional sex role attitudes.

Table 8.3
Effects of Traditional Sex Role Orientation on Spousal Marital Outcomes, Unstandardized Effects and Associated T-Values

Women's satisfaction	b	t	Men's satisfaction	b	t
Trad. orient., H	-.13	-1.64	Trad. orient., H	-.13	-1.64
Trad. orient., W	-.03	-0.36	Trad. orient., W	-.03	-0.36
Income	.08	1.33	Income	-.07	-1.37
Income * Trad. orient., H	-.03	-0.47	Income * Trad. orient., H	-.03	-0.54
Income * Trad. orient., W	-.04	-0.52	Income * Trad. orient., W	-.02	-0.25

$R^2 = .02$ $R^2 = .04$

Correlation (Eta1, Eta2) = .47 $\chi^2(11) = 15.35$ p = 0.17   RMSEA = .036   CFI = 1.00

Women's neg. com.	b	t	Men's neg. com.	b	t
Trad. orient., H	.14	1.78	Trad. orient., H	.14	1.78
Trad. orient., W	.20	2.46	Trad. orient., W	.20	2.46
Income	-.05	-0.82	Income	-.01	-0.15
Income * Trad. orient., H	-.07	-1.13	Income * Trad. orient., H	.06	0.81
Income * Trad. orient., W	.21	2.74	Income * Trad. orient., W	.02	0.24

$R^2 = .08$ $R^2 = .04$

Correlation (Eta1, Eta2) = .46 $\chi^2(11) = 16.05$ p = 0.14   RMSEA = .039   CFI = .99

Women's open com.	b	t	Men's open com.	b	t
Trad. orient., H	-.21	-2.62	Trad. orient., H	-.21	-2.62
Trad. orient., W	.06	0.72	Trad. orient., W	.06	0.72
Income	.07	1.39	Income	.07	1.39
Income * Trad. orient., H	.11	1.71	Income * Trad. orient., H	.06	0.87
Income * Trad. orient., W	-.03	-0.45	Income * Trad. orient., W	-.05	-0.56

$R^2 = .07$ $R^2 = .04$

Correlation (Eta1, Eta2) = .28 $\chi^2(13) = 21.19$ p = 0.07   RMSEA = .046   CFI = .99

Note: Trad. orient., H = traditional attitudes towards sex roles, husband; Trad. orient., W = traditional attitudes towards sex roles, wife
[a] t = 2.58 (p < .01); t = 1.96 (p < .05); t = 1.64 (p < .10)
[b] Correlation (Eta1, Eta2) = Correlation between husbands and wives' marital outcome variables

Role behavior

The last regression models test the effect of the performance of household and childrearing tasks on spousal marital outcomes. Our results show that spouses communicate more openly and are more satisfied when men do the greatest share of childrearing tasks. This finding confirms our expectations. As can be seen in Table 8.4, the effect of husbands' childrearing involvement on communicating more openly is even stronger the higher the couple's income level.

In contrast with identity theory, however, our results indicate that wives perceiving to spend more time at childrearing than their husbands communicate more negatively and are less satisfied. The latter effect, however, is moderated by the income level of the couple. The higher the family income is, the more husbands and wives report to be satisfied when women take the bulk of childrearing tasks at their expense.

When considering household labor, both spouses appear to be less satisfied with their marriage when husbands take main responsibility for these tasks. Women in higher income couples are even more dissatisfied in case husbands' doing the bulk of household tasks. Notice that the latter not only holds when husbands take primary care of the household in higher income families but also when women do that. Moreover, to the extent that the family income is higher, women communicate more negatively when doing most of the household tasks.

To test the independent effect of gender role identity, all gender aspects of interest were included in one model. The interaction effects were not brought into the analysis because they are not the point of interest here. Results are presented in Table 8.5. Our findings firstly demonstrate that husbands' expressiveness is positively associated with both spouses' marital satisfaction and open communication behavior. Wives' expressiveness too has a positive effect on their open communication behavior.

Second, it appears that instrumental wives communicate less negatively whereas husbands' negative communication is not meaningful related to this characteristic. In sum, our analysis seems to provide partially support for the idea that one's gender role identity in terms of expressiveness and instrumentality has an effect over and above role attitudes and role behavior.

Table 8.4
Effects of Perceiving to Take the Burden of Childrearing and Household Tasks on Spousal Marital Outcomes, Unstandardized Effects and Associated T-Values

Women's satisfaction	b	t	Men's satisfaction	b	t
Household, H	-.14	-1.84	Household, H	-.14	-1.84
Household, W	-.03	-0.38	Household, W	-.03	-0.38
Childrearing, W	-.19	-2.28	Childrearing, W	-.04	-0.55
Childrearing, H	.19	2.29	Childrearing, H	.19	2.29
Income	.05	0.84	Income	-.03	-0.58
Income * Household, H	-.22	-3.01	Income * Household, H	-.08	-1.17
Income * Childrearing, H	-.03	-0.52	Income * Childrearing, H	.07	1.20
Income * Household, W	-.28	-3.55	Income * Household, W	-.28	-3.55
Income * Childrearing, W	.10	1.92	Income * Childrearing, W	.10	1.92

$R^2 = .09$ $\qquad$ $R^2 = .08$

Correlation (Eta1, Eta2) = .39 $\quad$ $\chi^2(28)$ =32.23 $\quad$ p = 0.27 $\quad$ RMSEA = .022 $\quad$ CFI = 1.00

Women's neg. com.	b	t	Men' s neg. com.	b	t
Household, H	.10	1.24	Household, H	.10	1.24
Household, W	.10	1.04	Household, W	.10	1.04
Childrearing, W	.18	2.41	Childrearing, W	.18	2.41
Childrearing, H	-.02	-0.26	Childrearing, H	-.02	-0.26
Income	-.04	-0.73	Income	.00	-0.08
Income * Household, H	.07	1.00	Income * Household, H	.07	1.00
Income * Childrearing, H	.08	1.32	Income * Childrearing, H	.08	1.32
Income * Household, W	.02	0.20	Income * Household, W	.19	1.99
Income * Childrearing, W	.05	0.74	Income * Childrearing, W	-.08	-1.18

$R^2 = .06$ $\qquad$ $R^2 = .05$

Correlation (Eta1, Eta2) = .44 $\quad$ $\chi^2(29)$ =38.33 $\quad$ p = 0.12 $\quad$ RMSEA = .032 $\quad$ CFI = .99

Women's open com.	b	t	Men' s open com.	b	t
Household, H	-.04	-0.47	Household, H	-.04	-0.47
Household, W	-.04	-0.48	Household, W	-.04	-0.48
Childrearing, W	-.09	-1.28	Childrearing, W	-.09	-1.28
Childrearing, H	.25	2.96	Childrearing, H	.25	2.96
Income	.08	1.75	Income	.08	1.75
Income * Household, H	-.01	-0.08	Income * Household, H	-.01	-0.08
Income * Childrearing, H	.02	0.25	Income * Childrearing, H	.13	1.94
Income * Household, W	-.05	-0.62	Income * Household, W	-.05	-0.62
Income * Childrearing, W	.04	0.73	Income * Childrearing, W	.04	0.73

$R^2 = .08$ $\qquad$ $R^2 = .06$

Correlation (Eta1, Eta2) = .23 $\quad$ $\chi^2(33)$ =43.48 $\quad$ p = 0.10 $\quad$ RMSEA = .032 $\quad$ CFI = .99

Note. H = husband, W = wife

[a] t = 2.58 (p < .01); t = 1.96 (p < .05); t = 1.64 (p < .10)

[b] Correlation (Eta1, Eta2) = Correlation between husbands' and wives' marital outcome variables

This conclusion can be further founded by comparing the total model and the separate models, indicating that gender role identity overrules some effects that were significant in the separate models. For example, the positive effect of husbands' performance of childrearing tasks is no longer significant in understanding spousal open communication. Presumably, the positive association between husbands' participation in childrearing and spouses' open communication is due to the expressiveness of these husbands.

Also husbands' traditional sex role orientation is no longer significant in understanding spousal negative communication. Considering the correlational analysis, it appears that this characteristic is positively associated with women taking care of childrearing. The latter overrules the effect of husbands' traditionalism on spousal negative communication.

As can be seen in Table 8.5, husbands' expressiveness seems to take precedence over the negative influence of wives' childrearing involvement on spousal satisfaction. Indeed, the more expressive husbands are, the less women seem to take responsibility of childrearing ($r = -.11$, $p < .05$) and thus the more satisfied are women.

Table 8.5
Standardized Effects and Associated T-Values For the Models With All Gendered Characteristics

Women's satisfaction	β	t	Men's satisfaction	β	t
Inst, H	-.02	-0.39	Inst, H	-.02	-0.39
Inst, W	.09	1.49	Inst, W	-.05	-0.81
Expr, H	.09	1.87	Expr, H	.10	1.87
Expr, W	.07	1.42	Expr, W	.08	1.42
Trad. orient., H	-.07	-1.34	Trad. orient., H	-.08	-1.34
Trad. orient., W	.00	0.01	Trad. orient., W	.00	0.01
Household, H	-.10	-1.67	Household, H	-.11	-1.67
Household, W	.00	0.06	Household, W	.00	0.06
Childrearing, W	-.07	-1.41	Childrearing, W	-.08	-1.41
Childrearing, H	.08	1.64	Childrearing, H	.09	1.64

$R^2 = .07$

Correlation (Eta1, Eta2) = .40 $\quad \chi^2(75) = 57.94$

$R^2 = .09$

p = 0.94 $\quad$ RMSEA = .00 $\quad$ CFI = 1.00

Women's neg. com.	β	t	Men's neg. com.	β	t
Inst, H	.00	0.01	Inst, H	.00	0.01
Inst, W	-.14	-2.73	Inst, W	-.13	-2.73
Expr, H	-.06	-1.24	Expr, H	-.06	-1.24
Expr, W	.00	-0.01	Expr, W	.00	-0.01
Trad. orient., H	.02	0.41	Trad. orient., H	.02	0.41
Trad. orient., W	.12	2.28	Trad. orient., W	.11	2.28
Household, H	.06	0.95	Household, H	.06	0.95
Household, W	.03	0.53	Household, W	.03	0.53
Childrearing, W	.11	2.01	Childrearing, W	.10	2.01
Childrearing, H	-.02	-0.40	Childrearing, H	-.02	-0.40

$R^2 = .14$

Correlation (Eta1, Eta2) = .44 $\quad \chi^2(76) = 70.24$

$R^2 = .10$

p = 0.69 $\quad$ RMSEA = .00 $\quad$ CFI = 1.00

Women's open com.	β	t	Men's open com.	β	t
Inst, H	.06	1.33	Inst, H	.06	1.33
Inst, W	.01	0.29	Inst, W	.01	0.29
Expr, H	.13	2.70	Expr, H	.12	2.70
Expr, W	.16	2.70	Expr, W	-.01	-0.21
Trad. orient., H	-.12	-2.37	Trad. orient., H	-.11	-2.37
Trad. orient., W	.04	0.79	Trad. orient., W	.04	0.79
Household, H	-.04	-0.58	Household, H	-.03	-0.58
Household, W	.03	0.46	Household, W	.03	0.46
Childrearing, W	-.01	-0.19	Childrearing, W	-.15	-2.34
Childrearing, H	.08	1.50	Childrearing, H	.07	1.50

$R^2 = .12$

Correlation (Eta1, Eta2) = .20 $\quad \chi^2(74) = 55.91$

$R^2 = .10$

p = 0.94 $\quad$ RMSEA = .00 $\quad$ CFI = 1.00

Note: Inst, H = instrumentality, husband; Inst, W = instrumentality, wife; Expr, H = expressiveness, husband; Expr, W = expressiveness, wife; Trad. orient., H = traditional attitudes towards sex roles, husband; Trad. orient., W = traditional attitudes towards sex roles, wife

[a] t = 2.58 (p < .01); t = 1.96 (p < .05); t = 1.64 (p < .10)

[b] Correlation (Eta1, Eta2) = Correlation between husbands and wives' marital outcome variables

8.5. DISCUSSION

The central objective of this study was twofold. On the one hand, basic assumptions of identity theory were tested in relation to marital communication. On the other hand, we evaluated the extensions we made to identity theory. In accordance with a multifactorial perspective on gender, this extension firstly concerns the consideration of other gender characteristics beyond expressiveness and instrumentality. Secondly, not only marital communication but also marital satisfaction was taken into account. Finally, it was examined whether and to what degree family's income position moderates the linkages between gender characteristics and marital outcomes.

The strict assumption based on identity theory that wives and husbands are identified with one stereotypical sex trait is not supported. Spouses who define themselves in terms of their stereotypical qualities are also found to attribute qualities of the opposite sex to themselves.

Our study, however, provides evidence for the assumption underlying identity theory that one's *gender role identity* can explain spousal communication behavior beyond one's biological sex. It becomes clear that expressive individuals, husbands as well as wives, communicate more openly than less expressive spouses. According to identity theory, the explanation must be sought in the adoption of a more open and vulnerable attitude of lower status individuals in comparison to higher status people. In contrast with identity theory, instrumental wives and husbands do not communicate more negatively than do non-instrumental wives. Hence, it seems that identity theory holds with respect to our measure of open communication rather than to negative communication. This finding might be due to the different measurement of both communication styles. The former is formulated from the perspective of the respondent (e.g., "I often talk to my partner about personal problems") whereas the latter refers to the dyadic communication (e.g., "My partner often blames me when we are quarreling"). A measure of negative communication with the individual as the unit of analysis might have produced different results. Moreover, the measurement of communication through observational methods, as did Stets (1997) in his study on identity and marital interaction may also yield other results than when using self-report instruments.

The idea formulated by the multifactorial gender approach, indicating that besides expressiveness and instrumentality, also sex role attitudes and sex role behavior might be viewed as an expression of someone's gender identity is reasonably supported. As expected, it appears that husbands, embracing *sex role attitudes* that represent a superior status for men, communicate less openly.

Less consistent evidence, though, is obtained for *sex role behavior* in relation to communication. Performing a stereotypical feminine role like household labor does not systematically relate to communicating in a specific way. However, this does not hold with respect to the performance of childrearing tasks. The latter is associated with more negative communication by women but with more open communication by men. Husbands' open communication behavior is even stronger to the degree that the family income is higher.

As already indicated, men also communicate more openly when defining themselves in expressive terms and when orientated towards egalitarian sex roles. Thus, it may be speculated that being expressive, being egalitarian orientated towards sex roles and being responsible for taking care of the children is part of husbands' view on 'being feminine'. At least they act in accordance with it. Apparently, these phenomena share a common underlying meaning of interpersonal orientation resulting in more open communication behavior of husbands. By displaying this behavior, men transform the culturally steered expectations associated with their biological sex.

It is striking, however, that when women subscribe to attitudes and perform behavior, which is consistent with being feminine in our culture, this does not have a large impact on spousal marital outcomes. This conclusion is supported in previous research as well (Aube & Norcliffe, 1995). Despite the fact that expressive women also communicate more openly, their role attitudes or performance of stereotypical female tasks are not consistently related to their communication behavior. Thus it may be hypothesized that neither conventional role attitudes nor stereotypical female role behavior seem to be a relevant part of women's identity; at least this cannot be derived from their communication behavior. A similar conclusion was reached by Spence (1993). She asserts that gender oriented attitudes and behavior are part of men's overall assessment of how masculine they are whereas this does not hold for women.

Besides communication behavior, our study also addressed *marital satisfaction* as an outcome. Our findings lend some support to the multi-factorial gender idea that gender characteristics are differently related to marital communication and satisfaction. Our results suggest that gender role identity and attitudes are more closely tied up with marital communication while gender role behavior is more closely associated with marital satisfaction. Roughly spoken, however, the associations between gender characteristics and marital outcomes are relatively consistent.

Our study also obtained evidence for sex-specific experiences in the associations between gender and marital outcomes. For example, expressive husbands display more open communication behavior to the degree that the family income is higher whereas this finding does not hold for women endorsing expressive qualities (infra). Moreover, the positive effect of husbands' expressiveness on spousal satisfaction is stronger for women than for men.

In sum, our research findings account for the fact that marital behavior and marital experiences are not simply reflections of individuals' social position as man or woman (Stryker, 1980). The likelihood of displaying positive and negative communication behavior is linked with one's gender identity in terms of instrumentality and expressiveness but also closely associated with gendered meanings associated with other gender characteristics such as sex role attitudes and sex role behavior. By having (non)egalitarian sex role attitudes and doing specific family tasks, individuals might affirm gendered selves and produce gendered interaction (Coltrane, 2000).

This is not to say that all gendered characteristics meaningfully relate to spousal marital outcomes. Our study yielded several non-significant associations. For example, it appeared that in contrast to our expectations, instrumental husbands do not communicate more negatively nor do egalitarian women communicate more openly. In this respect, identity theory may possibly offer a way out by introducing the concept of *salience*. Salience indicates which identity is the most likely to be played out in a particular situation and thus the most likely to affect behavior in this situation. Because it is assumed that people are not always aware of this salience, one has to look at the behavior of individuals to be informed about the ranking (Stryker, 1980). In a similar vein, it can be argued that salience indicates which gender characteristics are the most likely to be played out in the marital context and to determine marital behavior. At present, this question as to whether some gender aspects may be higher in the salience hierarchy than other gender aspects is relatively unaddressed in the literature and awaits further investigation.

The different importance of gender characteristics becomes noticeable when considering the context-specificity of gender. This yielded several findings supporting the idea that spouses in higher income couples are less likely to act in accordance with cultural expectations associated with 'being male' or 'being female'. In other words, identity theory might be more valid in lower than in higher income groups. For example, the higher the income level of the couple, the less negative women communicate when adopting instrumental traits. Moreover, higher-income women communicate more negatively when spending much time on doing the household.

An intriguing finding, however, is that this reasoning does not hold when considering 'femininity' and marital outcomes. In higher income couples, it appears that expressive and childrearing husbands communicate even more openly, which is totally in line with identity theory. This result demonstrates that higher income couples appraise men acting feminine.

However, the appraisal of 'femininity' in higher income groups holds with respect to childrearing but not regarding domestic labor. Hence, despite the fact that expressiveness, childrearing as well as household labor may be associated with an interpersonal or relational orientation of the person involved, their effects on marital outcomes in higher income couples are distinct. Hence, this finding does not capture a tension between female discourse and day-to-day reality. Although a female *discourse* (i.e. role egalitarianism and expressive self-meanings), particularly on part of the husband, positively colors current partnership experiences in higher income layers whereas female daily *praxis* like doing the household is negatively valued, the latter does not hold when considering childrearing tasks.

The finding that childrearing has more positive effects on marital outcomes in higher layers, must be due to the different meanings attached to these tasks. The performance of both household labor and childrearing tasks is an imperative need and therefore less permissive. For lower income women, the performance of domestic labor may be less problematic because role expectations and the performance of expected behavior are more closely tied up within lower groups. Traditional notions on men as providers and women as homemakers may serve among lower class spouses as a comparison referent in perceptions of fairness (Perry-Jenkins & Folk, 1994). For higher income groups, however, considerations of career and self-development may be an excuse for being released from domestic labor (Pyke, 1996). Or, they have sufficient financial assets to pay for this service. By examining the income level as a moderating context, the different meanings attached to household chores and childrearing tasks became particularly apparent. Household labor is more practically orientated whereas childrearing is more emotionally laden. Women do not want to take the entire burden of this latter task any longer, increasingly expecting men to take part in childrearing tasks. Our finding that wives report more negative marital outcomes when they have childrearing responsibility whereas spouses report more positive marital outcomes when husbands are more involved with taking care of the children lends support to this idea. Hence, fathers' involvement in parenting rather than their household participation has become a salient and pivotal issue in couples' evaluations of their marriage (see also Kalmijn, 1999). Apparently, a 'hierarchy of care' is operating with taking care of children getting priority over performing household tasks (Knijn, 1997). This hierarchy is even more pronounced in higher income groups. In some respect, one can assert that husbands' performance of childrearing tasks is more valued in higher income groups because these strata appraise feminine features in men. Higher income groups may attempt to re-negotiate the masculine identity so that "doing fathering" is not considered to be contradictory to dominant images of "being man" (Morgan, 2004). However, the argumentation can be easily reversed. By socially allowing and expecting men to take care of children, parenting looses its sex-specific character. Hence, by limiting their involvement to activities that have increasingly become defined as sex-neutral (e.g., paying attention to children) and avoiding stereotypical female tasks (e.g., cleaning), men might affirm their masculinity and at the same time respond to new norms of parenthood. In a similar vein, higher income women might distinguish themselves from their female counterparts in lower income groups by a weaker identification with household labor and a somewhat stronger identification with childrearing.

We contend with Perry-Jenkins and Folk (1994) that, besides gender, social class remains another important identity steering spouses' marital behavior and affect. Turning attention to social class as playing a part in understanding the linkage between gender and marital outcomes can clarify the inconsistencies in past research about the role of expressiveness versus instrumentality and about the effect of household versus childrearing tasks.

Besides the attention paid to social class, an important strength of this study is the inclusion of husbands and wives into the same analysis, capturing the dynamic nature of partnership. In addition to the premises of identity theory, we found that expressiveness not only results in more open communication of the individual him/herself but also in that of his/her partner. Similarly, expressive husbands do not only communicate less negatively but so do their partners. This dynamic reveals that the effect of one specific gender quality of one of the partners not only positively contributes to marriage by that partners' behavior but also by the behavior evoked of the other partner.

Our research is limited on eight points in particular. First, the study deals with a sample of married couples that all have children. Therefore, the findings may be strongly related to the marital stage under study and not generalizable to newlywed couples or childless couples. Second, 'positive behavior' and 'negative behavior' between marital partners was indicated by a limited set of communication items. A more differentiated measurement of both behaviors may demonstrate that some gender characteristics are more or less likely to result in 'positive' or 'negative' behavior. Third, gender role behavior was not measured as the actual share of family work in terms of hours but as the perception of one's share. However, Yogev and Brett (1985), using a similar measurement, argue that the interpretation of the spouses with respect to housework and childcare behavior might be more important for examining marital outcomes. Fourth, it is worth mentioning that we did not tested causal relationships. For example, the finding that wives are happier if their husbands are more involved with childrearing might also be true in the opposite direction. However, indirect support for the former interpretation is provided by the long-term analysis of Amato and Booth (1995) showing that men with more egalitarian attitudes have less tensions and conflicts. Fifth, the women under study appear to be the most satisfied one's from the initial sample. They represent a group of 'marital survivors'. On the one hand, this might imply that some gender effects are already ruled out and thus fall beyond our scope; but on the other hand, it demonstrates the importance of particular gender characteristics in enduring marriages. Sixth, the family income position was used as an indicator for discerning higher and lower social classes. It reflects family's capacity of how many financial assets are available (to spend). This indicator must be distinguished from cultural indicators such as spousal educational level. The latter rather reflects someone's opinions, attitudes and beliefs and therefore touches upon a different aspect of social class. Future research may examine to what degree our results hold when using, for example, occupational status and educational level as indicators of class. The use of a class indicator for each spouse is advisable because in their study on the division of labor and marital assessments, Perry-Jenkins & Folk (1994) demonstrated that wives' class level rather than husbands' was related to the division of household labor. Seventh, a qualitative research design might supplement the present study by investigating the different meanings attached by husbands and wives to household and childrearing labor. Can we explain, for example, the different results regarding household tasks and parental tasks by the more instrumental meaning associated with the former and the more emotional connotation associated with the latter? In this respect, Vandemeulebroecke et al. (2000) demonstrated that wives consider household labor as 'care' whereas husbands consider their labor force participation as an expression of care. The question arises to what degree husbands and wives in higher and lower social classes differ in these connotations? Eighth, the variance explained in the different models is quite limited. When comparing the different models it appears that the included gender characteristics explain more variance in the distinct communication aspects than in marital satisfaction. This might suggest that these gender characteristics influence marital satisfaction indirectly by the communication behavior with which it is associated.

We see two avenues for future research that derive from the present effort. First, this study highlights the importance of measuring both gender identity and marital evaluations in multiple ways. To gain more insight in the role of gender in longer-term versus newlywed marriages, it is recommendable to unravel the complex issue of gender and marriage in different spousal samples. Using the framework of identity theory and the concept of salience in particular, a deeper understanding of gender in marriage may be accomplished. The second direction concerns the issue of conditionality. Future research should shed more light on the social contexts surrounding couples since it was demonstrated that valued gender-marriage outcomes differ for lower and higher-class spouses. The consideration of couples' income position enabled us to clarify the importance of women's instrumentality in higher social strata as well as the lower importance of their performance of stereotypical feminine role behavior like household labor. The question arises whether and to what degree women 'being masculine' can be seen as a social differentiation mechanism between higher and lower social strata in their evaluation of partnership. Conceivably, not only a 'new man' but also a 'new woman' is in the make.

9. Marital Relationships and Parenting Experiences in Established Marriages. Short-Term and Long-Term Interrelationships

9.1. INTRODUCTION

Parental and marital roles are one of the most salient sources of identity (Thoits, 1992). Therefore, experiences in the parent-child system are closely tied up with experiences in the marital system (Rogers & White, 1998). Nonetheless, the parent-child bound does not depend as much on individuals' role experiences as most other role relationships (Rogers & White, 1998). Whether parents are satisfied or not, has hardly any consequence for the persistence and stability of the parent-child relationship. This qualification notwithstanding, parenting satisfaction and childrearing experiences are an important issue for research. Parenting satisfaction does not only appear to be pivotal to the quality of parenting during marriage but also to parenting after divorce (Belsky et al., 1991). Besides, a better comprehension of parenting experiences is vital in light of the widely supported finding that parents are generally more distressed and unhappy than non-parents (Crnic & Acevedo, 1995; McLanahan & Adams, 1987; Twenge, Campbell & Foster, 2003; White, Booth, & Edwards, 1986).

The latter finding raises the question why parenthood, being socially valued and an important source of identity, is hardly reconcilable with individuals' well-being? Some explain this negative association by the high proportion of couples that remain unhappily together precisely because of the presence of children (Glenn & McLahan, 1982; White, Booth, & Edwards, 1986). However, other macro as well as micro-theoretical explanations might be put forward for the negative association between children and individuals' well-being. With respect to the former, the changing social and personal meaning of children is of special interest. The increase in childrens' affective-emotional value seems to be inversely proportional to their economical value, being prevalent in the 19th century. Some demographers interpret the trend in decreasing fertility, already started in the second half of the 19th century, as an important signal of larger parental investment in a smaller number of children. However, as the result of broad social transformations, a dominant parental model is absent, leaving open several ways of parenting, and enhancing the risk of 'parenting insecurity' (du Bois-Reymond et al., 1993). The latter is further fueled by a generational gap. Contemporary parents with adolescent children face the difficulty that the material and immaterial space of their children is very different from the one they had available during their childhood. Hence, parenting has become a difficult and tough psychological 'job', creating tension and strain.

The latter explanation is in line with a micro-theoretical approach of children's effect on marital relationships, focusing on roles and role changes. Indeed, the time men and women devote to parenting reduces the time they can spend at other relationships and activities of interest. Managing this time schedule may lead to role conflict and feelings of overload, resulting in lower satisfaction with marriage (O'Neill & Greenberger, 1994). Particularly employed women might be confronted with conflicting role expectations associated with their role as marital partner, mother and worker. This role perspective suggests that the negative effect of children on the marital system is due to the stress caused by the parental role.

The present study is directed towards this issue, attempting to gain a deeper insight in the interrelationships between parenting experiences and marital relationships. Assuming that parenting experiences actually affect the marital system, it is examined whether husband-wife communication can be considered as a mechanism linking aspects of parenting with marital satisfaction. Drawing on the Vulnerability-Stress-Adaptation (VSA)-model of Karney & Bradbury (1995), individuals' resources, which may affect both the parental and the marital system, are also taken into account. In a second part of the study, the cross-sectional analysis is extended with an examination of the long-term relationship between parenting and marital experiences. It is investigated whether experiences within the child-parent system are rather an antecedent or a consequence of experiences in the marital system. Because the majority of studies did not endeavor to establish the relative strength of the two directions, further investigating the nature of this relationship is indispensable.

9.2. SHORT-TERM RELATIONSHIPS BETWEEN PARENTING EXPERIENCES AND MARITAL RELATIONSHIPS

As indicated above, it is assumed that parenting may negatively affect the marital system due to the stress and difficulties with which it is associated. However, stress in general, and hence parental stress, is not deemed intrinsic to parenting but rather a response to it (McCubbin et al., 1980). It seems clear that not every individual is likely to perceive a similar situation as being equally stressful. In research on family stress, two types of stressors[12] are commonly dealt with: normative and non-normative stressor events. The former refers to predictable stressors that are associated with the stages of the life cycle (e.g., birth of a child, retirement) whereas the latter refers to events that occur unexpectedly (e.g., death of a child) (Burr, 1973; Hill, 1949; McCubbin & Patterson, 1983). In addition to these normative and non-normative events, there is also a third type of stressor, related to the (cumulative) demands with which families need to cope. This source of stress is engendered by the ongoing role strains and difficulties experienced in the daily family reality (Lavee, McCubbin, & Olson, 1987). However, unlike normative and non-normative events, strains have no discrete onset but rather result from unresolved tensions associated with the ongoing interpersonal relations among family members. In this respect, difficulties in performing one's parental role may produce specific tension or strain, impinging on the individual and the marital relationship. Lavee, McCubbin, and Olson (1987) even argue that strains might be more strongly associated with individuals' well-being than stressor events.

To understand why some people experience the parental role as more stressful than others and, to get a more solid grip on how this stressful experience relates to the marital relationship, this study draws upon the VSA-model of Karney & Bradbury (1995). In explaining marital quality and stability, this theoretical framework presupposes dynamic relationships between individuals' vulnerabilities, the stressful events couples encounter as well as their adaptive capacity (see Chapter 3). The conceptual model that will be tested in the present study is visualized in Figure 9.1. In the following, we elaborate upon the different hypothesized paths.

---

[12] Stressors are defined as "events that produce a change in the family social system" (Burr, 1973, p. 201).

Figure 9.1
The Hypothesized Model of the Relationship Between Parenting and Marital Satisfaction

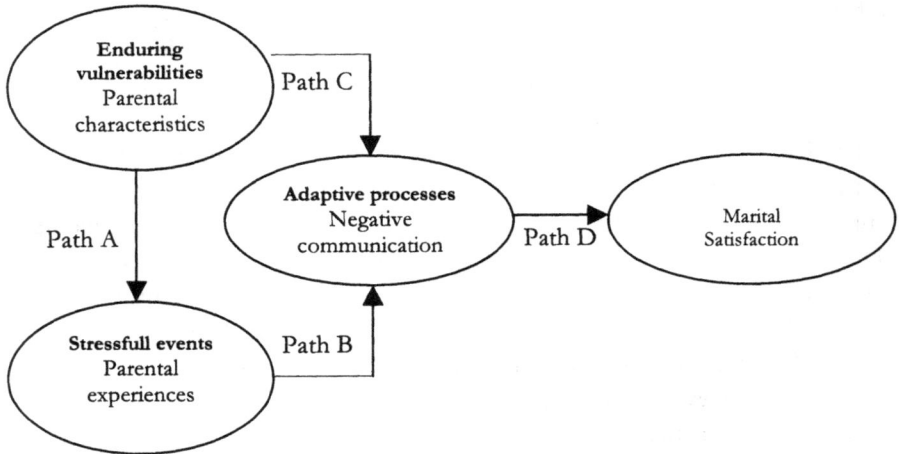

The effect of individuals' vulnerabilities on stressful events (Path A)

Path A implies that vulnerabilities, i.e. "stable demographic, historical, personality and experiential factors that individuals bring to marriage" (Bradbury, 1995, p. 461), have an influence on the degree to which individuals experience the parental role as a strain or as stressful. Three groups of vulnerabilities are discerned for the present study: (a) role demands, (b) life cycle and socioeconomic resources and (c) the spillover of multiple roles (Lavee & Sharlin, 1996; Rogers & White, 1998).

Role demands that may affect parenting experiences include the number and age of children. As to the former, research has shown that a larger number of children may put parents under greater pressure (Lavee & Sharlin, 1996; Umberson, 1989). McLanahan and Adams (1987), however, conclude that the mere presence of children is more important than their absolute number. Regarding the age of children, studies demonstrate that children under the age of 18 are less beneficial for parents' well-being than adult children (see Umberson, 1989). Rogers and White (1998), in contrast, found no significant association between child characteristics and parenting satisfaction, eliciting that role demands do not necessarily say anything about role commitment, or about the sacrifices one is willing to make in sustaining a role. Therefore, it can be argued that one's commitment to a role, rather than role demands, causes role performance to be less problematic, and hence increases the likelihood of role satisfaction.

Second, the VSA-model assumes that parenting strain may be relieved by the *resources* available to individuals. This idea is a longstanding view already accentuated in crisis theory and in the ABCX-model of stress[13] (Hill, 1949). It is asserted that the stability and quality of a family system is the result of both stressful experiences as well as the available resources to cope with these experiences (McCubbin & Patterson, 1982). As to the latter, some individuals may experience less strain or stress because they have more resources for performing their role well or because they dispose of resources preventing stressors to result in a major crisis (McCubbin et al., 1980). For example, role performance may improve by *age*. Umberson (1989) found that older parents, regardless of their childrens' age, report more parenting satisfaction. This might be due to the better financial and psychological equipment of older parents, suggesting that parenting becomes more positive and less stressful across the life course.

Greater *socioeconomic resources* (SES) may also be beneficial for adequate role performance (Rogers & White, 1998). This premise, however, is inconsistently supported. Some studies showed that economic distress adversely affects the marital relationship and exacerbates parental strain (Conger et al., 1990; Pittman, Wright, & Lloyd, 1989) whereas Twenge, Campbell, and Foster (2003) provide no evidence for this conclusion. In their meta-analysis, high SES groups showed more parental dissatisfaction than middle-class parents. Instead of an advantage, SES was found to be a source of role conflict in higher social strata. A similar conclusion was drawn by McLanaham and Adams (1987). The fact that higher educated parents in general, and women in particular, have more negative views about children is consistent with the idea that the opportunity cost of children is higher in these social groups. The presence of children may hinder higher-class

---

[13] The Family Stress or ABC-X model was initially developed by Hill (1949) in his study on separation and reunion of family members after the war. In the ABC-X model it is asserted that a crisis (X) is the result of stressor events (A) that interact with family's resources (B) and with the definition which families make of the event (C). The key idea is that a direct proportional association exists between the seriousness of the stress event and the crisis that it brings about.

women to develop successful careers and may require greater adjustments to loss of freedom and autonomy (Twenge, Campbell, & Foster, 2003). Rogers and White (1998) and Umberson (1989), in contrast, found no associations between income and education of the parents on the one hand, and the demandingness or quality of the parent-child relationship on the other hand.

Another important source of individuals' well functioning in social roles is *social support* (Cohen & Wills, 1985). Support in terms of social integration or embeddedness in a social network may provide a sense of stability and recognition of self-worth, helping individuals to avoid negative experiences. The availability of social support through means of feedback or active help may preclude individuals to appraise situations as stressful and demanding, alleviating the impact of potential stressful events (de Brock, 1994). Moreover, there are indications that women benefit more from social support than men because they generally dispose of more social support (Widmer, 2004).

Third, role stress can also be influenced by the *spillover or incompatibility of multiple roles*. The demands associated with the occupancy of multiple roles can elicit stress, which may undermine individuals' well-being (O'Neill & Greenberger, 1994). Traditionally, multiple roles have been considered as harmful because of the risk on competition and conflict (Goode, 1960). Today, there is growing recognition that multiple roles may be beneficial for one's self-esteem (Thoits, 1983). Although it is tempting to suppose that employed women in particular may benefit from this positive effect, research findings are inconclusive and even conflicting. Several researchers found only weak support for a specific link between parental experiences and women's employment (Guelzow, Bird, & Koball, 1991; Rogers & White, 1998; Scott & Alwin, 1989; Umberson, 1989). Scott and Alwin (1989), however, show that women enjoy less benefit than men from the roles of parent and worker. The latter effect should be due to the generally less intrinsically and financially rewarding jobs that women occupy as well as to the higher potential role conflict experienced by women. In contrast, Kessler and McRae (1982), and for the Netherlands also Vermulst and Gerris (1996) demonstrate that wives' employment enhances women's psychological and parental well- being.

In addition to the different factors related to parental strain it must be emphasized that parenting is also a gendered task. Consistent support is provided for the idea that parental experiences are *sex-specific*. In comparison to men, women experience both more strain and more reward from the parental role (Lavee & Sharlin, 1996; Scott & Alwin, 1989; Rogers & White, 1998). Because women's parental role is more burdensome, they may be exposed to a higher risk on psychological stress and therefore to more role strain (Scott & Alwin, 1989; Umberson, 1989). Paradoxically, women also report higher levels of parental role salience than men. This is particularly true for non-employed wives who do not have the extra identity of provider or worker. In this respect, it is also interesting to note that a sex-specific association is demonstrated regarding parental satisfaction and marital satisfaction. Rogers and White (1998) show that marital satisfaction is more strongly related to fathers' parenting satisfaction than to mothers'. This finding is consistent with previous work of Belsky et al. (1991), demonstrating for men a closer association between the marital and the parental system than for women.

The effect of stressful events on marital quality through adaptive processes (Path B)

Meta-analyses demonstrate meaningful spillover between the parental and the marital system (Erel & Burman, 1995). Feeling satisfied in one role is likely to spill over into satisfaction with other roles (Rogers & White, 1998). This idea is consistent with the well-established findings that parental satisfaction and marital satisfaction are strongly associated and that internal sources of (parental) stress negatively affect the marital relationship (Amato & Booth, 1996; Guelzow et al, 1991; Lavee, McCubbin, & Olson, 1987; Lavee & Sharlin, 1996; Rogers & White, 1998).

According to the VSA- model of Karney & Bradbury (1995), the spillover of the parental on the marital role is not a direct effect but runs through the behaviors that spouses exchange. It may be assumed that, when spouses experience strain in their parental role, their marital interaction in general and their marital communication in particular might be less relaxed and more prone for critical comments or blaming one another. Since we expect in our non-clinical sample not an extreme level of conflict but rather a normal range of social exchanges between spouses, marital communication, and negative marital communication in particular, might be preferred as a variable representing marital interaction. Therefore, it can be hypothesized that parenting satisfaction lessens negative communication whereas parenting stress enhances this behavior (Wise, 2003).

The effect of vulnerabilities on marital quality through adaptive processes (Path C)

Karney and Bradbury's model hypothesizes that vulnerabilities not only affect stressful events but also might influence marital satisfaction by means of the behavior that spouses exchange. It may be assumed that spouses with fewer role demands and more resources at their disposal, better perform their marital roles and hence, display less negative communication. The majority of literature, however, primarily attends to the effect of resources on marital satisfaction rather than on marital communication. Although findings cannot be completely used interchangeably, we presume that, for lack of specific findings, resources having a positive effect on marital satisfaction, also positively affect marital communication and vice versa.

With respect to *role demands*, there are no consistent findings to assume that the number and the age of children are inversely related to marital satisfaction. In accordance with the reasoning for parenting experiences, it could be assumed that the larger the *number* of children aged under 18, the more spouses are put under pressure and thus the more likely marital communication will be negative (Lavee & Sharlin, 1996; Umberson, 1989). Empirical support for this link, however, is weak. Abbott and Brody (1985), addressing wives' marital adjustment, found that mothers with two children reported lower marital satisfaction than childless mothers, whereas Stevens, Kiger, and Riley (2001) found no evidence for a direct association between number of children and marital satisfaction. As to *age* of the children, research lends support for increasing marital disagreements when adolescents are present (see Johnson et al., 1986). Like the presence of young children, adolescents demand that husbands and wives engage in a continuous dialogue regarding child-rearing practices, leading to higher levels of conflict and more negative evaluations of marital communication (Anderson et al., 1983).

Regarding the relationship between personal *resources* and marital outcomes it can be assumed that education and income have a positive effect on a person's capacity to perform marital roles. Particularly, spouses' level of education has been linked directly to the quality of their marital interactions (Griffin, 1993). Others refute this argumentation by stating that spouses with greater education also have higher marital expectations and, therefore, a greater chance on marital disagreements and negative perceptions of their marital communication (see Rogers & Amato, 1997). However, the effect of education might be sex-specific with higher educated women having a negative effect on marriage but higher educated men yielding positive effects because of their more egalitarian role attitudes (Amato & Booth, 1995). Considering age, fewer disagreements might be expected when spouses are older. On the one hand, these partners might have 'learned' to interact with each other in a satisfying way; on the other hand, compared to younger spouses, older partners might have experienced less disagreements during their childhood and now transmit this role model in their own relationship (Hatch & Bulcroft, 2004). Vannoy-Hiller and Philliber (1989), however, found opposite effects for husbands and wives when considering the association between age and marital satisfaction. Older husbands have a more favorable perception of their marriage whereas older wives appear to be less happy. The reason must be sought in contemporary role transitions. Probably, the fit between women's relationship expectations and experiences may more closely match for younger than for older women. Older men, in contrast, are expected to have higher quality marriages because they should less depend on establishing their identity as men when becoming older, therefore being more able to develop emotional relationships (Vannoy-Hiller & Philliber, 1989).

Besides socio-economic and life cycle variables, social support might also alleviate negative marital communication. Bryant & Conger (1999) demonstrate that social network support is not only important in the formation of a relationship but also remains beneficial for spousal marital satisfaction in long-lasting relationships. By channeling some problems to the network, spouses can relieve the burden on the other partner and hence contribute to a more positive interaction between the partners.

The effect of role *spillover* in terms of women's employment on the marital relationship is a controversial issue. Considering marital satisfaction, some studies failed to demonstrate a relationship (Glenn & Weaver, 1978) whereas others obtained evidence that wives' labor market participation reduces husbands' but not their own marital satisfaction (Booth, Johnson,

White, & Edwards, 1984; Greenstein, 1990; Kessler & McRae, 1982). Using panel data, Rogers (1999) found no support for the idea that changes in wives' income are related with changes in marital discord. Nonetheless, it can be expected that couples in which the wife is employed, experience more disagreements arising from their increased earning power and from role strain between family life and paid work (Hatch & Bulcroft, 2004).

The effect of adaptive processes on marital quality (path D)

The effect of marital communication on marital satisfaction is widely demonstrated. In the last decade, attention tends to shift towards explaining this link. Bradbury and Fincham (see Karney & Bradbury, 1995), for example, hypothesize that spousal appraisal of their interaction affects how they approach subsequent interactions. Consequently, the subjective interpretation of marital interaction is a pivotal factor in explaining the association between behavioral exchange and marital satisfaction. More specifically, it is found that having a negative perception of the marital communication in terms of "getting angry" or "interrupting each other" negatively affects spouses' marital experiences (Buunk & Nijskens, 1980; Gottman, 1991; 1993; 1994; Kerkstra, 1985). Therefore, we hypothesize an inverse association between one's perception of negative communication and one's marital satisfaction.

Husband-Wife dynamics

The family is a dynamic system of interacting individuals, mutually affecting each other in behavior and experiences. Therefore, mothers' experiences in the parent-child or the husband-wife system cannot be detached from those of their partners and vice versa. To fully capture this dynamic, both husbands and wives need to be included in one model, taking into account the parenting and marital experiences of the partner when examining the other partner. However, the majority of research on parenting only examined one of the spouses and rarely addressed this issue in a combined sample. An exception is the study of Lavee and Sharlin (1996) in an Israeli national representative sample of first marriages, indicating that marital partners affect one another in a circular way as regards parenting and marital experiences. However, to what degree particular aspects of parenting exert a stronger influence on husbands or on wives' marital experiences remain unaddressed in this study as well. Our research endeavors to examine this specific aspect for first marriages in the Netherlands.

9.3. LONG-TERM RELATIONSHIPS BETWEEN PARENTING EXPERIENCES AND MARITAL SATISFACTION

As indicated before, experiences in the parental sphere are likely to spill over in the marital sphere. In the model described in the previous section it is attempted to predict marital satisfaction using parental variables and marital communication as a mediating mechanism.

However, the causal nature of this spillover is less clear. Although there is ample evidence for spillover effects of the parental into the marital system (supra) and of the marital system into the parental system (Amato, 1996; Wallerstein, & Blakeslee, 1989), over-time associations between aspects of parenting and the marital system are scarcely explored. Although those studies do not prove causal relationships, it seems a reasonable suggestion to assume that changes in the marital relationships are a consequence or at least occur concurrently with changes in parenting (Mc Lanaham & Adams, 1987; Rogers & White, 1998).

Among other things, the impact of children on their parents may depend on the specific stage of the family life cycle. In particular, the stage in which children enter adolescence is accompanied by new demands, which might have a substantial impact on the marital system (Lavee, McCubbin, & Olson, 1987). Failure to meet the demands of developmental transitions might bring along a temporary or even structural disequilibrium. The higher salience of the parental role in this phase might result in parental satisfaction exerting a stronger influence on marital satisfaction than the other way around. A panel study of Rogers and White (1998), however, demonstrate that the reciprocal paths between parental satisfaction and marital satisfaction are both significant and equally strong. This finding was supported for both men and women. Because of the lack of attention paid to this issue, it remains to be seen whether this conclusion holds true in other samples and /or when other indicators of parenting are used.

9.4. PRESENT STUDY

This study builds upon previous research in several aspects. First, our study uses multifaceted assessments of parenting by including parental satisfaction, parenting stress and parental role restriction in one model. Second, this study goes beyond previous research in exploring whether negative communication mediates the effect of parenting aspects on marital satisfaction. Third, by examining over-time associations between parenting and marital satisfaction, our study may indicate whether marital satisfaction predicts parenting or whether the reverse is true. Fourth, simultaneous including mothers and fathers belonging to one dyad in the same analysis, allows us to assess the relative influence and sex-specificity of the distinct effects.

The major hypotheses to be tested in this study are addressed in the conceptual model given in Figure 9.2. As previous research has indicated, parenting aspects may be sex-specific. It is anticipated that women experience more role strain and parenting stress than men (*Hypothesis 1*) but also that they are more satisfied with the parental role than men (*Hypothesis 2*).

With respect to the determinants of parenting experiences in terms of *role demands*, our hypotheses are tentative because research only demonstrates weak support. It is firstly hypothesized that the more children are present, the lower one's satisfaction is with the parenting role and the higher one's parenting stress and perceived parental role restriction (*Hypothesis 3*). Because of the inconclusive findings, no specific hypotheses will be formulated with respect to the association between age of the children and parenting experiences, nor regarding role demands and negative communication.

Figure 9.2
Proposed Direct and Indirect Effects Between Resources, Parenting and Marital Satisfaction

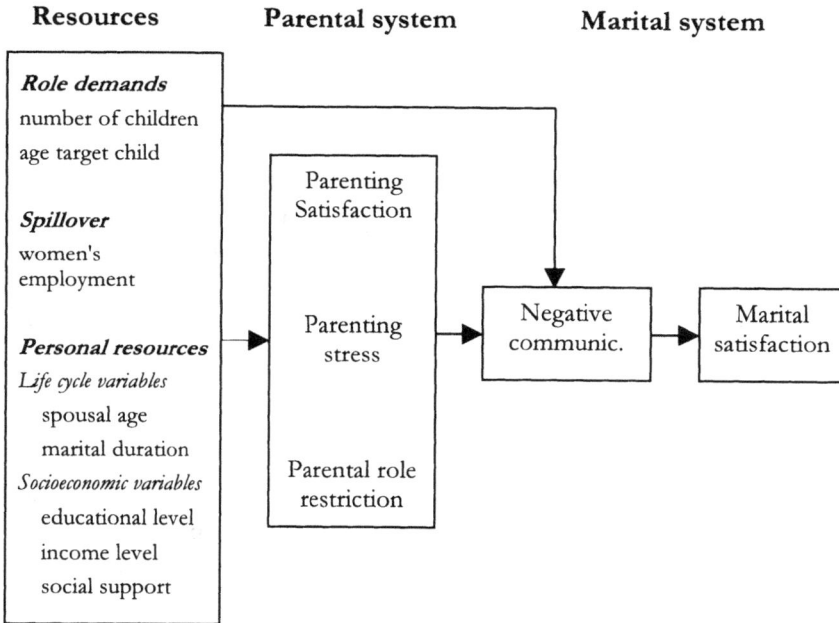

Regarding *socio-economic* resources as predictors of parenting, it is anticipated that higher educated husbands and wives report more negative parental experiences (*Hypothesis 4*). The same reasoning can be applied to marital outcomes with the qualification that higher educated husbands may have a more positive effect on marriage (*Hypothesis 5*) and higher educated women having a more negative effect (*Hypothesis 6*). Income is not expected to be a strong differentiating factor

Furthermore, we hypothesize that the more social support experienced by the individual, the more positive one's parental experiences are (*Hypothesis 7*) and the more positive spousal evaluation of marriage (*Hypothesis 8*).

As regards *life cycle* variables, it is anticipated that spouses report more parenting satisfaction and less parenting stress to the degree they are older

(Hypothesis 9). No specific hypothesis will be formulated as to the effect of age on role restriction. However, we expect a positive association between age and marital outcomes for husbands *(Hypotheses 10)*, but a negative association between these variables for wives *(Hypothesis 11)*.

Because of a lack of empirical support no specific hypothesis will be formulated for marital duration and parenting. However, it is anticipated that marital duration is negatively associated with marital outcomes, particularly for wives *(Hypothesis 12)*.

With respect to women's employment, we expect that women's participation in the labor market is associated with more positive parenting experiences *(Hypothesis 13)*. It is not clear however, how women's employment may impinge on marital experiences and therefore no specific hypothesis will be formulated.

Building on the premises of the vulnerability-stress-adaptability model, we expect that the stress and strain associated with parenting negatively affect marital satisfaction through the higher negative communication displayed by the spouses *(Hypothesis 14)*.

In the second part of the study, we attempt to elucidate the reciprocal relationship between the marital and the parental system. Using a cross-lagged model it is examined to what degree marital satisfaction affects parental experiences and conversely to what degree parenting influences marital satisfaction. Although two measurement points are not sufficient to clarify the causal nature of the relationship, this analysis may yet clarify whether the influence between the parental and marital system operates in two directions or in only one direction and whether differences are found between mothers and fathers. The cross-lagged relationships are addressed in Figure 9.3. The curved arrows denote the correlations between all husbands and wives' variables. Based on the findings of Rogers and White (1998) we expect a positive effect of marital satisfaction on parental satisfaction but also conversely a positive effect of approximately the same magnitude of parenting satisfaction on marital satisfaction *(Hypothesis 15)*. Because no research is directed towards this specific issue, no hypotheses will be formulated with respect to parenting stress and parental role restriction.

Figure 9.3
Conceptual Model for Long-Term Association Between Parenting
and Marital Satisfaction

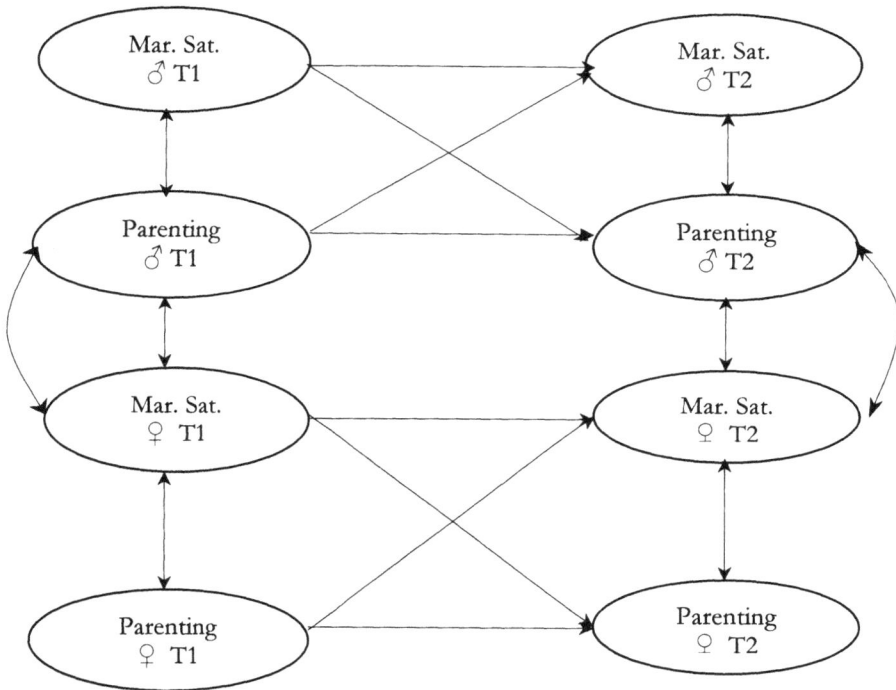

9.5. METHOD

9.5.1. Sample

The research sample consists of married men and women participating in the longitudinal research project "Child-rearing and Family in the Netherlands" (Gerris et al., 1992; 1993; 1998). Families were recruited using a multi-stage sampling method. In the first stage, a sample was taken of all Dutch municipalities distinguished by regional zone and degree of urbanization. In the second stage, a sample of children was taken in the selected municipalities. These children were selected in such a way that in each city as many boys as girls and as many children aged 9 to 12 as children aged 13 to 16 were chosen. These children as well as their parents were included in the research group. In 1990, this procedure resulted in a sample of 1829 families. The response ratio was 43 % (N = 788). More technical details on the database can be found in Chapter 3 and in Gerris et al. (1992; 1993; 1998). The data were gathered by means of structured interviews and questionnaires, completed by both the child and the parents.

Because previous studies speculate that the marital relationship may differ in first and higher order marriages (Booth & Edwards, 1992) and in order to establish a homogeneous research group, only first marriages in which both men and women have a Dutch nationality were selected. Therefore, higher order marriages and one-parent households were removed from the sample. This selection resulted in a research group of 646 couples with children. Couples had been married for about 17 years. Husbands were 42.5 years and wives were 40.0 years on average. Men reported higher levels of education than did women ($\chi^2(7)=328.65$, $p <$ .001). About one quarter of the male sample has a university degree, whereas for women this figure is approximately one out of eight. For husbands, 6% reported to have a lower school degree whereas for women this is 13%. Sex differences also exist with regard to employment activities. Whereas only 5% of the men are unemployed, this holds for about one out of two women. Our sample includes children across the age range of 9 -16 years old.

To test the cross-lagged models indicated above, we made use of the data of both the first and the second measurement wave. First-marriage couples that also remained married between the two measurement points (N = 386) were included in the cross-lagged analysis. Because of missing values on the variables of interest, the final sample for the cross-lagged analysis consisted of 288 couples. Using logistic regression it was examined to what degree this reduced number of observations deviate from the initial 646 couples at Time 1 as well as from the 386 couples participating at both Time 1 and Time 2. The logistic regression model included the control variables (year of marriage, spousal age, spousal educational level, number of children, year of birth of the child, family income) as well as the parenting aspects of both husbands and wives measured at Time 1. Comparing the 288 couples with the 358 couples that not remained in the study, it appears that the model was not significant with $\chi^2(14) = 8.04$, $p = 0.88$. The same conclusion can be drawn with respect to the characteristics of the 288 couples used in the cross-lagged analysis and the 98 couples who were dropped from the study because of non-response. This model was not significant with $\chi^2(14) = 18.02$, $p = 0.21$. Both comparisons indicate that the couples used in the cross-lagged analysis do not differentiate with respect to demographic and parenting characteristics from the *initial* couples and from the *both waves* couples.

9.5.2. Measures

Education was measured in response to the question "What is your highest educational level?" Nine levels were considered ranging from 1 = "elementary school" to 9 = "university education".

Income position is indicated by the net family income, measured in Dutch guilders. One guilder is approximately 0.45 Euro. Seven income groups were distinguished: 1 = "1100-1600", 2 = "1600-1800", 3 = "1800-2100", 4 = "2100-2500", 5 = "2500-3250", 6 = "3250-4500" and 7 = "more than 4500".

Age of the parents is indicated by year of birth. Similarly, *marital duration* is measured by year of marriage.

Age of the child is indicated by year of birth of the child. As became clear from the description of the sample, information is only gathered from one child, referred to as the target child. The mean age of the target child is 12.8 years ($SD = 2.20$). In one out of two families the target child included in the study is the oldest child whereas in another 37% of the families the child is second in rank. In most studies, however, the age of the youngest child is included in the analysis. This method could not be used in this study and has also its limitations because it is not known, for example, whether adolescent children are present in the family.

Number of children is a newly created variable, based on two questions. "How many brothers has N?" and "How many sisters has N?" with N being the target child.

Women's employment is dichotomized with 0 = not employed and 1 = employed. Because the Dutch labor participation of women is characterized by a very large proportion of part-time employment, no difference is made between full-time and part-time employment.

Social support measures the degree to which the spouse reports to receive or to have access to social support for personal problems he/she experiences both in the personal domain and in the parenting and family domain. The scale consists of eight 7-point Likert items ranging from 1 = "not at all applicable" to 7 = "very applicable" (e.g., "When I have problems, there are only few people who will help me"). Alpha is .77 for men and .75 for women.

The *Parenting Stress* scale is a 3-items scale (7-point Likert items) with alpha .77 for fathers and .81 for mothers. It refers to the degree to which the parent reports to experience child-rearing as a burden and as problematic (e.g., "raising my child(ren) frequently causes problems").

The *Parental Role Restriction* scale consists of 5 items measuring the degree to which the parent feels restrictions for their personal life from the parenting role. Alpha is .67 (fathers) and .69 (mothers). Response categories range from 1 = "not at all applicable" to 7 = "very applicable" (e.g., "Raising my children prevents me from doing things which are important to myself").

Parental satisfaction is measured by eleven 7-point Likert items, indicating the degree to which the parent values the upbringing of children as a task that gives satisfaction and new possibilities in life. (e.g., "Raising children is a rewarding task"). Alpha is .79 for women and .82 for men.

The *Negative communication scale* indicates to what degree certain forms of negative communication are characteristic of the marital relationship (e.g., "My partner often blames me when we are quarreling" or "My partner and I interrupt each other a lot when we are talking together"). The main focus of this scale is on the perception of one's partner's behavior. The scale consists of 7-point Likert items, ranging from 1 = "not at all applicable" to 7 = "very applicable". A higher score on the scale indicates more negative communication. For women the alpha reliability coefficient is .76, for men alpha is .81.

Marital satisfaction is measured by a scale consisting of 7 items (Gerris et al., 1992; 1993; 1998). Another study on this sample established the uniqueness and stability of concept of marital satisfaction as well as negative communication (Chapter 4). For formulating the items, satisfaction with the relationship and/or the partner was used as the guiding principle (e.g., "Generally, I'm dissatisfied with the relationship with my partner" or "If I could choose again, I would choose the same partner"). The scale consists of seven 7-point Likert items, ranging from 1 = "not at all applicable" to 7 = "very applicable". For women the alpha reliability coefficient is .85; for men this coefficient is .80.

9.6. RESULTS

Descriptive analysis

In a first step, we examined the correlations between the exogeneous and endogeneous variables included in our study. As can be seen in Table 9.1, husbands' parenting characteristics are less strongly associated with role demands and life cycle variables than are wives' parenting experiences. Husbands only report to feel more restricted by their parental role when they have to take care of more children ($r = .14, p < .001$). This association holds for women as well ($r = .12, p < .001$). Besides, correlations show that older women experience more restrictions than their younger counterparts ($r = -.11, p < .01$). Additionally, it is found that wives evaluate parenting as more problematic when married for a shorter duration ($r = .09, p < .05$).

The correlational analysis demonstrates that socioeconomic characteristics are more strongly related to parenting experiences than life cycle variables or children's characteristics. It seems that the higher the income level of the couple ($r = -.32, p < .001$) or the higher men are educated ($r = -.25, p < .001$), the less satisfied they are with childrearing. The latter is also true when their wives are employed ($r = -.10, p < .05$). For women too, it appears that the higher the income level ($r = -.19, p < .001$), or the higher they are educated ($r = -.27, p < .001$), the less satisfied they are with parenting. Higher educated women also feel more restricted by their parental role ($r = .11, p < .01$). Whether women are employed or not does not seem to be meaningfully related to women's experiences with childrearing. The availability of network support, though, positively relates to mothers' as well as fathers' parenting in terms of feeling less restricted by the parental role ($r = -.30, p < .001$ respectively $r = -.26, p < .001$), and the experience of parenting as less burdensome. ($r = -.18, p < .001$ respectively $r = -.16, p < .001$).

Considering the interrelations between parenting and marital characteristics, the results show that men report less negative communication and higher marital satisfaction to the extent that they experience less parental restriction ($r = .28, p < .001; r = -.26, p < .001$), less parenting stress ($r = .29, p < .001, r = -.22, p < .001$), and are more satisfied with parenting ($r = -.11, p < .01; r = -.22, p < .001$). Except for parenting satisfaction, which is unrelated to wives' assessment of negative communication, the same inferences can be drawn for women.

Considering the correlations between the parental characteristics under study, it appears that for both wives and husbands parenting satisfaction is negatively associated with parenting stress ($r = -.10, p < .01$ respectively $r = -.09, p < .05$), but unrelated to the restrictions experienced by parenting. Stronger associations, however, exist between the latter and parenting stress. The more parents feel restricted by their parental role, the more they experience parenting also as problematic ($r = .38, p < .001$ for men; $r = .26, p < .001$ for women).

Using paired T-tests the difference between husbands and wives' scores on the parenting and marital variables was examined. With respect to the latter no significant differences were found between spousal marital satisfaction ($t = 0.20, p = .94$) and negative communication ($t = 0.74, p = .46$). As Hypothesis 1 and 2 suggest, women are more satisfied with parenting than are men ($t = -3.76, p = .002$) but they also report to be more restricted by this role ($t = -8.58, p < .0001$) and to experience parenting as more burdensome and problematic ($t = -2.99, p < .003$).

Table 9.1
Correlations Between Life Cycle Variables, Socioeconomic Variables, Parenting and Marital Experiences, Women [above diagonal], Men [below diagonal]

	1	2	3	4	5	6	7	8	9	10	11	12	13	M	SD
1 Year marriage	1.00	.69***	-.13***	.54***	.04	-.04	.05	.05	-.07	-.06	.09*	-.10*	.07	72.6	3.37
2 Year birth	.63***	.75***	-.14***	.43***	-.15***	-.13**	.02	.07	.03	-.11**	.05	-.09*	.12**	49.9	4.17
3 Number children	-.13***	-.15***	1.00	.01	-.02	.03	.01	-.14***	.01	.12***	-.03	-.10*	.04	2.48	1.04
4 Year birth child	.54***	.41***	.01	1.00	.11**	.01	.04	-.00	-.05	.03	.03	-.02	.04	77.2	2.20
5 Education	-.01	-.11**	.06	.08*	.56***	.40***	.08*	.20***	-.27***	.11**	-.06	-.00	-.07*	3.13	1.63
6 Income	-.04	-.06	.03	.01	.57***	1.00	.13***	.27***	-.19***	.01	-.05	-.07	.01	6.28	1.34
7 Social support	.07	.14***	-.04	.06	.06	.12**	.37***	.07	.01	-.30***	-.18***	-.22***	.21***	5.08	1.09
8 Employment	.05	.04	-.14***	-.00	.07	.27***	.03	1.00	-.04	-.08	.01	-.01	.00	0.47	0.50
9 Par. Satisf	.01	.05	.03	.05	-.32***	-.25***	.04	-.10*	.32***	-.02	-.10**	-.03	.14***	4.77	0.92
10 Par. role restric.	-.01	-.04	.14***	.03	.05	.05	-.26***	.03	-.03	.26***	.26***	.28***	-.27***	3.06	1.03
11 Par. Stress	.07	.01	.04	.05	-.07	-.07	-.16***	.03	-.09*	.38***	.39***	.22***	-.17***	2.88	1.38
12 Negat. com.	-.01	-.01	-.04	-.00	.08	.01	-.22***	.04	-.11**	.28***	.29***	.47***	-.55***	2.73	1.07
13 Mar. satisf.	.05	.02	.01	.03	-.14***	-.07	.18***	-.04	.22***	-.26***	-.22***	-.55***	.47***	6.05	1.06
M	72.6	47.5	2.48	77.2	3.76	6.28	4.81	0.47	4.60	2.64	2.70	2.75	6.08		
SD	3.37	4.88	1.04	2.20	2.04	1.34	1.09	0.50	0.97	0.95	1.28	1.10	0.95		

* $p < .05$ ** $p < .01$ *** $p < .001$
Note. At the diagonal the correlations between husbands and wives' variables are presented

Path analysis

Using LISREL 8.5 (Jöreskog & Sörbom, 1996), we tested the structural model including the variables of both husbands and wives. An important underlying issue of structural equation modeling is that of statistical power. In our study we were faced with the problem that the sample size was too small for the parameters to be estimated (Mueller, 1996). Because of the high number of parameters to be estimated relatively to the number of observations, we could not include all manifest items of the latent constructs in our structural model. To maintain an acceptable subject-to-variable ratio we applied the technique of item parceling. Instead of using the original items as indicators for latent variables, parcels are used. The latter represent combinations of items underlying a latent variable. For each construct, two parcels were computed as the mean score of a subset of items. For marital satisfaction, a parcel of four items and one of three items was made; for negative communication two parcels of each three items were retained, for parenting satisfaction a parcel of six items and one of five was defined, social support was measured by two parcels of each four items, parental role restriction is represented by a parcel of three items and a parcel of two items, and finally for parenting stress a parcel of two items and a parcel consisting of the one remaining item was constructed. Theoretically, all parcels range from 1 to 7.

Applying the technique of item parceling, it is a necessary condition that the scales are unidimensional. For social support, unidimensionality was demonstrated in Gerris et al. (1992; 1993). Because the validity and reliability of the communication and satisfaction scales was established in Chapter 4, it is also considered sound to use item parceling for these scales. As to the parental variables, the unidimensionality was already demonstrated in Gerris et al. (1992; 1993; 1998) as well. However, because these scales are also used in the cross-lagged analysis, confirmatory factor analysis (LISREL 8.50) was used to demonstrate the reliability and stability of the three parental constructs and their indicators (parcels) for the couples who participated both times at the research project. Table 9.2 presents the standardized factor loadings and alpha coefficients for the latent constructs for both sexes at Time 1 as well as Time 2.

For the evaluation of this factor model (and the other models used below), two fit indices were considered: (1) the root mean square error of approximation (RMSEA), and (2) the comparative fit index (CFI). Models with a RMSEA value lower than .05 and a CFI value over .95 (or at least .90) are deemed acceptable (Mueller, 1996). The model with df = 209 showed a χ^2-value of 357.38 with a RMSEA of .051 and CFI = .93, indicating an acceptable fit. In the next step, the measurement invariance of the three concepts across time and across sex was tested with the aim to compare latent variables across time and between husbands and wives. For the marital satisfaction scales, measurement invariance was already established in a previous analysis (Chapter 4). To verify whether the parcels of the different parenting scales also show measurement invariance, factor loadings (lambda's) between the manifest parcels and their latent construct at Time 1 were equated with the corresponding loadings at Time 2. More-over, husbands and wives' parcels were also equated. This constrained model yielded a χ^2-value of 368.96 (*df* = 218) with RMSEA = .050 and CFI = .93. The increase in χ^2 was 11.58 (*df* = 9) with *p*= .234 showing that the model with equal factor loadings on equivalent concepts leads to a non-significant increase of χ^2. Therefore, it can be concluded that the three concepts of parenting are invariant across time and across sex.

Table 9.2
Lambda's of the Measurement Model With 24 Manifest Variables and 12 Latent Factors, According to Sex and Year

Factor and indicators	Time 1		Time 2	
	λ Men	λ Women	λ Men	λ Women
Parenting satisfaction	α = .82	.75	α = .76	α = .75
psat1	.90	.90	.88	.95
psat2	.77	.67	.69	.67
Parenting stress	α = .75	α = .77	α = .78	α = .78
pst1	.82	.89	.84	.83
pst2	.69	.67	.73	.78
Parental role restriction	α = .62	α = .63	α = .61	α = .63
prr1	.75	.77	.65	.70
prr2	.51	.63	.60	.65

Note: Standardized coefficients

At this stage, support was provided for using parcels in the path model. To test the path model as visualized in Figure 9.2, the set of exogenous variables as well as the set of endogenous variables were allowed to correlate. The baseline model shows a good fit with $\chi^2(328) = 487.99$, a RMSEA value of .028 and a CFI-value of .98. In a second step, non-significant gamma path coefficients (effect of exogenous on endogenous variables) and correlations were fixed to zero. The fit of this model is $\chi^2(416) = 559.78$, indicating that the increase in chi-square value did not worsen our model. To examine significant differences between husbands and wives, gamma and beta coefficients were constrained to equality if not significantly increasing the χ^2-value of the model. The final constrained model showed an excellent fit with $\chi^2(426) = 558.27$, a RMSEA value of .023 and a CFI-value of .98. Modification indices, however, showed that the χ^2-value of our model could be significantly reduced by defining a relation between parental satisfaction and marital satisfaction. This model yielded a $\chi^2(424) = 536.83$ with a RMSEA value of .021 and a CFI-value of .98. The squared multiple correlation for husbands' marital satisfaction was .49 and for wives' satisfaction .40.

Effect of resources on parenting variables

Table 9.3 presents the standardized effects between the exogeneous and the endogeneous variables in our model. With respect to the hypotheses regarding role demands, our results show that both mothers and fathers feel more restricted by their parental role to the degree that they have more children. Besides role restriction, fathers also experience more parental stress when having more children. No meaningful associations, however, were found between the number of children and spousal parenting satisfaction. Hence, the third hypothesis is true with respect to parental role restriction and fathers' childrearing stress but not to parenting satisfaction.

Additionally, our results demonstrate that fathers are more satisfied with parenting when the target child is younger. As our study only includes children aged between 9 and 16 years, this finding implies that men become less satisfied with their parental role when their children reach adolescence. This finding did not hold for women.

When considering socioeconomic resources available to spouses, our analysis lends support to hypothesis 4, assuming that education is negatively related to parental experiences. It was indeed found that the higher the educational level of the parents, the lower their satisfaction with parenting and the more they feel restricted by the parental role. The association between education and parenting is sex-specific since men's education is more strongly linked with their parenting satisfaction whereas women's education is more closely tied up to feelings of role restriction. In addition it was found that wives who are married with higher educated husbands also report more negative parenting experiences.

Our results support the seventh hypothesis, stating that the degree to which a spouse reports to receive or to have access to social support positively affects his/her experiences of raising children. Spouses not only experience parenting as less problematic and burdensome (parenting stress) but also as less restricting when having social support. This association was found to be stronger for women than for men.

Parental variables were not significantly associated with couples' income level or spousal age, refuting Hypothesis 9. Marital duration, in contrast, was negatively related to spousal parenting stress. The longer couples are married the less parenting appears to be a burdensome and problematic task.

With respect to the spillover effect of roles (hypothesis 13), our results show that wives feel less restricted by their parental role when they have a paid job. Neither husbands nor wives report more parenting stress or parental satisfaction when women participate at the labor market. Hence, hypothesis 13, stating that women's employment yields positive parental experiences, is supported for one specific aspect, i.e. parental role restriction.

Effect of resources on marital variables

Before evaluating the link between the parental and the marital system, we consider marital variables in relation to the above-described resources and role demands. In accordance with the VSA-model, it was anticipated that role demands, role spillover and personal resources indirectly affect marital satisfaction through (negative) communication. Six effects were found significant in this respect.

Table 9.3
Standardized Effects of Independent Variables on Parenting Experiences and Negative Communication

Path	β	t-value[a]
Year of marriage → Parenting stress, H	.07	2.12
Year of marriage → Parenting stress, W	.07	2.12
Number of children → Parenting stress, H	.08	1.93
Education, H → Parenting stress, H	-.07	-1.75
Education, H → Parenting stress, W	-.07	-1.75
Social support, W → Parenting stress, W	-.21	-4.18
Social support, H → Parenting stress, H	-.19	-3.73
Year birth child → Parenting satisfaction, H	.10	2.37
Education, H → Parenting satisfaction, H	-.30	-6.04
Education, H → Parenting satisfaction, W	-.16	-2.94
Education, W → Parenting satisfaction, W	-.21	-3.89
Number of children → Parental role restriction, H	.19	4.94
Number of children → Parental role restriction, W	.15	4.94
Wife's employment → Parental role restriction, W	-.12	-2.89
Education, H → Parental role restriction, H	.11	2.71
Education, H → Parental role restriction, W	.09	2.71
Education, W → Parental role restriction, W	.16	3.70
Social support, H → Parental role restriction, H	-.30	-5.24
Social support, W → Parental role restriction, W	-.39	-7.56
Year of marriage → Negative communication, W	-.17	-3.50
Number of children → Negative communication, W	-.13	-3.33
Number of children → Negative communication, H	-.13	-3.33
Year birth, H → Negative communication, H	.13	2.35
Year birth, W → Negative communication, H	-.14	-2.41
Year birth, C → Negative communication, W	.09	2.00
Education, H → Negative communication, W	-.13	-3.09
Education, W → Negative communication, W	.13	3.03
Education, W → Negative communication, H	.13	3.03
Social support, W → Negative communication, W	-.15	-2.86
Social support, H → Negative communication, H	-.20	-4.05

[a] $t = 2.58$ (p < .01); $t = 1.96$ (p < .05); $t = 1.64$ (p < .10)

First, our results show that women have a less negative perception of marital communication when married for a shorter duration, supporting Hypothesis 12. This finding does not hold for men.

Second, husbands' perception of marital communication depends on the age of the spouses. To the degree that wives are younger and husbands are older, men have a less negative perception of the marital communication. Hence, our study provides evidence for hypothesis 10 and 11.

Third, perceiving the marital communication as negative is inversely related to the number of children. Both husbands and wives have a less negative perception of the marital communication when more children are present.

Fourth, women also perceive the marital communication as more negative when their children are younger. Because the included children are between 9 and 16 years old, this finding implies that women have a more negative perception of the marital communication when having pre-adolescent children than having adolescent children.

Fifth, women perceive *less* negative communication when their husbands are higher educated whereas both partners perceive *more* negative communication when wives are higher educated. These findings support the fifth and sixth hypothesis, stating that husbands and wives' education have reverse effects on marital experiences.

Sixth, the receipt of or access to social support is associated with less negative communication, lending support for the eighth hypothesis. This finding holds for both husbands and wives but the effect is stronger for men.

The effect of parental experiences on marital experiences

Table 9.4 shows the standardized effects between variables of the parental and the marital system. The result for each aspect of parenting is discussed below.

It appears that *parenting stress* positively affects spousal perceptions of negative marital communication. Comparing these effects for husbands and wives, our findings demonstrate that the effect of parenting stress on negative communication is stronger for men than for women. In addition, husbands' parenting stress also affects their wives' perception of negative communication.

Table 9.4
Standardized Effects of Parenting on Marital Variables

Path	β	t-value[a]
Parenting stress, H → Negative communication, H	.33	4.97
Parenting stress, H → Negative communication, W	.10	3.01
Parenting stress, W → Negative communication, W	.11	3.01
Parenting satisfaction, H → Marital Satisfaction, H	.23	4.26
Parenting satisfaction, W → Marital Satisfaction, W	.17	3.28
Parental role restriction, H → Negative communication, H	.12	3.60
Parental role restriction, W → Negative communication, W	.31	4.45
Parental role restriction, W → Negative communication, H	.15	3.60
Negative communication, H → Marital Satisfaction, H	-.65	-14.52
Negative communication, H → Marital Satisfaction, W	-.08	-2.38
Negative communication, W → Marital Satisfaction, H	-.10	-2.38
Negative communication, W → Marital Satisfaction, W	-.58	-14.52

[a] t= 3.29 (p < .001), t = 2.58 (p < .01); t = 1.96 (p < .05); t = 1.64 (p < .10)

Reverse conclusions on sex-specificity can be drawn when considering *parental role restriction*. The negative effect of parental restriction on marital communication is stronger for women than for men. Additionally, our results show that wives' restriction by the parental role also negatively affects their husbands' communication perception.

Through their effect on negative communication, both parenting stress and parental role restriction indirectly affect spousal marital satisfaction. Note that spouses' negative communication does not only affect their own marital satisfaction but that of their partner as well.

Figure 9.4
Path Diagram of Couples' Resources, Parenting and Marital outcomes

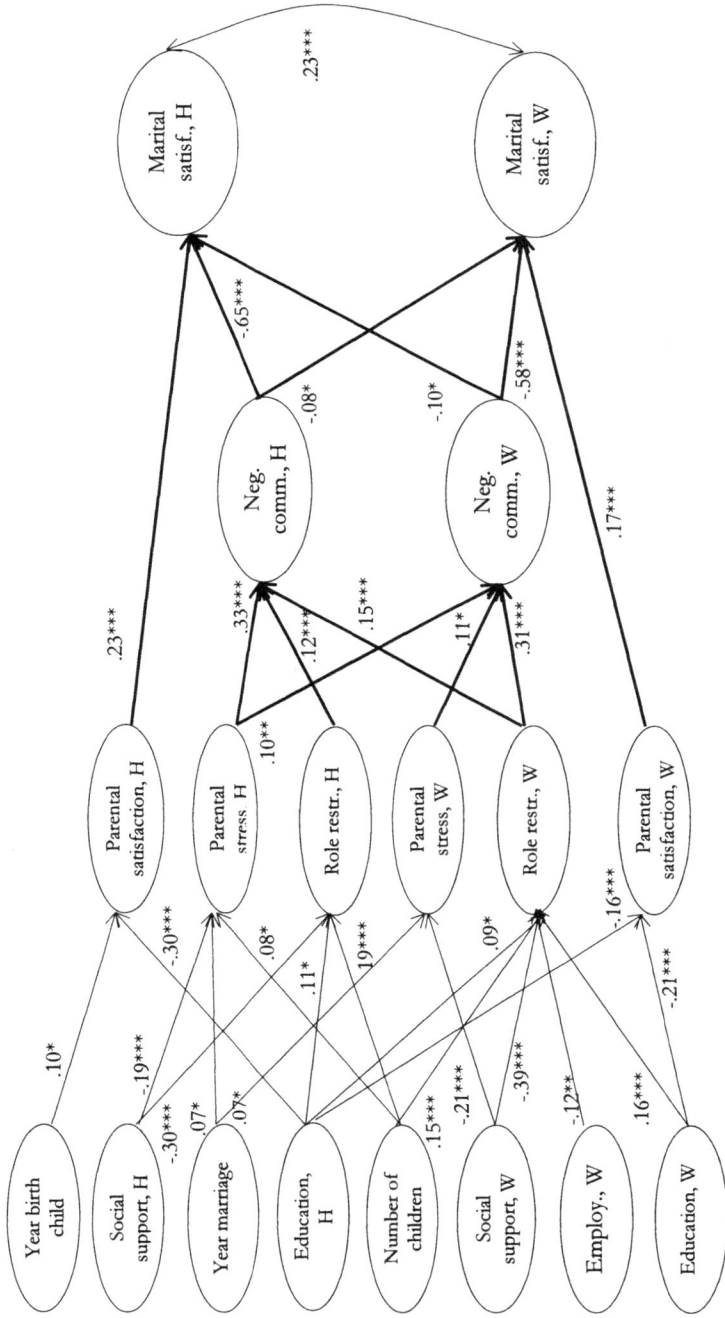

In contrast to the results for parenting stress and parental role restriction, it appears that the spillover of *parenting satisfaction* to marital satisfaction does not run through spousal negative communication. In this study, parental satisfaction has a direct effect on marital satisfaction. The more parents value the upbringing of children as a task that gives satisfaction and new possibilities in life, the more they are satisfied with their marital relationship. This association is sex-specific as the effect of parental satisfaction on marital satisfaction is stronger for men than for women.

Hence, our findings support Hypothesis 14, stating that parental role restriction and parenting stress are associated with the communication behavior displayed by the spouses. The hypothesis does not hold with respect to parental satisfaction. In Figure 9.4 the distinct paths described above are visualized. For reasons of comprehensibleness the effect of resources on negative communication were excluded from the presentation. For the sake of brevity, only the significant paths are presented.

Cross-lagged analysis

Couples that remain married between the two measurement points (N=386) were included in the cross-lagged analyses. Using LISREL 8.5 (Jöreskog & Sörbom, 1996) it is firstly assumed that marital satisfaction at Time 1 predicts marital satisfaction at Time 2 and similarly that parenting characteristics at Time 1 predict parenting characteristics at Time 2. Secondly, we test the assumption that parenting characteristics at Time 1 predict marital satisfaction at Time 2. A similar reasoning is held with respect to the effect of marital satisfaction at Time 1 on parental characteristics at Time 2. Controlling for the variables at Time 1, these reciprocal paths indicate the extent to which changes in one domain are related to changes in the other domain. Cross-lagged analyses are conducted jointly for husbands and wives. For the purpose of this study, variables at Time 1 were only allowed to affect one's own variables at Time 2 and not those of the partner.

The variables in this analysis are latent constructs measured by manifest scale items. Similarly to the short-term analysis, parcels are used to indicate the latent constructs in the cross-lagged analyses. The reason for using parcels in the long-term analysis is mainly due to the reduction in observations that participated twice. The covariance matrix of these parcels and seven control variables[14] was used as input matrix for the cross-lagged analysis.

Figure 9.5
Cross-lagged Model for Parental Role Restriction and Marital Satisfaction

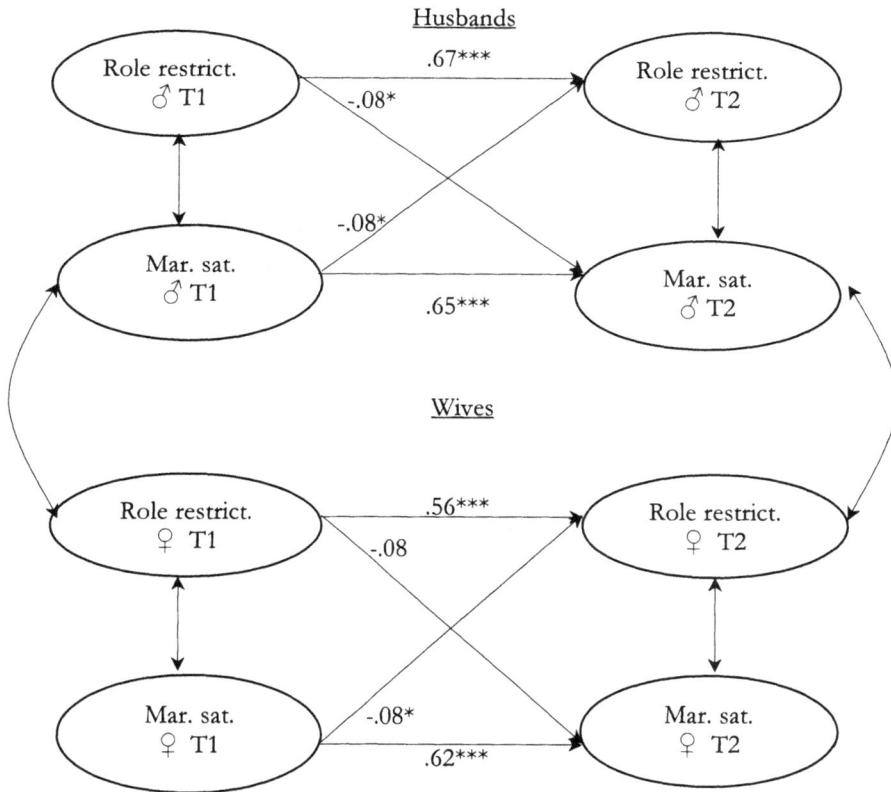

Note: The curved arrows denote the correlations between husbands' and wives' variables, which are not presented here for reasons of concision. Standardized parameter estimates.
* p < .05 *** p < .001

[14] Control variables include spousal age, age of the child, educational level of both spouses, year of marriage and the number of children.

Three separate cross-lagged models were tested, each including one of the three parenting aspects. Seven variables were included as exogenous variables in the cross-lagged analyses: marital duration, number of children, age of the target child, age of both spouses as well as their educational level. Non-significant gamma paths were constrained to zero. The involved factor loadings (lambda's) were constrained to equality across time and sex. Due to the time span of five years we did not expect error terms to be correlated over time. The endogenous variables of husband and wives were allowed to correlate at Time 1 as well as at Time 2.

Testing the cross-lagged model with parenting satisfaction as depicted in Figure 9.3, our analysis yields a χ^2-value of 300.56 with df = 198, RMSEA = .040 and CFI = .97, which fits very well. As expected, the results indicate that marital satisfaction as well as parenting satisfaction is stable across the two waves. However, neither for women, nor for men, cross-lagged effects were found significant. Omitting the cross-lagged relationships, the χ^2-value is 302.35 with df = 202, RMSEA = .039 and CFI = .97. The χ^2 difference equals 1.79 with df = 4 and p = .774 indicating that the cross-lagged effects have a non-significant contribution in the cross-lagged model. Hence, hypothesis 15 is not supported in our sample.

Considering parenting stress, the cross-lagged model showed χ^2-value of 292.69 with df = 200, RMSEA = .038 and CFI = .97, which indicates a good fit. Our findings demonstrate that marital satisfaction at Time 1 predicts marital satisfaction at Time 2. The same holds for parenting stress. Again, the cross-lagged effects did not appear to be significant. A model without the cross-lagged effects yielded a χ^2-value of 296.38 with df = 204, RMSEA = .038 and CFI = .97. The increase in χ^2 is 3.69 with df = 4 and p = .449 and thus not significant. As in the previous model, the cross-lagged relationships do not significantly contribute to a model already including the change in marital satisfaction and in parenting stress between Time 1 and Time 2.

Testing the cross-lagged model with marital satisfaction and parental role restriction, our baseline model showed a good fit with $\chi^2(197)$ = 257.30 and an RMSEA value of .031 and a CFI of .98. Both marital satisfaction and parental role restriction are stable across time. Additionally, our results demonstrate that the effect from marital satisfaction at Time 1 to parental role restriction at Time 2 is significant for women but failed to reach significance for men. To examine whether the cross-lagged relationship between marital satisfaction at Time 1 and parental role restriction at Time 2 is different for men and women and significantly different from the opposite relationship, a second model was tested. In this model, the path between marital satisfaction at Time 1 and parental role restriction at Time 2 as well as the path between parental role restriction at Time 1 and marital satisfaction at Time 2 is constrained to be equal between husbands and wives. This constrained model yields a $\chi^2(200) = 262.84$ with RMSEA = .031 and CFI = .98. The χ^2 difference equals 5.54 with $df = 3$ and $p = .136$ indicating that this equality constraint apparently not worsened our model. Considering the cross-lagged effects, our results show that both cross-lagged effects are significant at the .05 level for both men and women. The higher a spouses' marital satisfaction at Time 1, the lower he or she feel restricted by the parental role at Time 2. Conversely, the higher parental role restriction reported at Time 1, the lower one's satisfaction with marriage at Time 2. Because of the equality constraints, the negative effect of marital satisfaction on parental role restriction is equally strong as the opposite effect. Hence, we found no support for the assumption that parental role restriction is primarily a product rather than a cause of marital satisfaction. Moreover, our results suggest that changes in both concepts mutually influence each other in similar ways for men and women. The results are presented in Figure 9.5.

9.7. DISCUSSION AND CONCLUSION

Drawing upon the Vulnerability-Stress-Adaptation model of marriage (Karney & Bradbury, 1995), this study presented an integrated husband-wife model to explain how couples' parenting experiences are related to their marital experiences. The former were indicated by means of (1) spousal satisfaction with the parenting role, (2) feelings of restriction by the parental role and (3) the experience of parenting as problematic and burdensome, referred to as parenting stress. Because of the dynamic character of family life, we additionally performed cross-lagged analyses to capture the circular nature of parenting and spousal relationships.

To systematize our discussion, we first comment upon our findings with respect to the short-term relationships between the parenting and the marital system. Following on this, we consider the sex-specific character of parenting and the alleviating effect of resources on parenting and marital experiences. Each set of resources is separately addressed in relation to parental and marital variables. Finally, we discuss the interrelationship between parenting and marital satisfaction over time. To conclude, some limitations and strengths of our study are denoted.

Short-term relationships between parenting and the marital system

Referring to our first major question, evidence was obtained for a spillover effect of parental experiences on marital experiences. However, the way through which this effect comes about depends on the parental aspect under study.

We found support for negative communication being a mediating mechanism between parenting stress and marital satisfaction as well as between role restriction and marital satisfaction. It was shown that, on the one hand, spouses' perception of negative communication significantly relates to both spouses' marital satisfaction and, on the other hand, role restriction as well as parenting stress enhances this perception of negative communication behavior. Hence, our results demonstrate that spouses' feelings of parental role restriction as well as their parenting stress have a negative effect on both spouses' marital satisfaction because under these circumstances partners perceive their mutual communication as more negatively.

It should be noticed that the association between parental stress and negative communication is stronger for men than for women whereas the relationship between parental role restriction and negative communication is stronger for women than for men. These findings thus indicate that the restrictions experienced in the parental role have a larger impact on women's marital experiences than on men's. Reversely, the perception of childrearing as burdensome and problematic is more closely tied up with husbands' than with their wives' marital experiences..

Both sex-specific results offer additional insight in the two partner effects that were obtained in this respect. Indeed, it was found that the indirect effects of parenting stress and parental role restriction not only run through one's own perception of communication but also through the perception of the other partner. Wives' negative communication depends on their husbands' parental stress whereas husbands' negative communication depends on their wives' parental role restriction. Thus, both partner effects occur precisely with respect to those parental aspects, already being stronger associated with the communication perception of one of the partners involved. As aforementioned, it appears that in comparison to the other partner, husbands' parental stress and wives' parental role restriction are stronger related to their perception of negative communication. The finding that these already stronger effects also additionally influence the other partner indicates the strong impact of that specific aspect on the marital system.

Further, our results show that parenting satisfaction is directly related to spousal marital satisfaction and not indirectly through negative communication. Moreover, this effect is stronger for men than for women. Hence, for all the parental aspects under study, sex-specific findings were established. Taken these findings together, it appears that the spillover of parenting on partnership is the strongest for those aspects that are not traditionally defined as belonging to one's sex. For women, motherhood was traditionally assumed to be "natural" and high in priority. Therefore, it might be speculated that they were less likely to feel hindered by their parental role in both their personal development and in the maintenance of partnership. However, these expectations have changed and parenting might now interfere with personal fulfillment and developing high-quality partnership, explaining the stronger association between marital satisfaction and parental role restriction for women (Beck & Beck-Gernsheim, 1995). The reverse holds for men. Expectations about men's participation in child-rearing have risen. In this respect, men are more likely to be exposed to the advantages and disadvantages associated with parenting. However, because mother role expectations are more strongly inscribed in the social script than the father role, men are more susceptible to the side effects of this 'new' role. Therefore, the pain (i.e., parental stress) and pleasures (i.e., parental satisfaction) of parenting rather than feelings of role restriction have a stronger impact on husbands' marital experiences. To state it pithily, 'new' roles of men and women for which no strong guidelines are yet available, expose each sex to new risks and vulnerabilities, coloring the intimate bound between husbands and wives. Another possible explanation, fitting the above line of reasoning, is that women are better able to draw boundaries between their different roles *within* the family, but not as to roles *outside* the family.

Assuming that the assumptions of our theoretical model are feasible, the direct spillover effect of parenting satisfaction to marital satisfaction suggests that other adaptive mechanisms, not considered in this study, play a substantial part in the association between the parental and the marital system. Moreover, besides negative communication, other mechanisms may also account for the spillover of parental stress and role restriction on marital satisfaction. This theme needs to be further investigated in the future.

Sex-specificity of parental experiences

As expected, our results indicate that women experience more parenting stress and feel more restricted by the parental role than men. Nevertheless, they also report to be more satisfied with parenting than their husbands. These findings are in line with previous research and can be understood in terms of the different role experiences of men and women (Scott & Alwin, 1989). The high salience of the parental role for women may simultaneously account for their stronger appraisal of parenting (parenting satisfaction) and for the larger burden and sacrifices experienced in this respect. However, our results contrast with Stryker 's (1980) identity theory, suggesting that role salience makes the performance of a role less problematic. Insofar as a role is considered to be central to an individual's identity, the demands associated with it will be discounted or at least evaluated in a more positive light (O'Neill & Greenberger, 1994). Two qualifications need to be made in this respect. First, this reasoning can be easily reversed when considering our findings. Likewise, it may be speculated that the stress and strain experienced by women in their parental role may lead them to conclude that this specific role *must* be very important to them (Scott & Alwin, 1989). Second, our study deals with a particular generation that was socialized with a segregated sex role model but who developed their own marital relationships in a social climate, increasingly questioning traditional role expectations and opening up women's role repertoire. Moreover, negotiation between this generation and their children has become more difficult because these children enjoy material and immaterial possibilities that their parents, i.e. our generation of interest, are not acquainted with. Hence, women are confronted with several role expectations. On the one hand, women still take the burden of childrearing, which has become less obvious because of a lack of dominant models; on the other hand, women are faced with new opportunities and roles, competing with their mother role. There-fore, the mothers of this generation are particularly confronted with 'old models', explaining their parenting pleasure, and 'new realties' explaining their parenting pain.

The effects of role demands and role spillover on parental and marital experiences

Distinguishing three aspects of parenting, (1) parental satisfaction, (2) parenting stress and (3) parental role restriction, our study demonstrates that role demands and role spillover are weakly correlated with the distinc-tive aspects of parenting.

Men report lower parental satisfaction when children become older. Hence, the pre-adolescence phase of their children is more rewarding for fathers than the adolescence phase, probably because of the increasing autonomy demanded by adolescents. Moreover, research indicates that mothers are more important sources of support and more responsive to the desires of adolescents than are fathers, explaining why parenting give men less satisfaction in this specific stage (Vandemeulebroecke, et al., 2000). For women, role demands and the spillover of roles rather relate to their perception of the parental task as restrictive. It was found that employed wives feel less restricted by their parental role than non-employed wives. Hence, instead of role overload, it seems that women's possibility to perform multiple roles results in less parental role restriction. This might hold in particular for Dutch women who typically do not participate at the labor market when having children, or if they do, only work part-time.

The number of children yields mixed results for the parent-child and the husband-wife system. Our study shows that the more children are present in the family, the more both women and men feel hindered in the arrangement of their personal life, and hence the more negative their marital experiences. However, this effect on marriage is counterbalanced by the finding that the number of children is negatively related to husbands' and wives' negative communication, and thus positively affecting their marital experiences. It might be speculated that it is indeed more difficult for men and women to combine parenting with other desired activities to the extent that more children are present. However, at the same time marital partners might be 'forced' or have 'learned' to communicate in a more positive way in order to sustain the family system when handling the different problems and difficulties that children bring along. Future research needs to investigate this finding.

For mothers, it appears that not only the number of children but also the age of the target child predicts their perception of negative communication. It was found that women have a more negative perception of the marital communication when children are younger (min. 9 years old). In line of the aforementioned reasoning, it might be that in the phase of adolescence, mothers can alleviate the pressure, which the increased autonomy demand of their adolescents might have on the marital system, by becoming confidence-persons for their children. This finding also awaits further study.

The effect of spousal life course variables on parental and marital experiences

In contrast to previous findings, spousal age was not related to more positive experiences of parenting (Umberson, 1989). This might be due to the limited age range in our study. Our findings show, however, that the marital stage is more determining. The longer couples are married, the less parental stress is reported. Because this effect is controlled for the ages of the spouses, it points to the beneficial effect of the spousal bound. Sharing a marital reality together for a longer period in time may arm parents against experiencing parenting as being too stressful.

However, the duration of marriage seems to have an opposite effect on the marital system itself: wives perceive more negative communication the longer the couple is married. This finding supports the idea that marital quality declines gradually throughout the marital career and that women in specific tend to report lower marital quality. However, it might contrast with the earlier finding that women report less negative communication the older children are. It is abundantly clear that further investigation on time-period-cohort effects is required to elucidate these results.

This recommendation is further supported by the finding that husbands' negative perception of the marital communication depends on the age of the marital partners and not on the duration of being married. The effects however take the opposite direction. Husbands evaluate their marital communication more negatively to the extent that they are younger and their wives are older. This result lends support to the reasoning of Vannoy-Hiller and Philliber (1989) assuming that the discrepancy between expectations and relational experiences is larger for older women, whereas older men are more able to develop emotional relationships because in that life stage they less strongly depend on establishing their masculine identity. As emphasized before, future research needs to unravel the time, cohort and period effects that play a part in the explanation of these findings.

The effect of education and network support on parental and marital experiences

The educational and network resources available to a couple are vital in understanding parental and marital experiences. With respect to spousal educational level, it was found that husbands' education in particular was related to both spouses' parental experiences. The finding that lower-educated spouses have more positive experiences of parenthood in terms of parenting satisfaction and parental role restriction contrasts the commonly held idea that the more socio-economic resources available, the more adequate one's role performance is. An explanation for this finding needs to be sought in the higher opportunity costs of children for higher educated spouses as well as in the cultural orientation of higher educated people. Parenting might be a less far-reaching endeavor for lower class spouses because of their specific attitudes: higher educated spouses endorse less traditional family values than lower educated spouses. A post hoc analysis on our data indeed demonstrates for both husbands and wives, a positive association between one's appraisal of traditional family values on the one hand, and parenting experiences in terms of the three aspects of interest on the other hand. The less familial orientation of higher educated parents makes the parental role less salient and hence more problematic.

However, with respect to the performance of marital roles, different results are obtained when considering spousal educational level. We found that wives assess the marital communication less negatively when their husbands are higher educated. This might be due to the fact that these husbands are equipped with better communication skills than lower educated men and endorse more egalitarian sex role attitudes. The opposite result, however, holds with respect to women's education. The higher women are educated, the more negative both spouses evaluate their communication. This finding may reflect the lower contentment of higher educated women with partnership. Because higher education is associated with less traditionalism and a more emancipatory orientation, it may become more difficult for higher educated women to maintain satisfying marriages (Amato & Booth, 1995).

Besides spousal educational level, an important resource for parental and marital functioning is the availability of social support. Our results support the hypothesis that husbands and wives who have access to network support for personal problems, experience parenting as less problematic and less restrictive for their personal life. Some argue that this might be due to fact that 'integrated' individuals rely less heavily on their spouse for the fulfillment of a variety of needs (Booth, Edwards, & Johnson, 1991). Because some needs are already met by other social contacts, the expectations one has for the other partner may diminish. In addition, others assert that embeddedness may generate a confident feeling that one can count on the support of other people (Granovetter, 1985).

However, the strength of the associations between social support and parental experiences is sex-specific. The availability of network support appears to be more strongly associated to women's parental role restriction and childrearing stress than to men's. A plausible line of explanation could be that women enjoy more social support than men and therefore might also take more advantage of it. This reasoning, though, does not hold with respect to marital experiences because it seems that with respect to the latter, men profit more from social support than women. Again, this might be due to contemporary expectations on husbands' family involvement. Today, men are expected to invest more in both partnership and parent-hood. This investment is not obvious because men cannot rely on a dominant social script or pre-given model. However, as to parenthood they still can count on their female partners in case of problems and difficulties because the latter are still have the final responsibility. Things are different with respect to partnership since men have to take the responsibility themselves in this respect. Therefore, more than is the case for women, who are socialized to be 'relational gatekeepers', men can benefit from 'social others' in the development of partnership. In this respect, our study specifies the findings of van Yperen (1990) on social comparison and relationship satisfaction in the Netherlands. The author claims that women, as a result of their relational orientation, talk more about their relationships with others but are also more insecure in this respect because relational problems are made explicit. Our results suggest that women's 'insecurity' may be rather situated in the parenting domain whereas men's relate to the marital relationship.

All in all, the significant and persistent role of social networks throughout marriage was demonstrated for both husbands and wives. A similar conclusion was reached by Bryant & Conger (1999) showing that social support predicted a positive change in both husbands' and wives' marital experiences in long-term marriages. Our study corroborates this work and additionally identifies parenting as a mediating dynamic through which social support contributes to marital well-being.

Long-term interrelationship between parenting and marital satisfaction

Using cross-lagged analysis, a significant contribution of our study is the exploration of the long-term antecedent-consequence issue between the marital and the parental system in established marriages. Our exploration of three aspects of parenting, (a) parenting stress, (b) parenting satisfaction and (c) parental role restriction resulted in only significant cross-lagged effects between parental role restriction and marital satisfaction. This means that in established marriages, role restriction and marital satisfaction are both antecedent and consequence within a five years time interval. It might be interpreted that in established marriages, role restriction and marital satisfaction have become intertwined so strongly over time, that both are associated in a bi-directional way; or maybe even in a circular way. Given the conclusion that no cross-lagged effects for parenting stress and parenting satisfaction are found, parental role restriction might be one of the most relevant aspects of the parental system having a serious impact on the marital system over time. Therefore, parental role restriction seems to be the most important candidate for future explorations of long-term inter-relationships. The long-term finding of no significant effects between parenting stress and parental satisfaction, and marital satisfaction is in contrast with the short-term findings of significant associations between those variables. As to parental stress, this finding might be due to compensating effects. Some marital partners may suffer from parenting difficulties and problems whereas others may become strengthened by this situation in the long-term, offsetting the negative effects. The cross-sectional finding that marital duration was negatively associated with parenting stress supports the latter speculation.

The lack of cross-lagged effects between parenting and marital is in contrast with the work of Rogers and Whyte (1998). Using a four-years time span, these authors found significant cross-lagged effects between marital and parental satisfaction. The reason why this finding was not replicated may be due the longer period between the two measurement points or to the broader range in ages of the included respondents in the American study.

Therefore, it needs to be further investigated whether it holds that the rewarding aspects of parenting (parental satisfaction) or the problems induced by it (parenting stress), remain unimportant in the long-term evaluation of marital satisfaction within established marriages. Based on our study, however, it seems as if the mutual influence between the marital and the parental system over time hinges more strongly on the restrictive nature of the parental task, hindering individuals in their personal development.

Limitations and recommendations

Some caveats of our study should be noted. First, the spillover of multiple roles is measured in a very limited way, i.e. by means of women's employment. Other indicators such as the division of household and parenting labor between husbands and wives, indicating who takes the burden of family care, may be useful indicators too. Nonetheless, it can be argued that instead of measures of role spillover, a measure of role commitment may yield alternative and interesting results. Indeed, the sacrifices one is willing to make for performing different roles may deepening our insight in how role spillover, but also role demands, relate to parenting and hence to partnership.

Second, we need to learn more about communication as a mediating mechanism. As we used a limited conceptualization of spousal communication, it remains unclear which specific aspects are harmful and which interaction behavior can buffer the harmful effects of stress and strains on partnership. Moreover, other mechanisms are conceivable which may be responsible for the effect of parental experiences on marital satisfaction. For example, it is possible that the degree of cohesion brought about by parenting, is central in understanding the interrelationship between parenthood and partnership.

Thirdly, and related to the previous remark, it should be emphasized that social support was considered as a resource variable contributing to parental and spousal well-being. However, social support can also buffer stressful events by providing a solution to problems or by alleviating the importance of a problem. In this way, network support may reduce or eliminate the impact of stress (Cohen & Wills, 1985). This speculation must be investigated in future research.

Fourth, it is recommended to examine whether the sex-specific effects of the restrictive and stressful nature of the parental role might depend on spouses' family ideology. The "interactive effects of ideology" (Greenstein, 1996) may be especially important in understanding why some women (and men) experience more role restriction and stress than others.

Conclusion and implications

Our study yields some unique findings. First, the assumption that the marital system is an antecedent for parenting should be replaced by a bi-directional relationship. Neither parenting nor marital satisfaction should be dealt with only as an outcome variable. Second, and related to the previous remark, it may be that spousal communication, which we defined as a mediator between the parental and the marital systems, might also mediate the effect of the marital to the parental system. Third, besides our support of the widely held assumption that parenting is a gender-specific experience, our research design allowed to distinguish between gender-specific and gender-a-specific associations. Fourth, it was found that the associations between parenting characteristics and marital characteristics are stronger for men when considering parenting satisfaction and parenting stress. However, when taken parental role restriction into account the association between the parental and the marital system is stronger for women.

The findings presented here also have implications for couple intervention. Helping parents to function better in their parenting responsibilities may be an important avenue to improve marital relationships. As we also demonstrated that successful parenting provides a source for satisfying marriages by decreasing spousal perception of the marital communication as negative, interventions focused on improving couples' communication styles or the attributions associated with it, may also be an effective strategy.

PART III

Conclusions and Implications

10. Central Findings and Reflections

10.1. INTRODUCTION

· This study was about husbands and wives' marriages in the Netherlands, about 30 years after the onset of the so-called 'second demographic transition'. More specifically, attention was paid to the determinants and mechanisms underlying spousal satisfaction with marriage. The reason for this emphasis needs to be sought in the changing nature and significance of marital relationships. As a result of various social transformations, contemporary marriage is not only released from traditional cementing frames, but also faced with increasing quality-related demands of its members. Hence, more than ever, the survival of a union strongly depends on the nature of the conjugal relationship itself.

However, the loss of a clear-cut normative recipe specifying the 'ought' with regard to spousal behavior in marriages, makes it harder for partners to make their relationships work today, the more so since the latter is no longer exclusively built up around the complementary roles of husbands and wives. Relationships have turned into a private enterprise in which spouses are forced to work out their marital scripts on their own. Because there is no longer a generally agreed external moral code, making explicit one's positions and needs are at the core of modern marital relationships. The conjugal bond therefore serves the (difficult) purpose of taken into account and satisfying both partners' emotional needs. As the demographic picture demonstrates, this emotional fulfillment as a primary basis for marriage in modern society is at the same time a serious risk and a major gain, leading some to allege that the family is in decline whereas others consider it as a new opportunity in developing equal partnership.

The present micro-sociological study endeavors to deepen our insight into the factors that play a part in this emotional fulfillment, i.e. spousal marital satisfaction. Because of this broad research agenda, we sought to select significant topics penetrating the everyday reality of *all* married husbands and wives with children. The selected topics cover four general areas: spousal socio-cultural and economic embeddedness, marital communication, gender and parenting. To investigate how these areas affect husbands and wives' satisfaction with marriage, six major research questions are formulated. The *first* question deals with the valid and reliable measurement of our central object under study. Regarding the *second* question, an attempt is made to get a more profound grasp of the interrelationship between marital satisfaction and communication over time. The *third* research question addresses the extent to which spousal satisfaction is affected by women's economic position, and spouses' attitudes towards gender roles and family values. It is also examined whether women's economic resources are contingent upon these cultural orientations in influencing husbands and wives' satisfaction with marriage. The *fourth* question relates to spouses' gender role identity. More specifically, it is questioned how the incorporation of instrumental (masculine) and expressive (feminine) traits affects spousal marital experiences and how this effect is conditional upon the social position of the partners. The *fifth* question extends the previous research question by examining several gender-related characteristics in relation to marital satisfaction and marital communication. The *final* question assesses how the marital system hinges on parenting experiences. Both short-term and long-term associations were considered as well as the possibility that marital communication mediates the spillover effect of the parental system on the marital system.

To examine these questions, a Dutch longitudinal database of first married couples was used. At the first measurement point in 1990, 646 couples were eligible for inclusion in the study. All couples had children between 9 and 16 years old. Of this group, 386 couples participated a second time five years later. Hence, to some extent, our research deals with *marital survivors.* Considering the average marital duration of our research sample, i.e. 22 years at the second measurement point, the couples under study are likely to have weathered marital crises. This is not to say, however, that *only* the most satisfied couples are left because dissatisfied couples have their own reasons for remaining married. Nonetheless, it can be assumed that a considerable proportion of dissatisfied couples have already been filtered out of our sample. In this way, the results of the present study indicate which marital resources and processes play an important part in longer-term marriages, but they do not inform us about resources in other stages of the marital relationship or about the reasons why marriages do not succeed. The reader needs to keep this qualification in mind when interpreting and reflecting on the research findings.

In the following section, the central findings of this study are reviewed and reconsidered. To structure this review, findings are subsumed under four general headings. Besides unifying the distinct results of the individual chapters into a general conclusion, our results are interpreted in light of the discussion presented in the first chapter. The third section delineates theoretical, methodological and future research implications. Some thoughts of consideration of possible interest for policy makers are outlined as well. To conclude, a few final remarks are discussed in the last section.

10.2. CENTRAL FINDINGS RECAPITULATED AND RECONSIDERED

Our review of the central findings is built up around four broad themes: (a) spousal communication, (b) parenting, (c) spouses' economic and cultural position and (d) gender. Because they are already described at length in the individual discussions, a selection of the most important results will be touched upon in this section. The aim is to go through the different studies once again and to recapitulate the key results in order to arrive at more general considerations on what our findings add up to in light of the initial discussion on marriage in a changed social landscape (cf. Chapter 1).

10.2.1. Communication

Marital satisfaction and communication are considered as two key elements in understanding present marital behavior. Because of the weakening of traditional prescriptions and external rules, the role of communication moves from the periphery to the very heart of partnership. Husbands and wives create their unique and intimate *nomos* world through a continuous and open dialogue with each other (Berger & Kellner, 1964). By lack of external and structural standards on what a 'good' marriage should look like, marital partners use this dialogue to develop a satisfying partnership by their own internal standards.

Because of the utmost importance of communication and marital satisfaction, Chapter 3 made a promising effort in developing a short, reliable and valid instrument to assess both concepts. Two dimensions of communication were distinguished. For the first dimension, items were included to evaluate the degree to which certain forms of negative communication are characteristic of the marital relationship (negative communication). In a way, this scale measures the 'quality' of marital communication as perceived by the partners of interest. Because the theoretical literature assumes that current marital relationships are (or should be) characterized by more openness, a second dimension included items measuring the openly sharing of personal experiences (open communication).

The strong interwovenness of marital satisfaction and communication has led some authors to suggest that they are both indicators of an under-lying concept, 'marital quality'. However, replicating our results in inde-pendent samples and across time, our analysis demonstrates the conceptual uniqueness of marital satisfaction, open communication, and negative communication.

In a next step, the uniqueness of these concepts allowed investigating their interrelationship over a five years time interval. Despite the assumed central role of communication in developing satisfied partnerships, our results indicate that communication *does not* predict marital satisfaction. Instead, evidence was obtained for a reverse relationship with satisfied husbands being more inclined to share personal experiences with their partner. For women, no cross-lagged effects were demonstrated. Our sex-specific finding is striking in light of the widely held assumption that men are not as relationally attuned as women. In Chapter 1, it was elucidated that women are considered as the relational architects, being largely con-cerned with communication in and about their relationship. Hence, it would be expected that women's rather than men's communication behav-ior relates to their experiences of partnership. Our opposite conclusion that men's and not women's marital satisfaction predicts their open communi-cation over time therefore needs to be sought in the importance of femi-ninity in marriages. Compared to men, women score higher on open communication. Therefore, it looks as if men within successful marriages develop a communication style that their wives already tend to apply to a larger extent (Chapter 4).

With respect to negative communication, which primarily focuses on the communication *between* the partners, no long-term relationships with marital satisfaction were established. This finding indicates that negative partner communication is more consistently associated with concurrent marital satisfaction than with subsequent or prior assessments within a five years time interval (Chapter 4). As such, satisfaction *reflects* negative marital communication (and vice versa), rather than that they *influence* each other.

Because negative communication measures interactions between partners, it was considered a potential mechanism through which the partner and the parental system are linked with each other. In Chapter 1, it was elaborated that both parental and marital roles are salient sources of identity and therefore closely tied up with each other. Drawing upon the VSA-model of Karney and Bradbury, it was hypothesized that experiences in the parental role are likely to spillover onto the marital experiences through the behaviors that husbands and wives exchange. Three indicators for parental experiences were considered, i.e. satisfaction with the parental role, feelings of restriction by the parental role and experiencing parenting as problematic and burdensome. Evidence was found for parental role restriction and parental stress to have negative effects on both spouses' marital satisfaction because these characteristics cause partners to communicate more negatively with each other (Chapter 9). Hence, despite the failure to establish a *long-term* association between negative communication and marital satisfaction (Chapter 4), it can be asserted that marital communication is of vital importance in understanding husbands and wives' satisfaction with marriage in the short-term. The marital dialogue represents a central process through which partners not only make their internal relational standards explicit, but also ventilate their parental experiences. In this way, raising children may considerably weigh on the spousal system, burdening parents' enactment of their marital role.

10.2.2. Parenting

From the discussion in Chapter 1 the parallels between partnership and parenting became clear since both are increasingly driven by emotional motives and needs, instead of economic ones. Husbands and wives both expect to draw emotional-affective satisfaction from their parental role. Children may give partnership an extra dimension and may serve as an important anchor point because parenthood cannot fail in the same way as can partnership. However, like maintaining partnership, parenting also needs to meet stringent requirements, exerting pressure on individuals to favorably combine both parental, spousal and other tasks. As mentioned in the previous paragraph, children can therefore hindering individuals in their enactment of the marital role. Because of their close connection, the inter-relationship between the parental and spousal system was studied more profoundly in Chapter 9.

First, our findings show that wives experience more parental stress and role restriction but also seem to be more satisfied with the parental role than husbands. These sex-specific experiences are due to the central importance of motherhood in traditional images of femininity. Apparently, the high salience of the mother role simultaneously accounts for positive feelings but also for stress and strain. As the saying goes "no pleasure with-out pain". Indeed, the salience of the mother role may exert pressure on the accomplishment of the role and therefore on being 'responsible' for the problems and difficulties related to role performance. Because of the salience of the mother role, contemporary women also feel more restricted by their parental role than men. However, our study indicates that mothers' participation in the labor market can remedy this feeling of restriction. These findings are a good example of the negative side effects of role specialization as also voiced in the economic debate on the breadwinning role of men. Segregated sex roles may have positive effects because of the clear role delineation but at the same time cause men and women to be held *exclusively* responsible for the performance of their task.

Parental experiences are not only differentiated by sex but also accord-ing to the educational level of the parents. Less educated spouses report more positive parental experiences than higher educated partners. Thus, instead of benefiting from one's educational capital for performing the parental role, the opposite seems to be true. This effect might be due to children's higher opportunity cost for better educated spouses. Moreover, education is negatively related to familialism (cf. infra). In fact, the burden of parenting may be alleviated by holding a pro-family orientation, which is more likely to be true for lower educated spouses. Hence, adequately performing a role, or at least having a more positive perception of it, does not only relate to resources available to perform one's role but may also be linked to compatible orientations held towards the role. In this way, socioeconomic resources and cultural orientations can have contradictory effects on role performance and experiences.

More consistent, however, is the positive effect of spousal access to network support for alleviating the burdens of parenting. The beneficial effect of social support can be explained by the fact that one can rely on others to fulfill certain needs, lowering the expectations toward the partner. The beneficial effect of social support is sex-specific since access to network support has a stronger effect on women's than on men's feelings of parental role restriction and parental stress. This finding is not remarkable in light of the aforementioned conclusion that women also experience more stress and strain in their mother role and therefore can take more advantage of sources of support. Moreover, although the standard of motherhood may have become less imperative for an increasing number of women, the demand for ´psychologically´ responsible motherhood adds to contemporary women's feelings of insecurity (Brinkgreve, 1988). The availability of a social network can help to relieve these feelings.

Besides examining the differentiated parental experiences, we also investigated the impact of parenting on spousal marital experiences. Once more, the result is sex-specific. For husbands, experiences of parental stress are more closely tied up with their marital experiences than is true for wives, whereas for wives, experiences of parental role restriction (and not parental stress) are more strongly connected with marital experiences than those of their husbands. The partner effects that these aspects brought about as well, support the interwovenness between marriage and husbands' parental stress, and between marriage and wives' parental role restriction. Husbands' parental stress does not only affect their own perception of marital communication but also that of their wives. Similarly, wives' parental role restriction also impinges on their husbands' view of communication. In other words, the sex-specific spillover of parenting on marriage (i.e in terms of strength of association) precisely occurs for those parental domains with which the sexes are increasingly confronted as a consequence of changed sex role expectations. Indeed, women may feel ever more hindered by their parental role because other options became socially available in the life project of women. Reversely, because men are now socially allowed to take up parental roles, they are confronted with the problems and difficulties associated with it. In this respect, contemporary marriages suffer from the broadening of men and women's (mental) horizon.

Despite the stronger association between wives' marital experiences and their parental role restriction, our long-term analysis indicates for both spouses that feelings of parental restriction are cause as well as consequence of marital satisfaction in the long term; they mutually influence each other. For the other parental aspects, no cross-lagged effects were established. Hence, it looks as if the mutual influence between the marital and the parental system over time hinges more strongly on the restrictive nature of the parental task than on the rewarding or problematic aspects, indicating that husbands and wives meet difficulties in combining a demanding task like parenting with other self-fulfilling activities.

10.2.3. Spouses' Labor Market Resources and Their Cultural Orientations

Women's increased labor market resources are often considered as the essence of current marital vulnerability (cf. Chapter 1). It is argued that their enhanced economic status makes them less dependent on the marital institution and gives them more bargaining power within marriage. This so-called *female independence hypothesis* received some support in the present study when considering wives' education. Both spouses appear to be less satisfied with marriage when wives are better educated (Chapter 5). From Chapter 9, it became clear that this finding might be due to the more negative parental experiences of higher educated mothers and the negative effects of women's education on marital communication. Rather than benefiting from wives' (better) communication skills, it seems that couples whose wives are higher educated communicate more negatively. This might support the bargaining argument. It can be speculated that an increased educational level of women may put marriage under stress because these women have more verbal skills to make their needs and desires, which are more likely to be non-traditional, explicit. This assertiveness may unbalance the traditional positions of men and women within marriage and therefore enhances the chance of conflict and negative communication.

This speculation might also explain the finding that husbands belonging to higher income families tend to report stronger declines in marital satisfaction than those belonging to lower income families. Probably, the explanation must be sought in the social position of their wives since women in higher income families are higher educated than their female counterparts of lower income families. The stronger position of these wives (and the cultural and verbal characteristics associated with it) might be a threat for husbands' marital comfort.

When considering female employment instead of education, the female independence assumption was not strongly supported. Our study documents that women's labor market participation does not put husbands' marriage under pressure but rather affects women's. Considering the long-term analysis, our findings indicate that employed women do not experience more or less decrease in marital satisfaction than do non-employed women. Lower marital satisfaction, though, was reported by women who became unemployed between the first and second measurement point. The loss of work and hence the change in and adaptation to new roles rather than employment as such seem to affect women's satisfaction within the private sphere.

Nonetheless, an important finding of our cross-sectional analysis is that men can relieve the impact of women's outside employment on their wives' marital satisfaction by holding pro-family attitudes. The more husbands appraise traditional family values, the more positive wives' employment turns out to be for wives' satisfaction (Chapter 5). At first glance, the conclusion that husbands' endorsement of values such as "living for your family" and "having children", and not their egalitarian gender role orientation, provides a favorable context for women being satisfied when they are employed is remarkable. Instead of being irreconcilable, husbands' traditional family orientation is a gain for employed women. Other research suggests that this might be due to the higher motivation of these husbands to invest in and be committed to family life. Apparently, this commitment makes it easier for contemporary women to combine their family role with a role in the public sphere. To state it pithily, the more women withdraw from the private sphere, the more men need to enter this sphere for satisfying their wives. It looks as if the family role of the husband is also increasingly situated *within* the family than merely *outside* it. This contrasts with the situation of fifty years ago, about which Dumon (1977, p. 20) diagnosed that, "Strangely enough, the family role of the man-father [as provider and breadwinner] is situated outside the family".

The fading of domains exclusively reserved for one of the sexes, goes hand in hand with a cultural relaxation on what men and women 'ought' to do. An increasing preference for shared and equal responsibilities between husbands and wives results in wide social acceptance of performing a-stereotypical tasks. Moreover, the stronger emphasis put on autonomy and freedom of individuals, results in a weaker orientation on traditional family values. These cultural processes also affect the internal marital reality of husbands and wives and hence their evaluation of it. A major finding of the present study is that we have a stronger case for these *cultural* than for economic variables to be important determinants for marital satisfaction. Particularly, spouses' endorsement of traditional family values positively contributes to their own satisfaction with marriage. This is probably true because 'family' is a salient part of these spouses' identity, encouraging the sacrifices one is willing to make to develop a satisfying partnership.

In this respect, our study also showed that husbands' marital satisfaction depends on their wives' appraisal of traditional family values. This finding is not remarkable since it is not question of role change here. However, it might indicate the uncertainty accompanying women's changing role and expectations. The privilege of men to have structural power in society, now also becomes available for women. Even when women are solely housewives, no one can deny these changed expectations and the waning dominance of women's role of *family* maker. The *availability* rather than the actual employment of women might more strongly affect spousal marital experiences (Ruggles, 1997). Apparently, in a social area of insecurity and relationship fragility, successful partnership requires a pro-family orientation.

However, this reasoning is not true when considering sex role expectations. Women's orientation on egalitarian sex roles does not make their husbands more or less happy with their marriage. In contrast, women report to be more satisfied when their husbands value equal roles for men and women. In essence, however, a progressive gender role attitude on part of the husband refers to a pro-family-orientation as well. These men have adapted themselves to changed social circumstances in which men and women interact on equal terms and in which men may perform stereotypical female roles.

10.2.4. Gender

In reflecting upon the previous themes, gender manifests itself as a quintessential part of married life. Unlike biological sex, gender is created and recreated in interaction with others and as such is a social product (West & Zimmerman, 1987). Men and women do not only reproduce but can also transform gender through their behavior, attitudes and self-definitions (Connell, 1985; Hochschild & Machung, 1989). Particularly, because social prescriptions of what it means to be 'man' or 'woman' have become less restrictive, a whole plethora of gender expressions become available. Women can now display typical masculine behavior by taking a paid job and at the same time strongly incorporate female expressive qualities. In a similar vein, men can define themselves in stereotypical masculine qualities while also engaging in childrearing tasks. Hence, gender may operate in different ways within marriage. One of the questions in this study was to what degree and how gender, in the broad sense of the word, impinges on the marital system. This effect could be twofold. For one, different gender characteristics can be similarly related to specific marital aspects, and for another, the same gender characteristics can differently affect different marital aspects. The generation under study is particularly relevant in this respect because they were socialized with a sex-segregated social model that they questioned as adults later in life.

Drawing upon identity theory and the multifactorial theory of gender, the interrelationships between different gender characteristics and different marital characteristics were studied in Chapter 7 and 8. Three gender aspects were distinguished: (a) gender role attitudes, (b) gender role identity, i.e. incorporating stereotypical male and/or female qualities, and (c) gender role behavior, i.e. performing household and childrearing tasks. According to the multifactorial gender theory, these different gender aspects might be differently related to marital outcomes whereas identity theory hypothesizes that a female identity yields positive marital communication and therefore possibly also higher marital satisfaction. The reverse is assumed as to male identity.

Given the central importance of marital communication in understanding marital satisfaction, the relationship between gender and communication was firstly investigated. Considering gender role *identity* and gender role *attitudes*, our findings show that expressive spouses communicate less negatively and more openly, whereas egalitarian orientated wives and husbands communicate less negatively and the latter also more openly. Hence, adopting feminine orientated characteristics positively influences husbands and wives' communication behavior in marriage.

Considering gender role *behavior*, contrasting results were obtained. Wives taking the main responsibility of childrearing, communicate more negatively whereas husbands being responsible for childrearing communicate more openly. The former may fit the idea of women wanting no longer being the primary caretaker of children. For men, however, childrearing apparently creates possibilities to communicate more openly about their personal experiences. Taking these findings together, it can be asserted that, "being expressive", "having egalitarian sex role attitudes" and "taking care of children", are all part of husbands' view of being feminine because under these circumstances men display a more feminine communication style of openly sharing experiences. The latter is even more strongly pronounced for expressive husbands belonging to higher income groups. In this respect, "being expressive", "having egalitarian sex role attitudes" and "taking care of children", may signify new elements in the old image of masculinity as a way to adapt to new demands of partnership.

The assumption that gender operates differently within marriage also became clear when considering marital satisfaction. It was demonstrated that an important difference exists between the family *orientation* of women (cf. supra) and the family *role* of women. Whereas women's familialism (i.e. appraising traditional family values) positively affects both husbands and wives' marital satisfaction, it was found that having the main responsibility of *parenting* turns out negatively for women's experiences of partnership. This finding, along with the positive marital effects of husbands' parenting, might account for the fact that fathers are increasingly expected to take part in childrearing as well.

This norm, however, does not seem to exist as regards *housework*. The performance of domestic tasks by husbands has a negative influence on both spouses' evaluations of their marriage whereas wives' household labor does not have a significant impact on marital satisfaction. Hence, it seems that caring and household labor have become dissociated, with the former being more socially approved (Dumon, 1997). Household labor appears to be de-emphasized by spouses as a potential source of satisfaction in marriage.

The significance of social valued behavior for spousal marital experiences is brought further to a head when discerning higher and lower social classes. The present study shows that the impact of the approval and disapproval of *childrearing*, respectively *household* tasks, is even more pronounced in distinct income classes. Wives in higher income levels are less positive about their marriage when doing the lion's share of household labor whereas husbands and wives evaluate their marriage more positively when being responsible for parental tasks. Higher income classes may be able to 'buy' behavior that is less valued (e.g. household labor). In contrast, displaying behavior that is highly valued and emotionally loaded entails more positive consequences (in terms of marital satisfaction). Apparently, by taking more *marital advantage* of performing childrearing labor, higher income groups distinguish themselves from lower social classes. This might be due to the different meanings attached to having children. The salience of raising children in higher social classes becomes clear in both the positive consequences it has for marital satisfaction in higher income groups and the negative parental experiences reported by higher educated spouses. These findings might indicate that in higher social classes, children are a more deliberate choice than they are in lower social groups. Children are part of the whole set of choices one is 'forced' to make but for which one is also held responsible.

It is striking to note that higher income couples accentuate traditional female behavior in the sphere of parent-child relations, whereas the reverse holds for stereotypical female identity traits. Indeed, evidence was obtained for spouses to be more satisfied when women endorse more stereotypical male and less stereotypical female traits. Overall, it seems that motherhood, probably because of its social value, represents behavior that reproduces traditional femininity within higher income groups whereas household labor as well as gender identity traits represent domains through which higher income women produce a new image of femininity, i.e. not performing household labor and incorporating qualities that are traditionally associated with masculinity. Or an alternative reasoning may be true, i.e. child rearing might have increasingly become a sex-neutral task, not being specifically associated with femininity or masculinity, allowing men (and women) to respond to new (feminine) requirements.

In lower income groups, another picture can be drawn. By emotional disapproving (i.e. being marital dissatisfied) women who define themselves in stereotypical male traits, lower income husbands might define what is optimally masculine. Possibly, this attitude is also 'functional' for spousal satisfaction in the private sphere. It may allow lower income husbands to 'control' the sphere of partnership by preferring *not-masculine* women but rather women who are typified as stereotypically feminine.

Considering stereotypical feminine and masculine qualities in higher and lower social classes where the wife is employed, our findings show that wives' gender role identity is not a critical factor in understanding spousal marital satisfaction. In contrast, the focus is directed towards husbands' qualities. For being satisfied with one's marriage it appears that a strengthened economic position of women in higher social layers requires de-emphasizing husbands' stereotypical qualities whereas in lower social layers it demands an accentuation of these traits. In fact, 'masculine' men might be incompatible with women who display non-traditional female behavior, i.e. labor market participation.

However, it is remarkable that this incompatibility does not result from the smaller gap between husbands and wives' occupational status in higher social layers. Post-hoc analyses have shown that in spite of women's higher occupational status in higher social classes, the distance between both spouses' occupation is significantly larger in the higher than in the lower social strata. Hence, the economic power of higher-class husbands is relatively larger than that of their male counterparts in lower social classes. Perhaps, this gap might explain higher-class husbands' (unconscious) indulgence in the field of stereotypical identity traits. Indeed, subverting the male status position by less adhering to stereotypical male qualities is probably more far-reaching or threatening for lower-class men than for higher-class men. The latter may maintain a status difference by their relatively higher occupation. Although this assertion cannot be proved by means of this study, it is tempting to speculate.

This speculation notwithstanding, our study demonstrates that by far the most significant factor in spousal marital satisfaction in higher and lower social classes is husbands' incorporation of expressive qualities. Husbands who define themselves as "being kind", "not hiding emotions" and "expressing tender feelings", are more satisfied with marriage and so are their wives. This effect is probably due to the less negative and more open communication of these men. As indicated, the latter is of utmost importance in a social scenery characterized by less structural prescriptions. Accidents in communication may cause damage to the marriage and to its vital function of personal and emotional fulfillment (cf. Chapter 1). Our study shows that husbands' self-identification in terms of stereotypical female qualities positively fosters this behavior.

Overall, this gender discussion leads us to conclude that the onus is on the husband; the more so since our study shows that husbands' non-traditional sex role behavior and identifications are beneficial for higher-class marriages. Particularly, the belief that an essential role is reserved for men can be substantiated when considering the *principle of stratified diffusion,* stating that lower status groups have a tendency to imitate those above them (Cheal, 1991, p. 121). If it is true that important changes are likely to begin high up in the status hierarchy and gradually diffuse downwards, it can be expected that in the foreseeable future successful marriages will require more 'feminine' men and perhaps also more 'masculine' women.

10.3. CONCLUDING REFLECTIONS: STRENGTHS, UNRESOLVED ISSUES AND FUTURE DIRECTIONS

The present study significantly contributes to the study of marital satisfaction. The reason is twofold. For one, determinants and processes underlying spousal marital satisfaction in the Netherlands are not well corroborated. For another, our study extends prior research by the specific issues that were addressed and/or by the techniques that were used. In this section, we summarize the major strengths but also the shortcomings of this study. This task involves three steps. First, we reflect upon the methodological aspects characterizing the present study. Second, recent theorizing on marital satisfaction is evaluated in light of our findings. Finally, we discuss significant unresolved issues. Through the whole section, it is attempted to only deal with research caveats that go beyond those already made in the individual chapters of Part II.

10.3.1. Methodological Reflections

Two-Wave Design and Individual Trajectories. The use of a two-wave panel design in this study had major strengths. It allowed us to validate our central measures across time and to gain more insight in the short-term and long-term associations between marital satisfaction and relevant covariates. Moreover, by considering the same individuals for two periods in time, intra-individual changes in relation to marital satisfaction (change) were assessed. Nevertheless, the use of a two-wave panel design also has limitations. These have to do with the limited inferences that can be drawn about change in marriage. With two measurement points, the most complex line that can be fitted is a straight line (Rogossa, 1995). Hence, it can be assessed whether change has occurred but not whether the change is non-linear. At least three waves of data are required to better understand how and why marital satisfaction follows a particular pattern throughout the marital career. Doing so, the researcher also has the possibility to examine individual trajects throughout time (Bradbury, Fincham & Beach, 2000). In the present study, we reviewed marital processes with a fine-tooth comb, revealing differences in social class experiences and in husbands and wives' marital processes. Therefore, the evolution of a lower class wife's marital satisfaction may be very different from that of their male counterpart belonging to a higher social class. Especially in the light of an individualized 'self-made' life course, the use of traject-based models with multi-wave data is a promising research line for the future. The lesson that variables and strategies that make partners happy in the short term will not necessarily have the same impact in the long term, must researchers motivate to not only ask about what people makes happy, but also to deal with the issue of when and why (Holmes, 2000).

Dyadic Data and Partner Effects. A major advantage of this study is the availability of information from both husband and wife. Karney and Bradbury (1995) conclude, based on their meta-analysis that one out of three longitudinal studies on marital quality and stability fail to take sex differences into account. Because this is often due to the fact that data are only gathered by one of the partners, studies also fail considering partner effects in their analyses. Therefore, the strength of using couple data, as in our study, is twofold. For one, the availability of these data allowed us to evaluate sex-specific marital experiences. For another, information of the partner could be used to explain the marital outcomes of the other partner. To deal with husbands and wives' dependency, we exploited the capacity of *structural equation modeling* to use the couple as a unit of analysis. Hence, husbands and wives' information could be simultaneously included in one analysis with the purpose of testing for significant differences (Kenny & Cook, 1999). Illustrative for the argument that the consideration of both husbands and wives is a requisite for fully capturing the differences and similarities in spouses' marital experiences is the cross-lagged analysis described in Chapter 4. Conducting this analysis for husbands and wives separately, our results showed that the cross-lagged effect from wives' marital satisfaction to negative communication is significant as well. However, by including husbands and wives' information in one model, the long-term association between marital satisfaction and negative communication is no longer significant. This example shows that only studying information of one of the partners yield a biased view of the interpersonal nature of marital relationships.

Quantitative versus Qualitative Designs. The chosen method determines what sort of picture will be taken of marriage: a close-up or a wide-angle picture. To draw a comprehensive picture, however, both are needed. Using solely a quantitative design, the underlying meanings attached to some phenomena escape our notice. Therefore, qualitative research might supplement our research findings and deepen our insights obtained from quantitative studies. For example, face-to-face interviews enable the researcher to fully explore what it means for Dutch husbands and wives to perform household and childrearing tasks. Husbands might consider the performance of household tasks as an expression of their caring, and thus 'emotional' work, whereas women do not perceive it that way. Women may rather desire emotional work as defined in feminine terms. Similarly, it can be questioned to what extent different members distinguish between the task-related aspects of childcare and the more emotional components asso-

ciated with it. And what are the mechanisms behind the sex-specific parental experiences? Can it be assumed that women feel restricted because they
are 'expected' to prefer parenting above 'other' personal fulfillments
whereas men feel restricted because they are used to disregard the extra
responsibility of childrearing? These and other questions can be overcome
by extending quantitative research designs with a close-up approach from
qualitative research.

10.3.2. Theoretical Reflections

Throughout the chapters of Part II, several theoretical frames were considered useful candidates for investigating marital outcomes. Despite the use
of distinct theoretical perspectives, the various topics addressed throughout
this study could be thought within a more general model of marriage. One
model qualified for capturing the diverse relationships that were examined,
was the VSA-model of Karney and Bradbury (1995). As indicated, the VSA-
model is a rather abstract model, identifying four substantial domains to
understand the outcome of partner relationships: enduring vulnerabilities,
stressful events, adaptive processes and marital quality. Although this
model acknowledges the complexity and diversity of marriage as well as the
processes by which marriages change, the findings of the present study
recommend a further specification of this theoretical model.

First, the gender dimension is not explicitly addressed in the model.
Nonetheless, our study has shown several differences between husbands
and wives regarding enduring vulnerabilities (e.g. cultural orientations, gender role identity), stressful events (e.g. parental experiences) and adaptive
processes (e.g. open communication).

Second, the concept of 'enduring vulnerabilities' is ambiguous. According to Karney and Bradbury (1995, p. 461) this concept refers to "stable
demographic, historical, personality and experiential factors that individuals
bring to marriage". These characteristics should 'set the stage' for marriage.
As a consequence, the relevance of attitudes and characteristics acquired
during the marital course is absent from the model. Above and beyond the
premarital factors that spouses bring to marriage, they may also develop
characteristics throughout the marital career. For example, spouses' social
network may significantly affect the stressful events that the couple

encounters as well as the capacity to adapt to these events. Social support, however, is hard to think of as an enduring vulnerability. Hence, it seems that one important domain is missing in the VSA-model, i.e. *instable* personal characteristics. As became clear from our study, these characteristics, among which include social support or gender role attitudes, are also related to stressful life events and to spousal adaptive processes. However, in contrast to enduring vulnerabilities (e.g. family of origin experiences), these characteristics may alter during the marital course.

Third, the VSA-model shed insufficient light on moderating contexts. For example, the interrelatedness between husbands and wives' vulnerabilities and their adaptive processes may be contingent upon the specific social environments in which they act. This assertion was supported in the present study. Among others, it was demonstrated that husbands' and wives' gender role identity has a different impact on spousal marital satisfaction or communication within higher or lower social classes and according to the marital stage. With respect to the latter, it should be noted that the couples under study have already been married for some time. Therefore, the research problems addressed in this study might yield different results if examined among a sample of newlywed couples.

In sum, these findings indicate that the VSA-model may manifest itself differently within different social contexts. Therefore, attention needs to be paid to the specific conditions under which the relationships between specific vulnerabilities, stressful events, and adaptive processes hold. In this respect, the VSA-model might benefit from a social ecological thinking of marriage. The emphasis put by social ecology on the mutual interdependence between the marital partners as well as between the marital partners and the smaller and broader social environments in which they function, may bring the dynamically social nature of partnership into the VSA-model. I document this suggestion with two examples. First, the degree to which a spouse behaves negatively towards the other partner (adaptive processes) can be triggered by the social context. It might be more tolerated within middle classes than in lower social classes that women behave negatively towards their husbands, engendering different marital experiences and outcomes for the husbands and wives of interest. A second example relates to the aforementioned development of personal characteristics during marriage. Spouses may enter marriage with a particular orientation towards gender roles. This orientation can be re-adjusted by one or both of the spouses, for example, after the birth of the first child. This re-adjustment may in its turn affect subsequent marital satisfaction. Hence, as indicated above, the VSA-model seems to lack a fifth domain, i.e. 'individual characteristics', which are unsteady in nature. These characteristics may affect both stressful events and adaptive processes.

These caveats on gender differences and the moderating nature of marital relationships also imply that there is not a *single* theory of marital satisfaction. Our research suggests at least specifications with respect to sex, marital stage, cultural orientation, and socioeconomic context. In this respect, it is worthwhile to investigate and compare more homogeneous groups in order to examine the validity of theoretical models.

10.3.3. Towards a New Research Agenda for Studying Marital Satisfaction

In the different studies of Part II several recommendations for future research were addressed. Moreover, the speculations made when interpreting our research findings in the second paragraph of this section, each feeds the research agenda. The attempt of this paragraph is to exceed the individual chapters with the intention of formulating some general and promising research lines for the future. Four directions are outlined below. These concern research on indirect effects, conditional effects, partner incongruence and social networks.

Indirect Effects. Our study indicates that the widely held assumption that socioeconomic *background* factors are weakly correlated with marital satisfaction might be due to the focus on direct effects. Therefore, future research needs to more fully explore which background factors are *directly* or *indirectly* related to marital satisfaction. Our study showed, on the one hand, that economic factors in terms of income and income satisfaction might play an important part in understanding *change* in marital satisfaction; and on the other hand that several background factors directly relate to spousal marital communication. It looks as if: (a) education might have both direct and indirect effects through communication on marital satisfaction, (b) life cycle variables (e.g. age and marital duration) might have indirect effects through marital communication and (c) income and income satisfaction might rather affect marital satisfaction across time. Research that includes these different levels of background characteristics, communicational variables and marital satisfaction of both husbands and wives is scarce (see Kurdek, 1993). Therefore, it is recommended that future research further deciphers this complexity of direct and indirect effects between background factors and marital relationships.

This remark also holds with respect to *gender role identity*. The study reported in Chapter 6, using marital outcome variables other than marital satisfaction, supports the assumption that gender role identity has larger effects on marital communication than on marital satisfaction. Moreover, research needs to explore to what degree spouses' gender role identity affects marital satisfaction indirectly through spousal parental experiences. It can be speculated, for example, that husbands' expressiveness is beneficial for marriage because of its positive effects on parental experiences. In a similar vein, it can be examined whether the positive effect of women's 'masculine' qualities in higher social classes is due to the less negative parental experiences of these women. Perhaps, successful higher-class marriages increasingly require 'masculine' women because they are better able to cope with the difficult combination of raising children and participating in the labor market. Hence, the impact of gender role identity is probably greater than shown by research using a single indicator like marital satisfaction or studying direct effects only.

Conditional Effects. Although of significant importance to capture the complexity of marriage, moderating effects are rarely considered in previous research. Two directions seem promising. First, our study demonstrated that wives' satisfaction with the family income plays a part in understanding their subsequent marital satisfaction. This finding taps the issue of *relative deprivation* as accentuated in the theory of Easterlin (see Chapter 1). It is advisable to explore the causes of this effect. Thus far, we have no idea of the degree to which the effects of income satisfaction are limited to those who are confronted with 'objective' economic hardship or to those who do not face 'objective' economic hardship but have higher aspirations. And if the latter is true, why are women, more than men, sensitive to this relative deprivation? Therefore, it is recommendable to examine interaction effects between *objective* and *subjective* indicators of economic circumstances in future research.

Second, it needs to be examined to what degree the effects of gender role identity and parental experiences are contingent upon *cultural* orientations such as gender role and family attitudes. The latter may provide a different context in which particular aspects are evaluated. For example, the questions arises whether our results on the spillover of parental on marital experiences depends on the more or less traditional orientation of the spouses towards gender roles and family values. Since these cultural orientations underwent major shifts during the past decades, the question as to what extent they steer personal experiences in distinct areas of the private sphere becomes important.

Partner Incongruence. An important unresolved issue in this study is the incongruity *between* and *within* spouses with respect to gender and other characteristics. It is sometimes argued that the lag between husbands and wives' *role behavior* and the more advanced *beliefs* they hold in this respect lies at the core of current marital problems. Because an important difference might exist between what people think and what people actually do, examining the effects of discrepancies between, for example, gender role identity, gender role behavior (domestic labor and labor market participation), and gender role attitudes *within* individuals may contribute to a more full understanding of how marital reality is experienced by the partners. In view of the interdependence of marital partners, not only the within-individual but also the *between*-individual incongruences are relevant to consider. This becomes also clear in the benchmark paper of Karney and Bradbury (1995). Applying meta-analytical techniques, the authors estimated the aggregate effect size for frequently studied variables in longitudinal research on marital satisfaction. Personality homogamy was established as one of the strongest predictors. Besides personality, literature has demonstrated that spousal homogamy with respect to other characteristics, such as religion or socioeconomic background, is also beneficial for the satisfaction experienced by the spouses (Heaton, 1984; Medling & McCarrey, 1981). However, little attempt is made to consider homogamy as a multidimensional phenomenon. Doing so, insight would be gained in the relative importance of different dimensions of structural and cultural stratification for spousal marital satisfaction as well as in the different importance of homogamy dimensions within higher and lower social layers. Scrutinizing the effects of spousal congruence on structural, cultural and personality characteristics may contribute to our understanding of how 'similar' couples differently adapt to stressful events and everyday experiences than couples showing incongruent features.

Social Support. An important conclusion that can be drawn in the face of what some claim as a period of (negative) individualism is the importance of *social integration* in understanding satisfying marriages. Spouses who can fall back on network support have more positive parental experiences and perceive their marital communication and satisfaction as more positive as well. However, we have not analyzed the nature and mechanisms lying behind these positive effects. Several questions remain open. Has social support a direct effect or rather a buffering effect on marital satisfaction? Is the beneficial effect of social support merely due to the existence or to the number, frequency or intensity of the received social support? Does the emotional or rather the instrumental aspect of social support determine the beneficial effects on marriage? Besides, more attention needs to be paid to the social structures and processes that cause social support networks. For example, it must be investigated how the significance and usefulness of social support may vary across groups in different structural positions – for example men and women in lower and upper economic classes. Moreover, assuming that attitudes are formed through interaction, it can be questioned whether there is a link between diverse aspects of social support and cultural orientations in their effects on marital satisfaction? At least at a broader societal level, it can be speculated that the mechanisms through which large social transformations affect marital relationships might run through the social relations in whom marital life is embedded. Therefore, a much fuller understanding of these relations might be fruitful for capturing how major shifts in social life, as described in Chapter 1, affect the everyday life of husbands and wives.

10.3.4. Policy Thoughts

Although this study has not attempted to evaluate Dutch family policy or to derive policy implications, in this paragraph some tentative recommendations and general points of attention are made on the basis of our research findings. The ideas presented hereafter need to be seen as a potential breeding ground for policy initiatives rather than as concrete, delineated measures. The policy thoughts put forward concern (a) the spousal system and (its relation to) the parental system, (b) social diversity in private experiences and (c) the temporality of families.

Regarding the spousal system, our study points to the importance of stimulating husbands' taking over aspects of the stereotypical female role. It was found that men's expressiveness, open communication, and child rearing participation are important sources of spousal satisfaction with contemporary marriage. In this respect, the accentuation of the private female sphere and the public male sector as prevalent in 'modern' society, is questioned in developing a satisfying partnership in 'postmodern' society. Moreover, stimulating men fulfilling roles in the private sphere might overcome the problems faced by women in their role as primary caregiver. This became apparent in our research findings with regard to the parental system in specific. Because of a strong social orientation on women as primary caregivers, mothers feel more restricted and stressed by the parental role than fathers, indicating the negative side-effects of sex role specialization. Having a paid job, however, can alleviate women's feeling of parental role restriction. Hence, it seems that policy orientations on the public role of women and the private role of men need to go hand in hand.

However, stimulating and realizing this new orientation on sex roles is a difficult policy target because deep-rooted social images of womanhood and in particular manhood, lie at the core of this issue. It has to do with profound social expectations and habits ingrained with husbands and wives. Therefore, to realize such gender shifts, changes must take place both within the *structural* context (i.e. political and economic conditions), and within the prevailing *cultural* scripts.

As concerns the structural context, huge differences exist between husbands and wives' economic position in the Netherlands. For the couples studied in this research, this might be due to the higher educational levels of husbands in comparison to their wives. Consequently, husbands' participating in unpaid caring labor is relatively expensive because they can earn more by participating in paid labor. However, the different economic positions of Dutch husbands and wives could also result from the implicit family policy pursued by the Dutch government during the eighties. The availability of formal childcare and more flexible regulations of maternity leave since the nineties, has contributed to more flexibly combining private and public roles for women today. To also encourage fathers to take parental leave, the Netherlands adopted a system of equal and not transferable parent-specific allotments (Sigle-Rushton & Kenney, 2004). Nonetheless, this strategy seems to be counterbalanced by employers' attitudes (Duindam, 1993; European Commission, 1998). Fathers are afraid to be labeled as uncommitted when asking for parental leave or fear to let opportunities of promotion slip away. Therefore, the compatibility of the worker and the parental role, which is increasingly made possible for women, must also be (or remain) an explicit policy object that is directed towards men[1]. Moreover, a structural steering of balancing public and private responsibilities by means of family leave or flexible work hours, is in tune with current transformations in partnership and might alleviate dilemmas of care for wives and husbands. In this respect, Sigle-Rushton and Kenney (2004) demonstrate that in the Netherlands, which is dominated by the arrangement that women's economic role is secondary to their caring activities, there has already been some shift in preferences and priorities as to a more equitable distribution of working hours between men and women.

It goes without saying that the imbalance between the private and the public sphere is not only structural but also cultural in nature. Cultural images of womanhood and manhood are probably even harder to deal with than the just mentioned regulations in the structural context. As mentioned in the first chapter, the ideology that attended the division between family and workplace since the 19th century, reflects ideals of manhood and wom-

---

[1] Despite the fact that the enhancement of men's caring responsibility was pushed forward as the spearhead of the Dutch emancipation program in the nineties (*"Met het oog op 1995"*), Niphuis-Nell (1997) concludes that few catalysts exist to encourage men taking greater responsibility in unpaid labor.

anhood. Until today, men and women internalize that caring is a more feminine task and breadwinning is a more masculine task. However, this split and the symbolic meaning lying behind it, constrain the possibilities for care in marriage (Thompson, 1993). This becomes clear in research findings demonstrating that wives who earn more than their husbands tend to do more household and childrearing tasks than their female counterparts earning less (Hochschild & Machung, 1983). Thus, a two-way traffic seems to be going on. On the one hand, husbands are not eager to take part in unpaid caring labor, the more so since this labor is not socially high valued, but on the other hand, it is not evident or easy for women to depart from their traditional role. Or to voice Thompson (1993, p. 560), "The symbolic distinction between women and men preserves the notion of separate spheres, justifies the sexual division of labor, and creates personal dilemmas for couples". Influencing these symbolic distinctions can only be realized through different channels such as public campaigns, education and media.

A side effect of socially allowing 'new' sex roles is the lack of clear models at the moment. The cultural flexibility (and even expectation) that fathers take part in child rearing and that mothers also fulfill public roles, has created new risks and vulnerabilities for the spousal system. The longitudinal intertwinement of parental role restriction and marital satisfaction may lend support to this argumentation. It seems that husbands and wives, facing difficulties in living up to an extended role repertoire covering both the public and the private sphere, are more vulnerable in their marital relationship. Moreover, our study demonstrates that the spillover of parenting on partnership is the strongest for those aspects that are not traditionally defined as belonging to one's sex and for which no clear expectations are inscribed in the social script. Specifically, partnership seems to suffer from both husbands' exposure to the pleasures and pain of parenting as from wives' extended role repertoire resulting in feelings of parental role restriction. Hence, men and women seem to lack established role models to cope with new cultural expectations. (Local) initiatives to assist fathers and mothers in their parental responsibilities may therefore help to establish 'new' models.

Besides the idea of providing a structural and cultural environment that supports private roles for men and public roles for women, policy should, secondly, recognizes the social diversity of marital experiences. Our study clearly specifies the difficulty of treating men and women, and higher and lower social groups similarly in developing relationship-friendly policy measures. For example, instigating a more expressive self-definition on part of the husbands will yield more positive consequences for women's than for men's satisfaction. When considering different social layers, it appears that traditional notions of men as providers and women as homemakers are more likely to serve as a comparison referent of fairness in lower socioeconomic groups whereas higher social groups rather appraise a-stereotypical qualities and behavior. Hence, not every man or woman is waiting for a rethinking and reorganization of unpaid labor since stimulating an equal share in household labor is less valid for lower income spouses. Moreover, lower educated spouses experience parenting as less problematic, less restrictive and more satisfying than higher educated ones. Consequently, higher educated spouses are more likely to fall victim to a negative spillover of parenting on partnership. In this spillover, women are more affected by feelings of role restriction whereas men's marital relationship is more closely tied up to parenting stress. All in all, these research findings demonstrate that spousal resources for developing a satisfying partnership depend on the social categories to which they belong. These categories determine individuals' relational schemata and their specific experiences in the private sphere. Therefore, it is important that policy makers are directed towards the differences and specificities of their target groups, taking into account the social specificity of private experiences.

A third policy thought relates to the temporality of family experiences. Temporal aspects can refer to age-, period- and cohort-effects all clotting together in spousal experiences, but also to different marital stages (Becker, 1992; Kalmijn, 2002). As to age-, period- and cohort-effects, it was already mentioned that the spouses under study are part of the baby boom generation. This generation shares the common experience of being socialized with a traditional sex role model. However, the relational schemata adopted during childhood may not fit into the larger environment at the time individuals initiate and develop relationships themselves. The difficult exercise of adopting 'new' sex roles and living up to new partnership ideals may therefore be more pronounced in a generation that inherited an 'old' private story and therefore lacks appropriate behavior models. Our finding that older women have a more negative perception of the marital communication whereas older men do not might point towards a discrepancy between expectations and actual realizations in this specific female cohort.

As to marital stages, policy makers need to bear in mind that family roles and needs are dynamic as individuals move through their life and family career. Within a time period of five years, our longitudinal analysis indicates that the couples who go through a 'transition' of becoming more satisfied is a specific group characterized, among other things, by husbands' more open communication behavior, husbands' sex role egalitarianism, spouses' familial orientation and their experiences of less parental role restriction. This transition, however, needs to be interpreted within the specific family stage of these couples. Actually, the processes laid bare in this study operate in longer-term marriages but do not necessarily apply to newlywed couples. For example, our study indicates that husbands report lower parenting satisfaction as their children reach adolescence. To the degree their children are younger, fathers experience parenting as a more rewarding task. One of the elements playing a part in this experience might be the greater role of mothers as sources of support in this stage. Therefore, stimulating fathers' commitment in rearing their adolescent children might positively affect their parenting satisfaction and consequently their marital relationships. Thus, along with the longitudinal findings just mentioned above, it seems that affecting sex role standards can help longer-term couples to enhance their satisfaction with partnership. Research on newlywed couples might clarify the elements that are important in the earlier stages of the marital relationship. These temporal qualifications need to be taken into account when planning public initiatives such as the previously mentioned 'new man' campaigns. Acknowledging the rich diversity of families might be a difficult but focal policy point.

10.4. MARRIAGE IN MOTION: FINAL REFLECTION

Demographic figures indicate the waning quantitative significance of the marital institution. According to some authors, this paradoxically reflects the increased emotional importance of marital relationships. At the micro-level this qualitative importance becomes manifest in individuals' satisfaction with partnership. Gaining insight in forces contributing to husbands and wives' satisfaction with marriage was the central aim of the present study. Overall, three social movements came to the fore, reflecting the *time-specific* character of marital experiences.

First, segregated sex-role specialization as prevalent in the fifties, has negative rather than positive effects on spousal emotional life. Women's outside employment, be it primarily part-time in the Dutch case, does not seem to put marriage under pressure and make women feel less restricted in their parental role. Moreover, household labor is de-emphasized as a significant source of marital satisfaction.

Second, several findings lend support to the importance of pro-family orientations in maintaining rewarding partnership. Spouses' appraisal of traditional family values provides a cultural context benefiting spousal marital satisfaction, the more so when wives are employed.

Third, and related to the previous trend, is the overwhelming importance of 'feminine' husbands. Husbands incorporating stereotypical feminine qualities into their self-image take more part in childrearing tasks, communicate more openly, and hold more egalitarian attitudes towards sex roles. The former is essential given the fact that wives take the burden of parenting and experience more role restriction and parenting stress than men. The latter two, open communication behavior and egalitarian role attitudes are important because they represent both significant elements in new interpretations of (equal) partnership.

Hence, marital relationships are in motion and husbands and wives are permanently "doing marriage". The three movements described above, reflect a changing society where both men and women find themselves in circumstances, at which mid-century men and women, would have looked at suspiciously. Indeed, a successful marriage now seems to increasingly require a renouncement of traditional images of maleness and femaleness. We are standing, however, at the crossroad of 'old customs' and 'new ideals'. Hence, it can be expected that the picture drawn in the present study is a product of time and generation. Specifically, it is a time in which the generation under study holds other ideals and behaves differently than the ideals and behaviors with which it was raised, burdening husbands and wives with role ambivalences. Particularly, the finding of the close intertwinement of marital satisfaction and parental role restriction indicates the difficulty of combining new roles with deep-seated habits as well as the discrepancy between new roles and structural facilities making them possible. Hence, it looks as if marital vulnerability has not (only) to do with spouses decreased investment in relationships, as voiced in popular discourse, but with new (relational) ideals and attitudes not being in pace with structural opportunities.

Some authors define this situation as a kind of cultural lag (Jamieson, 1999; Vannoy, 1991). This lag also refers to the social boundaries limiting the choices individuals can make (see Chapter 1). Our study made clear that not everyone is losing sleep over these new ideals. Sharp social dividing lines exist between spouses, being still strongly orientated on traditional sex-specific images and those following new social avenues. Hence, the choices individuals recognize and make, the behavior that they display and the way they experience all this is inscribed in the social script of our society. It was shown that education continues to be an important element of social division within the private sphere. Therefore, theories (over-) emphasizing individuals' agency and their search for personal satisfaction might lose sight of the still important collective contexts in which the individual biography takes shape. Marital relationships are not pure but socially infected. Hence, examining gender and the diverse social contexts in which men and women develop their marriages, remains a fascinating research domain for the near future.

Research on the correlates and processes underlying partners' marital satisfaction is not only an important end in itself, but becomes particularly relevant from the perspective of the social advantages of established marriages. According to Latten (2003), relationship formation and maintenance has increasingly become an important factor in individual welfare. In fact, economic and other cumulative gains associated with staying married throughout the life course, has turned marriage into a status symbol disclosing new mechanism of inequality. In this respect, one can raise the question to what degree these intimate transformations in partnership will further result in class distinctions with stable and satisfied marriages being the pivotal issue at stake.

References

Abbott, D. A., & Brody, G. H. (1985). The relation of child age, gender and number of children to the marital adjustment of wives. *Journal of Marriage and the Family, 47*, 77-84.

Acitelli, L. K. (1992). Gender differences in relationship awareness and marital satisfaction among young married couples. *Personality and Social Psychology Bulletin, 18*, 102-110.

Aiken, L. S., & West, S. G. (1991). *Multiple regression: Testing and interpreting interactions*. Thousands Oaks: Sage.

Alders, M., Latten, J., Pool, M., & Esveldt, I. (2003). Het spitsuurgezin [The rushed family]. In N. van Nimwegen & I. Esveldt (Eds.), *Bevolkingsvraagstukken in Nederland anno 2003. Rapport no. 65* (pp. 105 - 136). Den Haag: NiDi.

Allan, G. (1993). Social structure and relationships. In S. Duck (Ed.), *Social context and relationships* (pp. 1-25). London: Sage Publications.

Allen, M. (1998). Methodological considerations when examining a gendered world. In D. J. Canary & K. Dindia (Eds.), *Sex differences and similarities in communication. Critical essays and empirical investigations of sex and gender in interaction* (pp. 427-444). New Jersey/London: Lawrence Erlbaum Associates Publishers.

Allison, P. D. (2001). *Missing data*. Sage University Papers on quantitative applications in the social sciences, 07-136. Thousands Oaks, CA: Sage.

Amato, P. (1996). Explaining the intergenerational transmission of divorce. *Journal of Marriage and the Family, 58*, 628-641.

Amato, P. R., & Booth, A. (1995). Changes in gender role attitudes and perceived marital quality. *American Sociological Review, 60*, 58-66.

Amato, P. R., & Booth, A. (1996). A prospective study of divorce and parent-child relationship. *Journal of Marriage and the Family, 58*, 256-365.

Amato, P. R., & Rogers, S. J. (1997). A longitudinal study of marital problems and subsequent divorce. *Journal of Marriage and the Family, 59*, 612-624.

Anderson, S. A., Russell, C. S., & Schumm, W. R. (1983). Perceived marital quality and family life-cycle categories: A further analysis. *Journal of Marriage and the Family, 45*, 127-139.

Antill, J. K. (1983). Sex role complementarity versus similarity in married couples. *Journal of Personality and Social Psychology, 45*, 145-155.

Ariès, P. (1980). Two successive motivations for declining birth rates in the West. *Population and Development Review, 6*, 645-650.

Arrindell, W. A. (1998). Femininity and subjective well-being. In G. Hofstede (Ed.), *Masculinity and Femininity. The Taboo Dimension of National Cultures* (pp. 44-54). London: Sage Publications.

Askham, J. (1976). Identity and stability within the marriage relationship. *Journal of Marriage and the Family, 38*, 535-547.

Aube, J., & Koestner, R. (1992). Gender characteristics and adjustment: a longitudinal study. *Journal of Personality and Social Psychology, 63*, 485-493.

Aube, J., & Norcliffe, H. (1995). Gender characteristics and adjustment-related outcomes: questioning the masculinity model. *Personality and Social Psychology Bulletin, 21*, 284-296.

Axelson, L. J. (1963). The marital adjustment and marital role definitions of husbands of working and nonworking wives. *Marriage and Family Living, 24*, 189-195.

Bandalos, D. L., & Finney, S. J. (2001). Item parceling issues in structural equation modeling. In G. A Marcoulides, & R. E. Schumacker (Eds.), *New developments and techniques in structural equation modeling* (pp. 269-296). New Jersey: Lawrence Erlbaum Associates Publishers.

Beach, S. R. H., Katz, J., Sooyeon, K., & Brody, G. H. (2003). Prospective effects of marital satisfaction on depressive symptoms in established marriages: a dyadic model. *Journal of Social and Personal Relationships, 20*, 355-372.

Beck, U. (1992). *Risk society, towards a new modernity.* London: Sage.

Beck, U., & Beck-Gernsheim, E. (1995). *The normal chaos of love.* Cambridge: Polity Press.

Becker, G. (1981). *A treatise on the family.* Cambridge: Harvard University Press.

Becker, H. (1992). *Generaties en hun kansen [Generations and their chances].* Amsterdam: Meulenhoff.

Becvar, D. S., & Becvar, R. J. (1996). *Family therapy. A systemic integration.* Boston: Allyn and Bacon.

Belsky, J., Youngblade, L., Rovine, M. & Volling, B. (1991). Patterns of marital change and parent-child interaction. *Journal of Marriage and the Family, 53,* 487-498.

Bem, S. L. (1985). Androgyny and gender schema theory. In T. B. Sonderegger (Ed.), *Nebraska Symposium on motivation: psychology of gender* (pp. 179-226). Loncoln: University of Nebraska Press.

Berger, P., & Kelner, H. (1964). Marriage and the construction of reality. *Diogenes, 46,* 1-24.

Bernard, J. (1972). *The future of marriage.* Harmondsworth: Penguin Books.

Bernard, J. (2002). The husband's marriage and the wife's marriage. In S. Jackson & S. Scott (Eds.), *Gender. A sociological reader* (pp. 207-219). London/New York: Routledge.

Bienvenu, M. J. (1970). Measurement of marital communication. *Family Coordinator, 1,* 26-31.

Billiet, J. (1993). *Ondanks beperkt zicht. Studies over waarden, ontzuiling, en politieke veranderingen in Vlaanderen [A limited view notwithstanding. Studies on values, desectarianization, and political changes in Flanders].* Brussel: VUBpress.

Billiet, J., & McClendon, M. J. (1998). On the identification of acquiescence in balanced sets of items using structural models, *Advances in Methodology, Data Analysis and Statistics, 14,* 129-150.

Blazina, C. (2003). *The cultural myth of masculinity.* Westport: Praeger Publishers.

Booth, A., & Edwards, J. N. (1992). Starting over: Why remarriages are more unstable. *Journal of Family Issues, 13,* 179-194.

Booth, A., Edwards, J. N., & Johnson, D. R. (1991). Social integration and divorce. *Social Forces, 70,* 207-224.

Booth, A., Johnson, D. R., White, L. K., & Edwards, J. N. (1984). Divorce and marital instability over the life course. *Journal of Family issues, 7,* 421-442.

Borscheid, P. (1986). Romantic love or material interest: choosing partners in nineteenth century Germany, *Journal of Family History, 11,* 157-168.

Bradbury, T. N. (1995). Assessing the four fundamental domains of marriage. *Family Relations, 44,* 459-468.

Bradbury, T. N., Cohan, L. C., & Karney, B. R. (1998). Optimizing longitudinal research for understanding and preventing marital dysfunction. In T. N. Bradbury (Ed.), *The developmental course of marital dysfunction* (pp. 279- 311). Cambridge: University Press.

Bradbury, T. N., Fincham, F. D., & Beach, S. R. H. (2000). Research on the nature and determinants of marital satisfaction: a decade in review. *Journal of Marriage and the Family, 62,* 964-981.

Brennan, R. T., Barnett, R. C., & Gareis, K. C. (2001). When she earns more than he does: a longitudinal study of dual-earner couples. *Journal of Marriage and the Family, 63,* 168-183.

Brinkgreve, C. (1988). De belasting van de bevrijding [The burden of emancipation]. *Amsterdams Sociologisch Tijdschrift, 15,* 171-207.

Brinkgreve, C. (1989). De herwaardering van de vrouwelijke zorg. Enkele sceptische notities [The revaluation of female care. Some skeptical considerations]. *Amsterdams Sociologisch Tijdschrift, 16,* 63-69.

Broman, C. (1988). Household work and family life satisfaction of blacks. *Journal of Marriage and the Family, 50,* 743- 748.

Bryant, C. M., & Conger, R. D. (1999). Marital success and domains of social support in long-term relationships: Does the influence of network members ever end? *Journal of Marriage and the Family, 61,* 437-451.

Brown, J. R., & Rogers, L. E. (1991). Openness, uncertainty and intimacy: An epistemological reformulation. In N. Coupland, H. Giles & J. M. Wiemann (Eds.), *"Miscommunication" and problematic talk* (pp. 146-165). Newbury, CA: Sage Publications.

Bubolz, M. M., & Sontag, M. S. (1993). Human ecological theory. In P. G. Boss, W. J. Doherty, R. LaRossa, W. R. Schumm & S. K. Steinmetz (Eds.), Sourcebook of family theories and methods. A contextual approach (pp. 419-447). New York/London: Plenum Press.

Burleson, B. R., Kunkel, A. W., Samter, W., & Werking, K. J. (1996). Men's and women's evaluations of communication skills in personal relationships: When sex differences make a difference – and when they don't. *Journal of Social and Personal Relationships, 13,* 201-224.

Burke, P. J. (1980). The self: measurement requirements from an interactionist perspective. *Social Psychology Quarterly, 43,* 18-29.

Burke, P. J., & Cast, A. D. (1997). Stability and change in the gender identities of newly married couples. *Social Psychology Quarterly, 60,* 277-290.

Burke, P. J., & Reitzes, D. C. (1981). The link between identity and role performance. *Social Psychology Quarterly, 44*, 83-92.

Burke, P. J., & Reitzes, D. C. (1991). An identity theory approach to commitment. *Social Psychology Quarterly, 54*, 239-251.

Burr, W. (1973). Families under stress. In W. R. Burr (Ed.), *Theory construction and the sociology of the family* (pp. 199-217). New York: Wiley.

Burris, B. (1991). Employed Mothers: The impact of class and marital status on the prioritizing of family and work. *Social Science Quarterly, 72*, 50-66.

Buunk, B., & Nijskens, J. (1980). Communicatie en satisfactie in intieme relaties [Communication and satisfaction in intimate relationships]. *Gedrag, 8*, 240-260.

Byrne, M. B. (1998). *Structural equation modelling with LISREL, PRELIS and SIMPLIS: basic concepts, applications and programming.* London: Lawrence Erlbaum Associates Publishers.

Campbell, D. T., & Kenny, D. A. (1999). *A primer on regression artefacts.* New-York: The Guilford Press.

Canary, D. J., & Dindia, K., (Eds.) (1998). *Sex differences and similarities in communication. Critical essays and empirical investigations of sex and gender in interaction.* London: Lawrence Erlbaum Associates Publishers.

Canary, D. J., & Stafford, L. (1992). Relational maintenance strategies and equity in marriage. *Communication Monographs, 59*, 243-267.

Canary, D. J., Stafford, L., & Semic, B. A. (2002). A panel study of the associations between maintenance strategies and relational characteristics. *Journal of Marriage and the Family, 64*, 395-406.

Cancian, F. M. (1989). Gender politics. Love and power in the private and public spheres. In A. S. Skolnick & J. H. Skolnick (Eds.), *Family in transition. Rethinking Marriage, Sexuality, Child Rearing and Family Organization*, (pp. 219-230). London: Scott, Foresman and Company.

Caughlin J. P. (2003). Family communication standards. *Human Communication Research, 29*, 5-40.

CBS (Centraal Bureau voor Statistiek) (2003). www.cbs.nl. Link http://statline.cbs.nl/StatWeb/table.asp

Cheal, D. (1991). *Family and the state of theory.* Hemel Hempstead: Harvester/Wheatsheaf.

Chodorow, N. (1978). *The reproduction of mothering.* Berkeley, CA: University of California Press.

Cohen, S., & Wills, T. A. (1985). Stress, social support and the buffering hypothesis. *Psychological Bulletin, 98*(2), 310-357.

Coltrane, S. (2000). Research on household labor: Modeling and measuring the social embeddedness of routine family work. *Journal of Marriage and the Family, 62*, 1208-1234.

Comaille, J. (1998). Family and democracy. In K. Matthijs (Ed.), *The family. Contemporary perspectives and challenges* (pp. 19-30). Leuven: Universitaire Pers.

Conger, R. D., Elder, G. H., Lorenz, E. O., Conger, K. J., Simons, R. L. Whitbeck, L. B., Huck, S., & Melby, J. N. (1990). Linking economic hardship to marital quality and instability. *Journal of Marriage and the Family, 52*, 643-656.

Connell, R. W. (1985). Theorising Gender. *Sociology, 19*, 260–272.

Coupland, N., Giles, H., & Wiemann, J. M. (1991). *"Miscommunication" and problematic talk.* Newbury, CA: Sage Publications.

Crnic, K., & Acevedo, M. (1995). Everyday stresses and parenting. In M. H. Bornstein (Ed.), *Handbook of parenting* (pp. 277-297). New Jersey: Lawrence Erlbaum Associates.

Crowley, M. S. (1998). Men's self-perceived adequacy as the family breadwinner: Implications for their psychological, marital, and work-family well-being. *Journal of Family and Economic Issues, 19*, 7-23.

Davis, J. A. (1984). New money, an old man/lady, and two's company. *Social indicators research, 15*, 319-350.

De Brock, A. J. L. L. (1994). *Ouderlijk opvoedkundig handelen: De invloed van ouder-, kind- en contextuele kenmerken [Parents raising children: The influence of parental, child and contextual characteristics].* Nijmegen: Universiteitsdrukkerij.

De Graaf, A. (2000). Scheiding: wie en waarom? [Divorce: Who and Why.]. *Demos, 16*, 25-27.

De Graaf, P. M., & Vermeulen, H. (1997). Female labour market participation in the Netherlands: developments in the relationship between family cycle and employment. In H.-P. Blossfeld & C. Hakim (Eds.), *Between equalisation and marginalisation. Women working part-time in*

Europe and the United States of America (pp. 191-209). Oxford: Oxford University Press.

Dempsey, K. (2002). Who gets the best deal from marriage: women or men? *Journal of Sociology, 38*, 91-110.

Dennis, J. M., & Li, R. (2003). *Effects of panel attrition on survey estimates.* Paper presented at the annual meeting of the American Association for Public Opinion Research in Nashville.

Denton, W. H., Burleson, B. R., & Sprenkle, D. H. (1994). Motivation in marital communication: comparison of distressed and nondistressed husbands and wives. *The American Journal of Family Therapy, 22*, 17-26.

Dillaway, H., & Broman, C. (2001). Race, class, and gender differences in marital satisfaction and divisions of household labor among dual-earner couples. A case for intersectional analysis. *Journal of Family Issues, 22*, 309-327.

Dindia, K., & Allen, M. (1992). Sex differences in self-disclosure: A meta-analysis. *Psychological Bulletin, 12*, 106-124.

Du Bois-Reymond, M., Peters, E., & Ravesloot, J. (1993). *Keuzeprocessen van jongeren. Een longitudinaal onderzoek naar veranderingen in de jeugdfase en de rol van de ouders [Choice processes of young people. A longitudinal study on changes in the juvenile phase and the role of parents].* 's Gravenhage: VUGA Uitgeverij.

Duindam, V. (1993). Wie maakt de nieuwe vader? [Who makes the new father]. In A. Meulenbelt (Ed.), *Het kind en het badwater* (pp. 49-74). Amsterdam: Van Gennep.

Dumon, W. (1974). Het gezin als instituut en als systeem [The family as institution and system]. *Praktische Theologie, 1*, 168-177.

Dumon, W. (1977). *Het gezin in Vlaanderen [The family in Flanders].* Leuven: Davidsfonds.

Dumon, W. (1991). Family policies in the EC countries: a general overview. In G. C. N. Beets e.a. (Eds.), *Population and family in the Low Countries 1991* (pp 1-16). Amsterdam/Lisse: Swets & Zeitlinger.

Dumon, W. (1997). The situation of families in Western Europe: A sociological perspective. In S. Dreman (Ed.), *The family on the threshold of the 21st century. Trends and implications* (pp. 181-200). New Yersey: Lawrence Erlbaum Associations.

Duncombe, J., & Marsden, D. (1993). Love and intimacy: the gender division of emotion and 'emotion work'. *Sociology, 27*, 221-241.

Duncombe, J., & Marsden, D. (1995). 'Workaholics' and 'whingeing women': theorising intimacy and emotion work – the last frontier of gender inequality. *Sociological Review, 43*, 150-169.

Erel, O., & Burman, B. (1995). Interrelatedness of marital relations and parent-child relations: A meta-analytic review. *Psychological Bulletin, 118*, 108-132.

Espenshade, T. (1985). Marriage trends in America: estimates, implications and underlying causes, *Population and Development Review, 12*, 193-245.

Esping-Andersen, G. (1999). Social foundations of post-industrial societies. Oxford: University Press.

European Commission (1998). *Men within family and work, European network on family and work,* No. 2/98. Luxembourg: European Commission.

Feldman, S. S., Biringen, Z. C., & Nash, S. C. (1981). Fluctuations of sex-related self-attributions as a function of stage of family life cycle. *Developmental Psychology, 17*, 24-35.

Felling, A., Peters, J., & Scheepers, P. (2000). *Individualisering in Nederland. Empirisch onderzoek naar omstreden hypotheses [Individualisation in the Netherlands. Empirical research about contested hypotheses].* Assen: Van Gorcum.

Ferree, M. M. (1990). Beyond separate spheres: Feminism and family research. *Journal of Marriage and the Family, 52*, 886-894.

Ferree, M. M. (1991). The gender division of labor in two-earner marriages: dimensions of variability and change. *Journal of Family Issues, 12*, 158-180.

Fincham, F. D., & Bradbury, T. N. (1987a). The assessment of marital quality: a re-evaluation. *Journal of Marriage and the Family, 49*, 797-809.

Fincham, F. D., & Bradbury, T. N. (1987b). The impact of attributions in marriage: A longitudinal analysis. *Journal of Personality and Social Psychology, 53*, 510-517.

Finkel, S. E. (1995). *Causal analysis with panel data.* London: Sage Publications.

Fisher, A. H. (2000). *Gender and emotion. Social psychological perspectives.* Cambridge: University Press.

Fitzpatrick, M. A. (1988). Approaches to marital interaction. In P. Noller & M. A. Fitzpatrick (Eds.), *Perspectives on marital interaction* (pp. 1-28). Philadelphia: Multilingual Matters Ltd.

Fitzpatrick, M. A., & Ritchie, L. D. (1994). Communication schemata within the family. *Human Communication research, 20*, 275-301.

Garrido, E. F., & Acitelli, L. K. (1999). Relational identity and the division of household labor. *Journal of Social and Personal Relationships, 16*, 619-637.

Gerris, J. R. M., Houtmans, M. J., Kwaaitaal-Roosen, E. M., Schipper, J. C., Vermulst, A. A., & Janssens, J. M. (1998). *Parents, adolescents and young adults in Dutch families. A longitudinal study. A description of Dutch family life in terms of validated concepts representing family living conditions, cultural activities, puberal timing, child-rearing, interpersonal relations and communications, personality dimensions, adolescent behaviour, marital relations, job experiences, household tasks and socio-cultural value orientations.* Nijmegen: University of Nijmegen, Institute of Family Studies.

Gerris, J. R. M., Vermulst, A. A., Van Boxtel, D. A. , Janssens, J. M. , Van Zutphen, R. A., & Felling, A. J. (1993). *Parenting in Dutch families. A representative description of Dutch family life in terms of validated concepts representing characteristics of parents, children, the family as a system and parental socio-cultural value orientations. Survey of child-rearing, family relations and family processes in 1990.* Nijmegen: University of Nijmegen, Institute of Family Studies.

Gerris, J. R. M., Van Boxtel, D. A., Vermulst, A. A., Janssens, J. M. , Van Zutphen, R. A. & Felling, A. J. (1992). *Child-rearing, family relations and family processes in 1990.* Nijmegen: Institute of Family Studies, University of Nijmegen.

Giddens, A. (1991). *Modernity and self-identity.* Cambridge: Polity Press.

Giddens, A. (1992). *The transformation of intimacy: Sexuality, love and eroticism in modern societies.* Cambridge: Polity.

Giddens, A., & Pierson, C. (1998). *Conversations with Anthony Giddens.* Nottingham: University of Nottingham.

Glenn, N. D. (1990). Quantitative research on marital quality in the 1980s: a critical review. *Journal of Marriage and the Family, 52*, 818-831.

Glenn, N. D., & McLanahan, S. (1982). Children and marital happiness: a further specification of the relationship. *Journal of Marriage and the Family, 44,* 63-72.

Glenn, N. D., & Weaver, C. N. (1978). A multivariate multisurvey study of marital happiness. *Journal of Marriage and the Family, 40*, 269-282.

Glorieux, I, & Vandeweyer, J. (2002). Het egalitaire gezin: nog niet voor morgen. Bevindingen uit het Belgische tijdsbudgetonderzoek [The egalitarian family is not for tomorrow. Results from the Belgian time budget study]. *Over.Werk*, *3*, 174-178.

Goldsmith, D. J., & Dun, S. A. (1997). Sex differences and similarities in the communication of social support. *Journal of Social and Personal Relationships*, *14*, 317-337.

Goode, W. J. (1960). A theory of role strain. *American Sociological Review*, *25*, 483-496.

Gottfried, A. E., Gottfried, A. W., & Bathurst, M. (1995). Maternal and dual-earner employment status and parenting. In M. H. Bornstein (Ed.), *Handbook of parenting* (Vol. 2) (pp. 139 – 160), New Yersey: Lawrence Erlbaum Associates.

Gottman, J. M. (1991). Predicting the longitudinal course of marriage. *Journal of Marital and Family Therapy, 17*, 3-7.

Gottman, J. M. (1993). A theory of marital dissolution and stability. *Journal of Family Psychology, 7*, 57-75.

Gottman, J. M. (1994). *What predicts divorce? The relationship between marital processes and marital outcomes.* New York: Erlbaum Hillsdale.

Gottman, J. M., & Krokoff, L. J. (1989). Marital interaction and satisfaction: a longitudinal view. *Journal of Consulting and Clinical Psychology*, *57*, 47-52.

Gottman, J. M., & Porterfield, A. L. (1981). Communication competence in the nonverbal behavior of married couples. *Journal of Marriage and the Family, 43*, 817-824.

Gove, W. R, Style, C. B., & Hughes, M. (1997). The effect of marriage on the well-being of adults. A theoretical analysis. *Jounal of Family Issues, 1*, 4-35.

Granovetter, M. (1985). Economic action and social structure: the problem of embeddedness. *American Journal of Sociology, 91*, 481-510.

Gray, J. (1992). *Men are from Mars, women are from Venus.* New York: Harper Collins Publishers.

Greenstein, T. N. (1990). Marital disruption and the employment of married women. *Journal of Marriage and the Family, 52*, 657-676.

Greenstein, T. N. (1996). Husbands' participation in domestic labor: interactive effects of wives' and husbands' gender ideologies. *Journal of Marriage and the Family, 58*, 585-595.

Griffin, W. A. (1993). Transitions from negative affect during marital interaction: husband and wife differences. *Journal of Family Psychology, 63*, 221-233.

Guelzow, M G., Bird, G. W., & Koball, E. H. (1991). An exploratory path analysis of the stress process for dual-career men and women. *Journal of Marriage and the Family, 53*, 151-164.

Gupta, S., Smock, P. J., & Manning, W. D. (2004). Moving out: Transition to nonresidence among resident fathers in the United States. *Journal of Marriage and the Family, 66*, 627-638.

Halman, L. (1991). *Waarden in de westerse wereld. Een internationale exploratie van de waarden in de westerse samenleving [Values in the Western world. An international exploration of values in Western society]*. Tilburg: Tilburg University Press.

Halman, L., & Ester, P. (1995). Modernization and the nature of individualism. *Sociale Wetenschappen, 38*, 28-53.

Hatch, L. R., & Bulcroft, K. (2004). Does long-term marriage bring less frequent disagreements? Five explanatory frameworks. *Journal of Family Issues, 25*, 465-495.

Heaton, T. B. (1984). Religious homogamy and marital satisfaction reconsidered. *Journal of Marriage and the Family, 46*, 729-733.

Hill, R. (1949). *Families under stress*. Wesport, CT: Greenwood.

Hochschild, A., & Machung, A. (1989). *The second shift*. New York: Avon Books.

Hofstede, G. (1998). *Masculinity and femininity. The taboo dimension of national cultures*. London: Sage Publications.

Holman, T. (2001). *Premarital prediction of marital quality or breakup: research, theory, and practice*. New York: Kluwer.

Holmbeck, G. N., Paikoff, R. L., & Brooks-Gunn, J. (1995). Parenting adolescents. In M. H. Bornstein (Ed.), *Handbook of parenting* (Vol. 1) (pp. 91 - 118). New Jersey: Lawrence Erlbaum Assoc.

Holmes, J. G. (2000). Social Relationships: the nature and function of relational schemas. *European Journal of Social Psychology, 30*, 447-495.

Hondius, D. (2003). Gemengde huwelijken, gemengde gevoelens [Mixed marriages, mixed feelings]. *Demos, 19*, 68-69.

Honeycutt, J. M., & Wiemann, J. M. (1999). Analysis of functions of talk and reports of imagined interactions during engagement and marriage. *Human Communication Research, 25,* 399-419.

Hooghiemstra, E. (1997). Partnerrelaties [Partnerships]. In M. Niphuis-Nell (Ed), *Sociale atlas van de vrouw. Deel 4. Veranderingen in the primaire leefsfeer* (pp. 187-222). Rijswijk: Sociaal en Cultureel Planbureau.

Houck, J. W., & Daniel, R. W. (1994). Husbands' and wives' views of the communication in their marriages. *Journal of Humanities Counseling, Education & Development, 33,* 21-32.

Hu, L., & Bentler, P. M. (1999). Cutoff criteria for fit indexes in covariance structure analysis: conventional criteria versus new alternatives. *Structural Equation Modeling, 6,* 1-55.

Huston, T. L. (2000). The social ecology of marriage and other intimate unions. *Journal of Marriage and the Family, 62,* 298-320.

Huston, T. L., & Geis, G. (1993). In what ways do gender-related attributes and beliefs affect marriage? *Journal of Social Issues, 49,* 87-106.

Inglehart, R. (1977). *The silent revolution: changing values and political styles among western publics.* Princeton: Princeton University Press.

Jaccard, J., Turrissi, R., & Wan, C. K. (1990). *Interaction effects in multiple regression.* Newbury Park, CA: Sage.

Jackson, S., & Scott, S. (Eds.) (2002). *Gender. A sociological reader.* London: Routledge.

Jacobs, T. (2000). *Gezinsontbinding in Vlaanderen. Persoonlijke relaties in beweging [Family dissolution in Flanders. Personal relations in motion].* Antwerpen: UIA.

Jacobson, N. S., & Moore, D. (1981). Spouses as observers of the events in their relationship. *Journal of Consulting and Clinical Psychology, 49,* 269-279.

Jamieson, L. (1999). Intimacy transformed? A critical look at the 'pure relationship'. *Sociology, 33,* 477-494.

Jamshidan, M. (2004). Strategies for analysis of incomplete data. In M. Hardy & A. Bryman (Eds.), *Handbook of data-analysis* (pp. 113-130). London: Sage Publications.

Janssen, J. P. G. (2003). Twee geloven op één kussen [Two religions on one pillow]. *Demos, 19,* 29-32.

Johnson, D. R., White, L. K., Edwards, J. N., & Booth, A. (1986). Dimensions of marital quality: Toward methodological and conceptual refinement. *Journal of Family Issues, 7,* 31-49.

Jonker, J. M. L. (1990). *In de ban van het gezin: enige beschouwingen over de betekenis van primaire netwerken als vangnet [Under the spell of the family. Considerations on primary networks as safety net]* Nijmegen: Catholic University of Nijmegen.

Jöreskog, K. G., & Sörbom, D. (1989). *LISREL 7. User's reference guide.* Chicago: Scientific Software, Inc.

Jöreskog, K. G., & Sörbom, D. (1993). *LISREL 8: Structural equation modeling with the Simplis command language.* Hillsdale, NJ: Lawrence Erlbaum Associates Publishers.

Jöreskog, K. G., & Sörbom, D. (1996). *LISREL 8: User's Reference Guide.* Chicago, Ill: Scientific Software, Inc.

Kalmijn, M. (1999). Father involvement in childrearing and the perceived stability of marriage. *Journal of Marriage and the Family, 61*, 409-421.

Kalmijn, M. (2002). Sociologische analyse van levensloopeffecten: een overzicht van economische, sociale en culturele gevolgen [Sociological analysis of life course effects: an overview of economic, social and cultural consequences]. *Bevolking en Gezin, 31*, 3-46.

Kalmijn, M., de Graaf, P. M., & Poortman, A. (2004). Interactions between cultural and economic determinants of divorce in the Netherlands. *Journal of Marriage and Family, 66*, 75-89.

Kalmijn, M. & Jansen, M. (2000). *Investments in family life: The impact of value orientations.* Paper presented at the Workshop 'Value orientations and life course decisions', Royal Academy of Arts and Sciences. Brussels, Belgium, September 4-5.

Karney, B. R., & Bradbury, T. N. (1995). The longitudinal course of marital quality and stability: A review of theory, method and research, *Psychological Bulletin, 118*, 3-34.

Katsurada, E., & Sugihara, Y. (2002). Gender-role identity, attitudes toward marriage, and gender-segregated school backgrounds. *Sex Roles, 47*, 249-258.

Kellerhals, J. (1998). The family and the construction of adult identity. In K. Matthijs (Ed.), *The family. Contemporary perspectives and challenges* (pp. 73-90). Leuven: Universitaire Pers.

Kenny, D. A., & Cook, W. (1999). Partner effects in relationship research: conceptual issues, analytic difficulties and illustrations. *Personal relationships, 6*, 433-448.

Kerkstra, A. (1985). *Conflicthantering bij echtparen [Conflict management among couples]*. Amsterdam: VU-Uitgeverij.

Kessler, R. C., & McRae, J. A. Jr. (1982). The effect of wives' employment on the mental health of married men and women. *American Sociological Review, 47*, 216-227.

Kim, H. K., & McKenry, P. C. (2002). The relationship between marriage and psychological well-being. A longitudinal analysis. *Journal of Family Issues, 23*, 885-911.

Kline, R. B. (1998). *Principles and practice of Structural equation modeling*. New York: The Guilford Press.

Knijn, T. (1997). Keuze voor en beleving van moederschap en vaderschap [Choice for and experience of motherhood and fatherhood]. In M. Niphuis-Nell (Ed.), *Sociale atlas van de vrouw. Deel 4. Veranderingen in de primaire leefsfeer.* Rijswijk: Sociaal en Cultureel Planbureau.

Koestner, R., & Aube, J. (1995). A multifactorial approach to the study of gender characteristics. *Journal of Personality, 63*, 681-710.

Komarowsky, M. (1964). *Blue-collar marriage*. New York: Random House.

Kreppner, K. (2000). The child and the family: interdependence in developmental pathways. *Psicologia Teoria e Pesquisa, 16*, 11-22.

Kroska, A. (1997). The division of labor in the home: A review and reconceptualization. *Social Psychology Quarterly, 60*, 304-322.

Kuijsten, A., & Schulze, H-J. (1997). The Netherlands: the latent family. In F-X Kaufman, A. Kuijsten, H -J Schulze & K. P. Strohmeier (Eds.), *Family life and family policies in Europe. Structures and trends in the 1980s* (pp. 253-301). Oxford: Clarendon Press.

Kurdek, L. A.(1991). Marital stability and changes in marital quality in newly wed couples: a test of the contextual model. *Journal of Social and Personal Relationships, 8*, 27-48.

Kurdek, L. A. (1993). Predicting marital dissolution: A 5-year prospective longitudinal study of newlywed couples. *Journal of Personality and Social Psychology, 64*, 221-242.

Kurdek, L. A., & Schmitt, J. P. (1986). Relationship quality of partners in heterosexual married, heterosexual cohabitating, and gay and lesbian relationships. *Journal of Personality and Social Psychology, 51*, 711-720.

Laermans, R. (1993). Meer individuele mogelijkheden, minder sociale dwang? [More individual options, less social constraints]. In W. Dumon,

G. Fauconnier, R. Maes & E. Meulemans (Eds.), *Scenario's voor de toekomst* (pp. 137-151). Leuven: Acco.

Lamke, L. K., Sollie, D. L., Durbin, R. G., & Fitzpatrick, J. A. (1994). Masculinity, femininity and relationship satisfaction: the mediating role of interpersonal competence. *Journal of Social and Personal Relationships, 11*, 535-554.

Lammertyn, F. (1998). Le nouveau social: maatschappij op zoek naar nieuwe vormen van sociale bescherming [Le nouveau social. A society in pursuit of new forms of social protection]. *Gids op Maatschappelijk Gebied, 11*, 819-845.

Latten, J. (2003). Dynamiek in relaties en welvaart: over singleplateau, stellenberg, gezinsdal en eenouderravijn [Dynamics in relationships and welfare: about single plateau, couples' mountain, family's valley and one-parent ravine], *Bevolking en Gezin, 32*, 35-56.

Latten, J. (2004). Trends in samenwonen en trouwen. De schone schijn van burgerlijke staat. [Trends in cohabitation and marriage. The pretence of civil status]. *Bevolkingstrends, 4*, 46-60.

Latten, J., & De Graaf, A. (1997). *Fertility and family surveys in countries of the ECE region. Standard country report. The Netherlands.* United Nations Economic Commission for Europe, Economic Studies No. 10c. New York/Geneva: United Nations.

Lavee, Y., McCubbin, H. I., & Olson, D. H. (1987). The effect of stressful life events and transitions on family functioning and well-being. *Journal of Marriage and the Family, 49*, 857-873.

Lavee, Y., & Sharlin, S. (1996). The effect of parenting stress on marital quality. *Journal of Family Issues, 17*, 114-136.

Lesthaeghe, R. (1987) Gezinsvorming en -ontbinding: de twee transities, *Tijdschrift voor Sociologie, 8*, 9-33.

Lesthaeghe, R. (1993). Gezins- en partnerrelaties: demografische evolutie [Family- and partner relationships: demographic evolutions]. In R. Cammaer & L. Boeykens (Eds.), *Man-vrouw-mens. Fysiek, psychisch, cultureel mens-zijn als man en vrouw* (pp. 97-118). Leuven: Acco.

Lesthaeghe, R. (1999). The second demographic transition in western countries: an interpretation. In K. Oppenheim Mason & A. M. Jensen (Eds.), *Gender and family change in industrialized countries* (pp. 17-62). Oxford: Clarendon Press.

Lesthaeghe, R., & Surkyn, J. (1988). Cultural dynamics and economic theories of fertility change. *Population and Development Review, 14*, 1-45.

Lesthaege, R., & van de Kaa, D. (1986). Twee demografische transities? [Two demographic transitions?]. In D. van de Kaa & R. Lesthaeghe (Eds.), *Groei en krimp* (pp. 9-24). Deventer: Van Loghum Slaterus.

Lewis, J. (2001). *The end of marriage.* Cheltenham: Edward Elgar Publishing.

Lewis, R. A., & Spanier, G. B. (1979). Theorizing about the quality and stability of marriage. In W. R. Burr, R. Hill, F. I. Nye & I. L. Reiss (Eds.), *Contemporary theories about the family: Research-base theories* (pp. 49-65). New York: Free Press.

Locksley, A. (1982). Social class and marital attitudes and behavior. *Journal of Marriage and the Family, 44*, 427-440.

Lye, D. N., & Biblarz, T. J. (1993). The effects of attitudes toward family life and gender roles on marital satisfaction. *Journal of Family Issues, 14*, 157-189.

Macionis, J. J. (1997). *Sociology.* New Jersey: Prentice Hall.

Margolin, G., Hattem, D., John, R. S., & Yost, K. (1985). Perceptual agreement between spouses and outside observers when coding themselves and a stranger dyad. *Behavioural Assessment, 7*, 235-247.

Marusic, I. (1998). Relations of masculinity and femininity with personality dimensions of the five-factor model. *Sex roles, 38*, 29-44.

Matthews, L. S., Wickrama, K. A. S., & Conger, R. D. (1996). Predicting marital instability from spouse and observer reports of marital interaction. *Journal of Marriage and the Family, 58*, 641-655.

Matthijs, K. (1986). *Echtscheiding als sociaal proces [Divorce as a social process].* Leuven: Departement Sociologie/Sociologisch Onderzoeksinstituut-SSD/31.

Matthijs, K. (2000). Vernieuwingsdrang, bindingsangst en statusstrijd in de postmoderne private ruimte [Neophilia, bounding fear and status battle in the postmodern private sphere]. In R. Burggraeve, L. Dhaene, L. Vints, M. Cloet, K. Dobbelare & L. Leijssen (Eds.), *Levensrituelen: het huwelijk* (pp.104-122). Leuven: Universitaire Pers Leuven.

Matthijs, K. (2001). *De mateloze negentiende eeuw. Bevolking, huwelijk, gezin en sociale verandering [The excessive Ninetheenth Century. Population, family and social change].* Leuven: Universitaire Pers Leuven.

Matthijs, K. (2003). Demographic and sociological indicators of privatisation of marriage in the 19th century in Flanders. *European Journal of Population, 19*, 375-412.

Matthijs, K., & Van den Troost, A. (1998). The perception of private lifeforms. An empirical survey by Louvain students. In K. Matthijs (Ed.), *The family: contemporary perspectives and challenges. Festshrift in honor of Wilfried Dumon* (pp. 111-133). Leuven: University Press.

McCubbin, H. I., Joy, C. B., Cauble, A. E., Comeau, J. K., Patterson, J. M., & Needle, R. H. (1980). Family stress and coping: a decade review. *Journal of Marriage and the Family, 42*, 855-871.

McCubbin, H. I., & Patterson, J. M. (1982). Family adaptation to crises. In H. I. McCubbin, A. E. Cauble & J. M. Patterson (Eds.), *Family stress, coping and social support* (pp 26-47). Springfield: Charles C. Thomas Publishers.

McCubbin, H. I., & Patterson, J. M. (1983). The family stress process: The Double ABCX model of adjustment and adaptation. *Marriage and Family Review, 6*, 7-37.

McDowell, L. (2001). Father and Ford revisited: gender, class and employment change in the new millennium. *Transactions of the Institute of British Geographers, 26*, 448-464.

McLanahan, S., & Adams, J. (1987). Parenthood and psychological well-being. *Annual Review of Sociology, 13*, 237-257.

Medling, J. M., & McCarrey, M. (1981). Martital adjustment over segments of the family life cycle: the issue of spouses' value similarity. *Journal of Marriage and the Family, 43*, 195-203.

Meeks, B. S., Hendrick, S. S., & Hendrick, C. (1998). Communication, love and relationship satisfaction. *Journal of Social and Personal Relationships, 15*, 755-773.

Miller, P. J. E., Caughlin, J. P., & Huston, T. L. (2003). Trait expressiveness and marital satisfaction: the role of idealization process. *Journal of Marriage and the Family, 65*, 978-996.

Mills, M. (2000). *The transformation of partnerships*. Amsterdam: Thela Thesis.

Mirowsky, J., & Ross, C. (1987). Belief in innate sex roles: sex stratification versus interpersonal influence in marriage. *Journal of Marriage and the Family*, *49*, 527-540.

Morgan, D. (2004). Men in families and households. In J. Scott, J. Treas & M. Richards (Eds.), *The Blackwell Companion to the sociology of families* (pp. 374-393). Malden: Blackwell Publishing.

Moors, G. (2001). Family theory: role of changing values. In N. J. Smelser & P. B. Baltes (Eds.), *International encyclopedia of the social and behavioral sciences* (pp. 5397-5401). Amsterdam: Elsevier.

Mueller, R. O. (1996). *Basic principles of structural equation modeling. An introduction to Lisrel and EQS*. New York: Springer-Verlag.

Mugenda, O. M., Hira, T. K., & Fanslow, A. M. (1990). Assessing the causal relationship among communication, money management practices, satisfaction with financial status and satisfaction with quality of life. *Journal of Family and Economic Issues, 11*, 343-360.

Mulac, A., Bradac, J. J., & Gibbons, P. (2001). Empirical support for the gender-as-culture hypothesis. An intercultural analysis of male/female language differences. *Human Communication Research, 27*, 121-152.

Navran, L. (1967). Communication and adjustment in marriage. *Family Process, 6*, 173-184.

Nesselroade, J. R., & Baltes, P. B. (Eds.) (1985). *Longitudinal research in the study of behaviour and development*. New York: Academic Press.

Niphuis-Nell, M. (1997). Beleid inzake herverdeling van onbetaalde arbeid [Policy on the reorganisation of unpaid labor]. In M. Niphuis-Nell (Ed.), *Sociale atlas van de vrouw. Deel 4: Veranderingen in de primaire leefsfeer.* (pp. 287-334). Rijkswijk: Sociaal en Cultureel Planbureau.

Niphuis-Nell, M., & de Beer, P. (1997). Verdeling van arbeid en zorg [Division of labour and care]. In C. S Van Praag & M. Niphuis-Nell (Eds.), *Het gezinsrapport. Een verkennende studie naar het gezin in een veranderende samenleving* (pp. 43-113). Rijswijk: Sociaal en Cultureel Planbureau.

Noller, P. (1981). Gender and marital adjustment level differences in decoding messages from spouses and strangers. *Journal of Personality and Social Psychology, 41,* 272-278.

Noller, P., & Feeney, J. A. (1994). Relationship satisfaction, attachment and nonverbal accuracy in early marriage. *Journal of Nonverbal Behavior, 18,* 199-221.

Noller, P., & Fitzpatrick, M. A. (1990). Marital communication in the eighties. *Journal of Marriage & the Family, 52,* 832-843.

Norton, R. (1983). Measuring marital quality: a critical look at the dependent variable. *Journal of Marriage and the Family, 45,* 141-151.

OECD (1996). *Organisation for Economic Co-operation and Development.* Employment Outlook, July, 1996. Paris: OECD.

O'Heron, C.A., & Orlofsky, J. L. (1990). Stereotypic and nonstereotypic sex role trait and behavior orientations, gender identity, and psychological adjustment. *Journal of Personality and Social Psychology, 58,* 134-143.

Olson, D. H., McCubbin, H. I., Barnes, H., & Hill, R. (1983). *Families: what makes them work?* California: Sage Beverly Hills.

O'Neill, R., & Greenberger, E. (1994). Patterns of commitment to work and parenting: implications for role strain. *Journal of Marriage and the Family, 56,* 101-118.

Ono, H. (1998). Husbands' and wives' resources and marital dissolution. *Journal of Marriage and the Family, 60,* 674-690.

Oppenheimer, V. K. (1994). Women's rising employment and the future of the family in industrial societies. *Population and Development Review, 20,* 293-342.

Oppenheimer, V. K. (1997). Women's employment and the gain to marriage. The specialization and trading model. *Annual Review of Sociology, 23,* 431-453.

Oppenheimer, V. K. (2001). Family theory: competing perspectives in social demography. In N. J. Smelser & P. B. Baltes (Eds.), *International encyclopedia of the social and behavioral sciences* (pp. 5367-5373). Amsterdam: Elsevier.

Orden, S. R., & Bradburn, N. M. (1969). Working wives and marital happiness. *American Journal of Sociology, 74,* 392-407.

Orlofsky, J. L., & O'Heron, C. A. (1987). Development of a short-form sex role behavior scale. *Journal of Personality Assessment, 51,* 267-277.

Orlofsky, J. L., & Stake, J. E. (1981). Psychological masculinity and femininity: relationship to striving and self-concept in the achievement and interpersonal domains. *Psychology of Women Quarterly, 6,* 218-233.

Paetsch, J. J., Bala, N. M., Bertrand, L. D. & Glennon, L. (2004). Trends in the formation and dissolution of couples. In J. Scott, J. Treas & M. Richards (Eds.), *The Blackwell Companion to the sociology of families* (pp. 306-321). Malden: Blackwell Publishing.

Pattyn, B., & Van Liedekerke, L. (2001). *Angst en onzekerheid in de moderne samenleving [Fear and insecurity in modern society]*. Discussietekst voor seminarie van Multatuli-lezing. Leuven: K.U.Leuven.

Parmelee, P. A. (1987). Sex role identity, role performance and marital satisfaction of newlywed couples. *Journal of Social and Personal Relationships, 4*, 429-444.

Parott, W. G. (2000). The nature of emotion. In A. Tesser & N. Schwarz (Eds.), *Handbook of social psychology. Intraindividual processes* (pp. 375-390). Oxford: Blackwell Publishers.

Pease, A. (1999). *Why men don't listen and women can't read maps*. Utrecht: Het Spectrum.

Perry-Jenkins, M., & Folk, K. (1994). Class, couples and conflict: effects of the division of labor on assessments of marriage in dual-earner families. *Journal of Marriage and the Family, 56*, 165-180.

Peters, J., & Felling, A. (2000). Individualisering van waardeoriëntaties [Individualisation of value orientations]. In A. Felling, J. Peters & P. Scheepers (Eds.), *Individualisering in Nederland aan het einde van de twintigste eeuw. Empirisch onderzoek naar omstreden hypothesen* (pp. 21-34). Assen: Van Gorcum.

Peters, J., & Gerris, J. R. M. (1995). Familialisme: sociaal-culturele verschuivingen in de jaren tachtig en de samenhang met gezin en opvoeding [Familialism: socio-cultural transformations during the eighties and the association with family and child rearing]. In J. R. M. Gerris (Ed.), *Gezin: onderzoek en diagnostiek* (pp. 21-34). Assen: Van Gorcum.

Peterson, C. D., Baucom, D. H., Elliot, M. J., & Farr, P. A. (1989). The relationship between sex-role identity and marital adjustment. *Sex Roles, 21*, 775-788.

Plewis, I. (1985). *Analysing change. Measurement and explanation using longitudinal data*. New York: John Wiley & Sons.

Pittman, J. F., Wright, C. A., & Llyod, S. A. (1989). Predicting parenting difficulty. *Journal of Family Issues, 10*, 267-286.

Popenoe, D. (1993). American family decline, 1960-1990: A review and reappraisal. *Journal of Marriage and the Family, 55,* 527-555.

Prince-Gibson, E., & Schwartz, S. H. (1998). Value priorities and gender. *Social Psychology Quarterly, 61,* 49-67.

Pyke, K. D. (1996). Class-based masculinities. The interdependence of gender, class, and interpersonal power. *Gender and Society, 10,* 527-549.

Ridgeway, C. L., & Smith-Lovin, L. (1999). The gender system and interaction. *Annual Review of Sociology, 25,* 191-216.

Rispens, J., Hermanns, J. M. A., Meeus, W. H. J. (Eds.) (1996). *Opvoeden in Nederland [Child Rearing in the Netherlands].* Assen: Van Gorcum.

Rogers, S. J. (1999). Wives' income and marital quality: Are there reciprocal effects?. *Journal of Marriage and the Family, 61,* 123-132.

Rogers, S. J., & Amato, P. R. (1997). Is marital quality declining? The evidence from two generations. *Social Forces, 75,* 1089-1100.

Rogers, S. J., & Amato, P. R. (2000). Have changes in gender relations affected marital quality? *Social Forces, 2,* 731-753.

Rogers, S. J., & White, L. K. (1998). Satisfaction with parenting: the role of marital happiness, family structure and parent's gender. *Journal of Marriage and the Family, 60,* 293-309.

Rogossa, D. (1995). Myths and methods: "Myths about longitudinal research" plus supplemental questions. In J. M. Gottman (Ed.), *The analysis of change* (pp. 3-66). New Jersey: Lawrence Erlbaum Associates.

Rubin, L. B. (1976). *Worlds of pain: life in the working-class family.* New York: Basic Books.

Rubin, L. B. (1983). *Intimate strangers.* New York: Harper & Row

Ruggles, S. (1997). The rise of divorce and separation in the United States, 1880-1990. *Demography, 34,* 455-466.

Sabatelli, R. (1988). Measurement issues in marital research: a review and critique of contemporary survey instruments. *Journal of Marriage and the Family, 50,* 891-915.

Scanzoni, J. (1979). Social processes and power in families. In W. R. Burr, R. Hill, F. I. Nye & I. L. Reiss (Eds.), *Contemporary theories about the family* (Vol. 1) (pp. 295-316). New York: Free Press.

Scanzoni, J. (1987). Families in the 1980s. Time to refocus our thinking. *Journal of Family Issues, 8,* 394-421.

Schumm, W. R., Paff-Bergen, R. C., Hatch, F. C. O., Copeland, J. M., Meens, L. D., & Bugaighis, M. A. (1986). Concurrent and discriminant validity of the Kansas marital satisfaction scale. *Journal of Marriage and the Family, 48,* 381-387.

Scott, J. (1995). Using household panels to study micro-social change. *The European Journal of Social Sciences, 8,* 61-74.

Scott, J., & Alwin, D. F. (1989). Gender differences in parental strain. Parental role or gender role? *Journal of Family Issues, 10,* 482-503.

Segal, L. (1990). *Slow motion: Changing masculinities, changing men.* New Brunswick, NJ: Rutgers University Press.

Shelton, B. A., & John, D. (1996). The division of household labor. *Annual Review of Sociology, 22,* 299-322.

Shorter, E. (1975). *The making of the modern family.* New York: Basic Books.

Sigle-Rushton, W. & Kenney, C. (2004). Public policy and families. In J. Scott, J. Treas & M. Richards (Eds.), *The Blackwell Companion to the sociology of families* (pp. 457-4771). Malden: Blackwell Publishing.

South, S. J. (2001). Time-dependent effects of wives' employment on marital dissolution. *American Sociological Review, 66,* 226.

Spanier, G. B. (1976). Measuring dyadic adjustment: new scales for assessing the quality of marriages and similar dyads. *Journal of Marriage and the Family, 42,* 15-27.

Spence, J. T. (1984). Gender identity and its implications for the concepts of masculinity and femininity. In T. B. Sonderegger (Ed.), *Nebraska symposium on motivation: Vol. 32. Psychology of gender* (pp. 59-95). Lincoln: University of Nebraska Press.

Spence, J. T. (1993). Gender-related traits and gender ideology: evidence for a multifactorial theory. *Journal of Personality and Social Psychology, 64,* 624-635.

Spence, J. T., & Helmreich, R. L. (1978). *Masculinity and femininity: their psychological dimensions, correlates and antecedents.* Austin: University of Texas Press.

Steenkamp, J. B. E. M., & Baumgartner, H. (1998). Assessing measurement invariance in cross-national consumer research. *Journal of Consumer Research, 25,* 78-89.

Stets, J. E. (1995). Role identities and person identities: gender identity, master identity and controlling one's partner. *Sociological perspectives, 38*, 129-150.

Stets, J. E. (1997). Status and identity in marital interaction. *Social Psychology Quarterly, 60*, 185-217.

Stets, J. E., & Burke, P. J. (1996). Gender, control and interaction. *Social Psychology Quarterly, 59*, 193-220.

Stets, J. E., & Burke, P. J. (2000). Femininity/masculinity. In E. F. Borgatta & R. J. V. Montgomery (Eds.), *Encyclopedia of Sociology* (pp. 997-1005). New York: Macmillan.

Stevens, D., Kiger, G., & Riley, P. J. (2001). Working hard and hardly working: domestic labor and marital satisfaction among dual earner couples. *Journal of Marriage and the Family, 63*, 514-527.

Straver, C. J., van der Heyden, A. M., van der Vliet, R. W. F. (1994). *De huwelijkse logica [The marital logic]*. Leiden: DSWO-Press, Rijksuniversiteit Leiden.

Stryker, S. (1968). Identity salience and role performance: the relevance of symbolic interaction theory for family research. *Journal of Marriage and the Family, 30*, 558-564.

Stryker, S. (1980). *Symbolic interactionism: a social structural version*. Menlo Park, CA: Benjamin/Cummings.

Stryker, S. (1992). Identity theory. In E. F. Borgatta & M. L. Borgatta (Eds.), *Encyclopedia of sociology* (pp. 871-876). New York: MacMillan Publishers.

Suitor, J. J. (1991). Marital quality and satisfaction with the division of household labor across the family life cycle. *Journal of Marriage and the Family, 53*, 221-230.

Tamir, L. M., & Antonucci, T. C. (1981). Self-perception, motivation and social support through the family life course. *Journal of Marriage and the Family, 43*, 151-161.

Taris, T. (2000). *A primer in longitudinal data analysis*. London: Sage Publications.

Thoits, P. A. (1983). Multiple identities and psychological well-being: A reformulation and test of the social isolation hypothesis. *American Sociological Review, 48*, 147-187.

Thoits, P. A. (1992). Identity structures and psychological well-being: gender and marital status comparsions. *Social Psychological Quarterly*, *55*, 236-256.

Tichenor, V. J. (1999). Status and income as gendered resources: the case of marital power. *Journal of Marriage and the Family*, *61*, 638-650.

Thompson, L., & Walker, A. J. (1989). Gender in families: Women and men in marriage, work and parenthood. *Journal of Marriage and the Family*, *51*, 845-871.

Thornton, A., Alwin, D. E., & Camburn, D. (1983). Causes and consequences of sex role attitude and attitude change. *American Sociological Review*, *48*, 211-227.

Twenge, J. M. (1999). Mapping gender. The multifactorial approach and the organization of gender-related attributes. *Psychology of Women Quarterly*, *23*, 485-502.

Twenge, J. M. Campbell, W. K., & Foster, C. A. (2003). Parenthood and marital satisfaction: a meta-analytic review. *Journal of Marriage and the Family*, *65*, 574-583.

Tyrell, H., & Schulze, H-J. (1997). Stability as a cultural ingredient of parenting: a collision within the coupling of partnership and parenthood. Preliminary draft for book project *Stability and complexity: perspectives for family policy*.

Umberson, D. (1989). Relationships with children: explaining parents' psychological well-being. *Journal of Marriage and the Family*, *51*, 999-1012.

Van Ammers, E., Dekovic, M., Gerrits, L. A. W., Groenendaal, J. H. A., Hermanns, J. M. A., Meeus, W. H. J., Noom, M. J., Rispens, J., Vergeer, M. M. (1998). *Opvoeden in Nederland: Schalenboek [Childrearing in the Netherlands: measures book]*. Utrecht: University of Utrecht.

Van de Kaa, D. J. (1987). Europe's second demographic transition. *Population Bulletin*, *42*, 1-59.

Van de Kaa, D. J. (2001). The second demographic transition. In N. J. Smelser & P. B. Baltes (Eds.), *International encyclopedia of the social and behavioral sciences* (pp. 3486-3488). Amsterdam: Elsevier.

Vandemeulebroecke, L., De Munter, A., Jacobs, T., & Van den Bosch, L. (2000). *Waardering, verdeling en overdracht van de 'vrouwelijke zorg' in de opvoeding [Appraisal, division and transmission of 'female care' in child rearing]*. Onderzoeksrapport. Leuven: Centrum voor Gezinspedagogiek.

Vandenberg, R. J., & Lance, C. E. (2000). A review and synthesis of the measurement invariance literature: suggestions, practices and recommendations for organizational research. *Organizational Research Methods, 3*, 4-70.

Van den Troost, A. (2000). De relationele markt anno 2000. Een exploratie van waardeoriëntaties en vormgeving [The relational market anno 2000. An exploration of value orientations and relational style] *Tijdschrift voor Sociologie, 2*, 131-157.

Van den Troost, A., Vermulst, A. A., Gerris, J. R. M., & Matthijs, K. (2001). *Measurement invariance of marital quality and satisfaction*. Research report of the Department of Sociology (K.U.Leuven) and Orthopedagogy (KUNijmegen).

Van der Avort, A. (1987). *De gulzige vrijblijvendheid van expliciete relaties [The greedy non-commitment of explicit relationships]*. Tilburg: University Press.

Van der Lippe, T. (1997). Verdeling van onbetaalde arbeid, 1975-1995 [Division of unpaid labour, 1975-1995]. In M. Niphuis-Nell (Ed.), *Sociale atlas van de vrouw. Deel 4. Veranderingen in de primaire leefsfeer* (pp. 117-157). Rijswijk: Sociaal en Cultureel Planbureau.

Vanhove, T., & Matthijs, K. (2002). *The socio-demographic evolution of divorce and remarriage in Belgium*. Unpublished paper presented on 'Divorce in cross-national perspective: a European research network', November 14th - 15th, Firenze.

VanLanningham, J., Johnson, D. R., & Amato, P. (2001). Marital happiness, marital duration, and the U-shaped curve: evidence from a five-wave panel study. *Social Forces, 78*, 1313-1341.

Vannoy-Hiller, D., & Philliber, W. W. (1989). *Equal partners. Successful women in marriage*. London: Sage Publications.

Vannoy, D., & Philliber, W. W. (1992). Wife's employment and quality of marriage. *Journal of Marriage and the Family, 54*, 387-398.

Van Praag, C. S. (1997). Demografie [Demography]. In C. S Van Praag & M. Niphuis-Nell (Eds.), *Het gezinsrapport. Een verkennende studie naar het gezin in een veranderende samenleving* (pp. 9-42). Rijswijk: Sociaal en Cultureel Planbureau.

Van Praag, C. S., & Niphuis-Nell, M. (Eds.) (1997). *Het gezinsrapport. Een verkennende studie naar het gezin in een veranderende samenleving [The family report. An exploratory study on family in a changing society].* Rijswijk: Sociaal en Cultureel Planbureau.

Vansteenwegen, A. (1988). *Liefde is een werkwoord [Love is a Verb].* Tielt: Lannoo.

Van Stokkom, B. (1997). *Emotionele democratie. Over morele vooruitgang [Emotional democracy. About moral progress].* Amsterdam: Van Gennep.

Van Yperen, N. (1990). *Sociale vergelijking en sociale uitwisseling in huwelijksrelaties [Social comparison and social exchange in marital relationships].* Nijmegen: s.n.

Veenhoven, R. (1984). *Conditions of happiness.* Dordrecht: Kluwer Academic.

Vermulst, A. A., & Gerris, J. R. M. (1996). Gezin en opvoeding bij kostwinners en tweeverdieners. Beschikbaarheid, opleiding en achterliggende gezinswaarden van vaders en moeders. [Family and child rearing in one-earner and two-earner households. Availability, education and family values of mothers and fathers]. In J. R. M. Gerris (Ed.), *Gezin: welzijn, gezondheid en hulpverlening* (pp. 38-56). Assen: Van Gorcum.

Walker, A. J. (1999). Gender and family relationships. In M. Sussman, S. K. Steinmetz & G. W. Peterson (Eds.), *Handbook of marriage and the family* (2nd edition) (pp. 439-474). New York: Plenum Press.

Wallerstein, J. S., & Blakeslee, S. (1989). *Second chances: men, women and children a decade after divorce.* New York: Houghton Mifflin Company.

Weeda, C. J. (1981). Huwelijkskwaliteit en echtscheiding [Marital quality and divorce]. In C. J. Weeda (Ed.), *Huwelijk, gezin en samenleving. Centrale problemen, alternatieven en overzichten* (pp. 73-98). Assen: Van Gorcum.

Weigel, D. J., & Ballard-Reisch, D. S. (1999). How couples maintain marriages: A closer look at self and spouse influences upon the use of maintenance behaviours in marriages. *Family Relations, 48,* 263-269.

Weigel, D. J., & Ballard-Reisch, D. S. (2001). The impact of relational maintenance behaviours on marital satisfaction: A longitudinal analysis. *The Journal of Family Communication, 1,* 265-279.

West, C., & Zimmerman, D. H. (1987). Doing gender. *Gender and society, 1,* 125-151.

White, L. K. (1983). Determinants of spousal interaction: Marital structure or marital happiness. *Journal of Marriage and the Family, 45,* 511-519.

White, L., Booth, A., & Edwards, J. (1986). Children and marital happiness: Why the negative correlation. *Journal of Family Issues, 7,* 131-147.

White, L., & Rogers, S. J. (2000). Economic circumstances and family outcomes. A review of the 1990s. *Journal of Marriage and the Family, 62*, 1035-1051.

Whyte, M. K. (1990). *Dating, mating and marriage.* New York: Aldine de Gruyter.

Widmer, E. (2004). Couples and their networks. In J. Scott, J. Treas & M. Richards (Eds.), *The Blackwell Companion to the sociology of families* (pp. 356-373). Malden: Blackwell Publishing.

Willekens, F. (2001). Theoretical and technical orientations toward longitudinal research in the social sciences. *Canadian Studies in Population, 28*, 189-217.

Wise, S. (2003). *Family structure, child outcomes and environmental mediators. An overview of the development in diverse families study.* Melbourne: Australian Institute of Family Studies.

Wood, J. T. (1993). Engendered relations: interaction, caring, power and responsibility in intimacy. In S. Duck (Ed.), *Social context and social relationships* (pp. 26-54). London: Sage Publications.

Wothke, W. (2000). Longitudinal and multigroup modeling with missing data. In T. D Little, K. U. Schnabel & J. Baumert (Eds.), *Modeling longitudinal and multilevel data. Practical issues, applied approaches and specific examples.* New Jersey: Lawrence Erlbaum Associates Publishers.

Wouters, C. (1985). Formalisering en informalisering. Veranderingen in omgangsvormen tussen de seksen in Nederland, 1930-1985 [Formalisation and informalisation. Transformations in social manners between the sexes in the Netherlands, 1930-1985]. *Sociologisch Tijdschrift, 12*, 133-162.

Wright, P. H. (1998). Toward an expanded orientation to the study of sex differences in friendship. In D. J. Canary & K. Dindia (Eds.), *Sex differences and similarities in communication. Critical essays and empirical investigations of sex and gender in interaction* (pp. 41-63). New Jersey/London: Lawrence Erlbaum Associates.

Yogev, S., & Brett, J. (1985). Perceptions of the division of housework and child care and marital satisfaction. *Journal of Marriage and the Family, 47*, 609-618.

PRINTED ON PERMANENT PAPER • IMPRIME SUR PAPIER PERMANENT • GEDRUKT OP DUURZAAM PAPIER - ISO 9706

N.V. PEETERS S.A., WAROTSTRAAT 50, B-3020 HERENT

www.ingramcontent.com/pod-product-compliance
Lightning Source LLC
Chambersburg PA
CBHW060146280326
41932CB00012B/1651